9   8   7   6   5   4   3   2   1
Digit on the right indicates the number of this printing

Library of Congress Control Number: 2004093566

ISBN 0-7624-1971-7

Cover designed by Doogie Horner
Interior designed by Doogie Horner
Edited by Greg Jones
Typography: Times NR, Vinyl, Bulldog, Trade Gothic, and City

We would like to thank the following DC Comics artists for their contributions to this book:
Jack Burnley, Stan Kaye, George Klein, Sheldon Moldoff, Al Plastino, Fred Ray, Kurt Schaffenberger,
Joe Shuster, John Sikela and Curt Swan.

This book may be ordered by mail from the publisher.
Please include $2.50 for postage and handling.
But try your bookstore first!

Running Press Book Publishers
125 South Twenty-second Street
Philadelphia, Pennsylvania 19103-4399

Visit us on the web!
www.runningpress.com

Visit DC Comics on the web:
http://www.dccomics.com
AOL Keyword: DCCOMICS

FOR MY SUPERBOY and WONDER WOMAN.

CONTENTS

ACKNOWLEDGMENTS AND SOURCES

This book would not exist but for the vision of two super editors, Greg Jones at Running Press and Chris Cerasi at DC Comics, and two super DC Comics experts, Richard Bruning and Steve Korté, Men of Steel all.

The primary sources for this book are six-plus decades of Superman comics, but I am also deeply indebted to the following insightful, meticulous, and endlessly entertaining books, which are indispensable to anyone deeply interested in comics generally and Superman in particular:

Superman: The Ultimate Guide to the Man of Steel, by Scott Beatty (London and New York: Dorling Kindersley, 2002)

Superman: The Complete History, by Les Daniels (San Francisco: Chronicle Books, 1998)

Superman at Fifty: The Persistence of a Legend, edited by Dennis Dooley and Gary Engle (New York: Collier, 1988)

The Great Superman Book: The Complete Encyclopedia of the Folk Hero of America! by Michael L. Fleisher (New York: Harmony Books, 1978)

Help Wanted: Super Hero (No Experience Necessary)

Not very long ago, the United States Army changed its recruiting slogan. For years, men and women, ages seventeen to thirty-four, were invited to "Be All That You Can Be." Now they are enticed to become "An Army of One." The change was probably a good idea, because it was all too easy to take the first slogan the wrong way. Doubtless, the army brass and their Madison Avenue lieutenants intended the phrase to sell an opportunity to realize your full potential: *all that you can be.* However, the unintended implication was not of boundless potential, but of certain limitation: be all that you can be *and not a bit more.* For some, joining the army is the first step in a great life; for many others, it is, quite simply, all they can be.

At least, that seemed to be the flip side of the old slogan.

But why? Why should a cynical double meaning lurk in what was intended to be an idealistic expression of service and self-realization?

The cynicism nestles not in the phrase, but in ourselves. We aren't ambushed by the army's slogan, but by our own expectations—or, more precisely, by our own diminished expectations. Most of us most of the time are conditioned to see limits rather than potential. Most of us most of the time are conditioned to expect little from ourselves and even less from others. Your computer freezes. With infinite resignation, you dial the manufacturer's tech support number, not daring to expect actual help, but anticipating an eternity of on-hold melody as you wait to be connected to an entry-level employee who knows little more about your computer's malady than you do. If it so happens that you are answered promptly and productively, your reaction is less likely to be satisfaction and relief than shock.

In the workplace it's much the same. Recent years have conditioned us to expect less and less from what we do for a living. Where our mothers and fathers had honest-to-goodness offices, most of us are lucky to find ourselves in a cubicle. Whereas a worker of the previous generation could reasonably look forward to starting at Acme Widget, work hard, move up, and, after twenty-five or thirty years, retire from Acme an executive with a fully vested pension, a young person today expects to change firms, voluntarily or not, more than a few times. It used to be that the prospect of getting laid off was an almost unthinkable catastrophe. Now it's par for the course. Once upon a time, a firm really was, well, *firm,* something destined to outlast employees, owners, and stockholders alike. These days, many companies prove as impermanent as the walls of the cubicles around which they're built.

It is no wonder that so many of us believe we live in an age not just of diminished expectation, but of diminished opportunity. Jobs—good jobs—are hard to land and of a long career with the firm that gave you your start. However, becoming an Office Superman will give you the tools you need to help build an exceptional career wherever you are today, tomorrow, or the next day. Here's the real beauty part: The ability to make yourself indispensable to the enterprise is completely portable. You may *lend* it to the enterprise, but it *belongs* to you, and you pack it up and take it with you, from one challenge to the next.

We've said that two things come to mind whenever Superman is mentioned: strength and flight. Here's a third: disguise. The cape and tights of the super hero are hidden under the business suit of a hard-working reporter. Adversity, it is said, is just opportunity in another set of clothes. Siegel and Shuster found opportunity in adversity when they carved Superman out of the stuff of worldwide depression and approaching war. Likewise, the Office Superman never turns away from adversity. Instead, he tears it off, sheds it, and finds the opportunity within. Be all that you *can* be? The Office Superman makes it his business to strip away the destructive doubleness from this army-surplus motto by rewriting it just a little bit: *Be all that you* choose *to be.*

Choose now to fly with the Man of Steel through the pages that follow.

1

WHIP OFF THE GLASSES, TEAR OFF THE SUIT

LET ME TELL YOU ABOUT MY FIRST TIME. I must have been four or five years old when I first saw, as through a Philco television, darkly, George "Superman" Reeves rescue Noel "Lois Lane" Neill and Jack "Jimmy Olsen" Larson from whatever lethal trap into which their journalistic curiosity had led them. By that time, *my* first time, Superman comics had been around for about eighteen years (having debuted in 1938) and *Adventures of Superman* had been playing on TV for four. The show, among broadcast television's first crop of programming, premiered in the fall of 1952, less than a month after I was born. I loved the show, and I watched it for years in reruns—it's *still* in reruns on the cable nostalgia channels—even after I was old enough to start reading the comic books. But let me tell you a little more about my first time. Everyone—or at least everyone around my age—knows the show's opening voice-over by heart the way the generation before mine knew by heart "The Gettysburg Address":

Faster than a speeding bullet! More powerful than a locomotive! Able to leap tall buildings in a single bound!

Look! Up in the sky. It's a bird. It's a plane. It's Superman!

Yes, it's Superman, strange visitor from another planet who came to Earth with powers and abilities far beyond those of mortal men. Superman—who can change the course of mighty rivers, bend steel in his bare hands, and who, disguised as Clark Kent, mild-mannered reporter for a great metropolitan newspaper, fights a never-ending battle for truth, justice, and the American way.

There it is. I remember every word. But when I heard these words the first time, I riveted on the phrase "disguised as Clark Kent." To me, at age four or five, this clearly implied not that Clark Kent was Superman's alter ego, but that Clark Kent was a real person, whom Superman sometimes disguised himself as. It took me, well, let's say a year or two to figure out that Clark Kent and Superman were one and the same, so that, for the first year or two that I watched the show, I always wondered whether I was looking at the *real* Clark Kent or Superman *disguised as* Clark Kent.

Put it another way: Superman disguised as Clark Kent is Superman disguised as himself, and, conversely, we could say that Clark Kent is also sometimes disguised as himself—that is, as Superman. As a preschooler, *I* may not have known who the "real" Clark Kent was, but Clark Kent/Superman was never in any doubt. Whether clad in the outer garments of the mild-mannered reporter or in the inner costume of Superman, he had the same powers and abilities far beyond those of mortal men.

After so many years piled up between "my first time" and now, this seems to me a key lesson of Superman. *Know who you are.* That's lesson number one. Lesson two? *Know that you are more than you think you are.*

Under that business suit of yours is a super man of business, an achiever capable of more than you may believe. This chapter tells you how to whip off the glasses and tear off the suit to get in touch with the Office Superman that you are.

The Stretch Factor

There are essentially two accounts of the origin of Superman's superpowers. For about the first ten years of Superman comics, the explanation was that the people of Krypton were a "super race" and that, as the sole survivor of that race, Superman has the powers shared by all of his fellow Kryptonians. Beginning in the late 1940s, however, the explanation changed. In the newer version, the people of Krypton were perfectly ordinary beings, but because of great differences between the gravity on Krypton and that on Earth, what was ordinary on Krypton became extraordinary on Earth. Superman's muscles were suited to the much greater gravitational force of Krypton. On Earth, with much less gravity, his strength was greatly magnified. Later issues of the comics added atmospheric considerations to the gravitational ones. As Superman's father, Jor-El, explained in a 1957 comic, "when a native Kryptonian is elsewhere, free of Krypton's unique atmosphere and tremendous gravitational pull, he becomes a superman!"

Just as the story of the source of Superman's powers evolved over time, so did the nature of those powers. When the Man of Steel debuted in *Action Comics* #1 (June 1938), he couldn't fly, but he could "leap $\frac{1}{8}$th of a mile" and was capable of hurdling a "twenty-story building." He was strong, but not unimaginably so, merely capable of raising "tremendous weights." Was he "faster than a speeding bullet"? No, but he was "faster than an express train." Most of us grew up thinking that Superman was invulnerable to everything except kryptonite, but in *Action Comics* #1 we are told that "nothing less than a bursting shell could penetrate his skin." Amazing durability, to be sure, but not invulnerable. Over the years, the creators of the Superman stories increasingly added to the super hero's powers. By the 1970s, Superman had penetrated to the core of the Sun without acquiring so much as a tan, he proved himself capable of flying thousands of times the speed of light, and he even used his prodigious lung capacity to blow out a star as if it were a candle.

Most of us have become all too familiar with inflation, not just in the realm of economics, but in just about everything, including, especially, entertainment. Each new action-adventure flick ups the ante with bigger explosions, faster and more reckless car chases, and oceans of blood and gore where mere lakes had earlier sufficed. It is no different with the comics, but it is also true that Superman's powers grew in proportion to the challenges with which he was confronted. In the earliest days, most of Superman's adversaries were gangsters, more or less common criminals. Over the years, however, the foes have become far more formidable, with whole worlds, even galaxies at stake. Thus Superman's powers did not grow arbitrarily, but increased in proportion to increased challenges and ever more desperate and demanding situations. In fact, while Superman's powers and the adversaries against which he uses them have become increasingly formidable, the creators of the Man of Steel never gave him an easy time, not even at the beginning. They always compelled their super hero to do his utmost, to risk failure, to stretch.

No mystery here, of course. A daring effort on the knife edge of danger—this is the essence of a good story. Had *Action Comics* #1 presented Superman in a cakewalk, there would have been no *Action Comics* #2, let alone more than six decades (and counting!) of Superman comics, movies, and TV shows.

But *why* are we so irresistibly compelled by stories of pushing the envelope? The poet Robert Browning said it a long time ago: "A man's reach should always exceed his grasp, or what's a heaven for?" It is in our best human nature to stretch, and acknowledging this is the first step toward discovering the Superman within.

Set Goals Worth Achieving

Stretching is always good exercise, but the effort has little meaning if you aren't score. I want to be in sales!" then the exercise has still succeeded in helping you make a choice.

In fact, if, after going through this exercise, you are still undecided, why not flip a coin? Seriously. This doesn't mean you've given up on making a choice. After all, you aren't *really* letting the coin choose. It works like this. You're struggling to choose between sales and accounting. Heads it's sales; tails, accounting. You flip and come up tails. You stare at the coin and say, "But I really want to be in sales!" The coin toss isn't important. What matters is how you respond to it. *That*, and not the coin toss, is your choice.

Audit Yourself

I have to admit that if I were suddenly given the superpower of flight, I would be tempted sometimes to fly around just for fun, aimlessly and without destination. This, however, is not something Superman really does. When he flies, it is always with a purpose and a destination firmly in mind. Of course, getting to where you want to go requires knowing where you are right now.

As important as it is to set worthwhile goals, it is equally important to form a realistic picture of where you're at before you begin your journey. You can put the picture together this way:

1. List your achievements for the week: projects begun, projects completed, bills paid—anything you feel good about.
2. On a piece of paper, write the following in a column: Personal Finances, Job Satisfaction, Career Potential, Education, Family, Relationships. Beside each category, write a number from 1 to 5 that expresses how you feel about each.

     1 = I feel terrible.

     3 = Could be better, could be worse.

     5 = I feel great about this.
3. Make a list of the things you most enjoy doing.
4. Make a list of things you do routinely but hate doing.
5. Make a list of your business and professional assets—not money resources, but personal skills, experience, and talent.
6. Make a list of your "external" business resources, including money resources available (you may have to complete number 8 first) and business contacts you have, including potential partners, colleagues, bosses, subordinates, and customers.
7. Make a list of your business and professional liabilities, faults, weaknesses, or areas that require improvement.
8. Assess your current financial situation. Draw up a balance sheet showing assets and liabilities. Include regular income and expenses, assets (such as house, car,

stocks), debts (such as outstanding loans), and bank account balances. Jot down everything you spend in a week's time. Write down anticipated major expenses coming up in the next year. Don't forget to make a separate list of things that you regularly use your credit cards for. Write down how much money you save and/or invest annually.

To get to point B, you need to know the location of point A.

Devote serious time to this self-audit, and you will have a clear picture of point A, your present location.

Explore the Gap

Once you have defined a worthwhile goal or a set of goals and after you have painted an accurate picture of your present circumstances, you should be able to see the gap that separates you from your goal. Superman could leap this in a single bound. You, however, need to determine what's necessary to fill the gap or to bridge it.

Some of this will be obvious. If, for instance, your professional goal is to make the leap from bookkeeper to accountant, you know that a certain amount of further education is required. It should be a simple matter to determine what college or continuing education coursework is necessary to get yourself certified. Acquire the academic credits, and most of the gap will be filled.

However, determining some of the things you need will not be so obvious or easy. Probably the most effective way to begin the process of reaching your goal is by exercising your imagination. Visualize your goal. At present, you are an entry-level bookkeeper with your firm. Your goal is to become manager of the accounting department. Sit back, close your eyes, and start imagining what that would be like. Go ahead and imagine the perks and the professional satisfaction, but don't forget also to picture the responsibilities, the crises, the fact that a lot of people will come to you desperately looking for solutions to their problems.

Most of us are taught from an early age that daydreaming is a waste of time and something to be avoided. Let your mind wander at school, and the teacher will send a sharp word your way. You need to overcome this early negative training. Give yourself permission to daydream. Devote some serious time to visualizing your goal and everything that achieving your goal entails. It is always easier to address issues and solve problems that you can actually *see*. See them now.

Balance your imaginary journey with whatever hard information you can obtain. Research your options. To achieve A, I need to do B, C, D, and E. Read about people who have already attained your goal. Seek such people out and talk to them. They don't have to be friends or acquaintances. Look up the director of the accounting department in your firm or in some other firm, call her, tell her that you are currently a bookkeeper at XYZ Incorporated and that your professional goal is to become an accounting director. "It would really help me to focus my career if I could speak with you about what you do." Don't think of this request as asking a favor or, much less, creating an imposition. The fact is that most people who have achieved something actually *want* to help others, and they are also flattered that you value their knowledge, experience, and achievement.

The Failure to Plan Is a Plan for Failure

Once you have established some worthwhile goals, make a plan to achieve them. Used at whim or randomly, even Superman's superpowers would accomplish little and might well end up wrecking a lot. It is amazing how few of us devote serious time to planning for success. At best, a minority of us plan to avoid failure, but this is a negative rather than a positive plan. It is about avoidance, not achievement. And this, inadequate though it is, is more planning than the majority does. Most of us simply take whatever paths offer least resistance at a given time or place. We may count the absence of adversity as proof of success, but it is proof only of having avoided both failure *and* success.

Begin by focusing and defining. Make use of the steps and procedures we've discussed earlier in this chapter. Part of the process of focusing and defining is prioritizing. Create a schedule, a time plan for the day, the week, the month. Start managing your time. This will accomplish three things:

First: It will provide an inventory of tasks that you need to do, will help ensure that each gets its fair share of time, and will reduce the chances of important activities falling between the cracks.

Second: You keep some account of your money, your personal funds, what you spend, what you bring in, what you have on hand. You do this because money is scarce and valuable. Well, time's even more scarce and more valuable. So it is imperative that you account for it. At the very least, doing so will continually remind you of the value of your time.

Third: Managing time gives you a great measure of control over your life and, equally important, gives you the feeling—the positive, empowering feeling—of being in control of your life.

Another important part of planning is getting the help and support you need. Civilization and all the progress and goodies that go along with it are based on a simple assumption: Relatively little is achieved by working alone. In his earliest days, Superman was a solo super hero, but by the mid-1950s he was part of the Justice League of America, a team of super heroes who, together, could accomplish more good than any of them could achieve alone.

Acquire the habit of asking for help. Do not make yourself a prisoner of an I-can-do-it-alone attitude. Collaborate. Your colleagues do not want to do your work for you, but just about everyone derives satisfaction from helping. They are flattered and honored by being asked. They feel good when they have contributed to a successful outcome. Don't wait for a crisis to ask for help. Identify sources of advice and instruction. Talk to them. Make them your mentors.

The final part of any plan for success is, quite simply, to plan for *success* rather than to just look out for failure. If you spend your time cringing in anticipation of disaster, you will not be able to recognize opportunity when you meet it. Think in positive terms. Look for opportunity. Expect success.

Execute and Persist

As you'll see in the next chapter, the first character Jerry Siegel and Joe Shuster called Superman was a breadline derelict named Bill Dunn who receives, as the result of a scientific experiment, extraordinary mental powers. Siegel and Shuster soon abandoned this character and, after years of work, came up with a new Superman, whose superpowers were not primarily mental (though he does have some of those), but paramountly physical. A man of action, Superman's creators realized, is far more attractive than a man who thinks but does not act. To be sure, Superman is thoughtful. He even has a super-secluded Fortress of Solitude to which he resorts when he needs a quiet place for contemplation. But he is above all an *action* hero, a doer.

Take stock, evaluate, formulate, and plan. These steps are essential to reaching the Superman within you. But they mean nothing if they remain unacted upon. No plan should be made without the intention of acting on it. Action *may bring* failure. Inaction *is* failure.

Expect success. Act on opportunity. Failure to do so does not merely pass up an opportunity—which is bad enough—but, most of the time, it makes that opportunity available to someone else. You lose not only a personal competition, but also forfeit a contest against everyone who competes for the same position, salary, and advancement you're looking for.

Whatever else action may be, it is *change*. You can put up a display of frenetic activity and get nowhere, of course, but real action, purposeful action, always entails change. Be willing to change and be prepared for change. Clinging to the status quo does not build a career and is not the way of the Office Superman. The Man of Steel is never afraid to whip off the glasses, tear off the suit, and take a well-planned leap.

C H A P T E R

2

BACKSTORY

NO ONE IS BORN A BUM, A CRIMINAL, OR A CEO. Everyone is taught an array of roles by role models. This is absolute truth and cannot be disputed. However, there are varying degrees involved.

True, people are born into different socioeconomic situations and are endowed by genetics with this or that natural asset or liability. Some people are born rich or poor, born into a family of business leaders or into a family of criminals, born with a gene for genius or with one that puts a serious cap on mental capacity. And, yes, the circumstances of time and place also play their part. As Depression- and war-era president Franklin Roosevelt said, "To some generations much is given. Of other generations much is expected."

Genetics, family economic status, and the opportunity of a particular time and place we customarily lump under the rubric "luck," and either you got it or you ain't. But *luck* is just a label, and the trouble with a label is that it is so easily mistaken for an answer. Branch Rickey, the legendary president and general manager of the Brooklyn Dodgers in the 1940s, a man who dared to change the world by crossing professional baseball's supposedly sacrosanct "color line" when he hired infield great Jackie Robinson, dismissed "luck" as the "residue of design." Luck matters, but

Cleveland was predominantly Jewish, and, as Jews, Siegel and Shuster had religion and culture in common with many of their classmates, too. But if it was hard times for most of the world, it looked to be especially hard times for Jews, as anyone could predict who eyed the rise of Adolf Hitler across the Atlantic.

Whoever you were and however you sliced it, it was tough living in Cleveland and it was tough to be a Jew in 1931, but there was nothing special about any of that. In fact, on the face of it, there was nothing special at all about Siegel and Shuster. Neither was an athlete, neither was particularly good-looking, and neither was a shining star where academics were concerned. Many youngsters at Glenville were obvious overachievers, full of ambition to become lawyers, doctors, and, well, all-round successes. Siegel and Shuster's classmates included the great psychologist Albert Maslow (creator of the clinical theory of "transactional analysis"), the playwright Jerome Lawrence (co-author of *Inherit the Wind* and *Auntie Mame*), journalist Charlotte Plimer (who would turn *Seventeen* magazine into an unprecedented teen sensation), and Seymour Heller, the legendary big-time show-biz manager, whose most famous client was Liberace.

What did Siegel and Shuster want to be in 1931? They couldn't say. Maybe it was because they didn't yet know. Or maybe because they didn't have the nerve to say it. Because what they wanted to be was what they were *right now:* dreamers.

They worked together on the school newspaper, the *Glenville Torch,* Siegel writing and Shuster drawing cartoons. They also shared a passion for science fiction, and, in the pages of the *Torch*, Siegel even announced the impending publication of his new magazine, *Science Fiction: The Advance Guard of Future Civilization,* setting a target circulation of five million. In the meantime, he wrote comic pieces and lurid mysteries for the *Torch*, then created Goober the Mighty, a parody of Tarzan, who, as he flexes his muscles, declares in his debut appearance, May 7, 1931, "By Jove, one year from now I'll be the strongest man on Earth!" The kids at Glenville loved it, thought it was hilarious, but Siegel had his eye on a bigger audience. He kept writing science fiction stories, submitted them to the pulp magazines he and Shuster read and reread, and, time after time, was rejected.

In October 1932, Siegel came out with the first issue of *Science Fiction.* If it didn't fulfill the dream of a five million circulation, the mimeographed magazine at least made a down payment on it. Shuster designed an impressive cover featuring a *moderne*-style graphic, and he provided illustrations throughout. In January 1933, the third issue featured a short story Siegel called "The Reign of the Superman."

Fantasy and Reality

This story was not exactly the birth of Superman, certainly not as we would come to know him. As written by Siegel and illustrated by Shuster, the character of Bill Dunn is a bald megalomaniac whose ambition is to initiate the reign of the superman, namely himself, in order to dominate not merely the world, but the universe.

It was a fantasy born both of the Great Depression and the emerging Age of Great Dictators. Bill Dunn wasn't born a megalomaniac, but is transformed into one by a latter-day Dr. Frankenstein named Professor Ernest Smalley. Looking for a subject on which to experiment, Smalley finds Dunn in a Depression breadline, takes him to his laboratory, and there exposes him to a mysterious chemical refined from an element found in a meteor that had fallen from outer space. The effect is sort of kryptonite-in-reverse. The chemical does not weaken Dunn, but gives him super-powers. His new-found strength is not physical, however, but mental. Dunn escapes from Smalley and finds that he can use telepathy to control the thoughts of anyone he wishes.

At first, "the Superman" acts much as Siegel or Shuster might have. He dreams. He focuses his prodigious mental powers on outer space to watch a war between bizarre creatures on the planet Mars. But then he gets down to earth and down to business. He begins to exercise his telepathic powers to obtain wealth, first through outright theft and then by means of a program of rigged gambling schemes and stock manipulation. When Professor Smalley fathoms Dunn's nefarious plots, he decides that the only way to combat him is to administer the chemical to himself. Before he can carry this out, however, Dunn kills him, then ups the ante on his evil doing. If, in drawing Dunn, Shuster had in mind the look of another would-be world ruler, the bald and jut-jawed Benito Mussolini, Siegel now furnished a plot truly worthy of the Italian strongman. Dunn exercises his mental powers to destroy a great international peace conference, reasoning that a world-engulfing war is just the ticket to create the chaos that will make the planet ripe for his conquest. Today Germany, Hitler declared, tomorrow—the world! For Siegel and Shuster's Bill Dunn, it is the world today, and tomorrow—the universe!

Fortunately for all creation, the effects of Professor Smalley's chemical prove temporary. They wear off, and Dunn, no longer super, exits the stage, presumably to resume his place in the breadline.

If Cleveland had been Hollywood, this disappearance, a highly indefinite ending, would have telegraphed the single glowing word *sequel*. But Siegel and Shuster never used the character again. As if he had known Dunn would be a one-shot, Jerry Siegel didn't even sign his own name to his creation. He called himself Herbert S. Fine (a combination of his mother's maiden name and the first name of the cousin who had introduced him to Joe Shuster).

Instead of another evil Superman, Siegel and Shuster briefly toyed with the idea million (for starters!) were high school seniors who struggled to make ends meet with a delivery job and by selling ice cream on the corner. The Depression was relentless. If the Siegel household was struggling, the Shusters were downright desperate. The heat had been turned off in their apartment, and Siegel remembers his severely nearsighted, bespectacled friend wrapped in several sweaters, hunched over his drawing board, myopic eyes a few inches from the work, his drawing medium whatever he could scrounge: red-brown blotchy butcher paper or the back of a scrap of wallpaper remnant. At the moment and under such circumstances, the pair had little more than a glimmer of a character cobbled together from various comic strip characters, including Popeye the Sailor Man and pieces of book and movie heroes such as the Scarlet Pimpernel, Zorro, and Robin Hood. As for the name, "the Superman," that had been borrowed, too, though from sources of a different class.

The word *Übermensch* was coined by the German philosopher Friedrich Nietzsche in his *Thus Spake Zarathustra*, published in four parts between 1883 and 1885. Sometimes translated as "Overman" but more usually as "Superman," this figure was Nietzsche's idea of the superior human being, whose imagination, will, and creativity place him above the general run of humanity and beyond the reach of ordinary petty morality. In 1903, the Irish playwright George Bernard Shaw published *Man and Superman,* a play based in part on Nietzsche's philosophy. Siegel may have picked up the word from one of these sources, perhaps in a high school literature class, or he may simply have pulled it out of the air. Because, by 1933, that is where it was. Adolf Hitler and his Nazis had selectively appropriated the ideas of Nietzsche and frequently spoke of the "German race" as a race of *Übermenschen*, Supermen.

The irony of a Jewish American high schooler calling his fictional super hero by a name bandied about by Nazis is hard to miss, especially when we consider that many of the Superman comics of the World War II years would pit the Man of Steel against these very *Übermenschen*, Nazi agents and villains. In a world filled with news of anti-Semitic Nietzsche-quoting Nazis, was there something self-consciously personal about Siegel's growing obsession with the Superman idea? Maybe. Siegel and Shuster surely longed for comic book success to pull them out of Depression poverty. Perhaps Siegel also wanted to "steal" Superman from the thugs who were already menacing the Jews of Europe. We don't know. Siegel never said. But we do know that, about 1934, a year after the crushing disappointment of Consolidated Book, the whole Superman idea suddenly got very personal, and, as soon as it did, Superman—*our* familiar Superman—erupted almost fully formed from the mind of Jerry Siegel and the cartooning pen of Joe Shuster.

In 1983, an interviewer asked Siegel about the origin of Clark Kent. Shuster was a "mild-mannered" guy who wore thick glasses. Was *he* the model? "Clark Kent grew not only out of my private life," Siegel responded, "but also out of Joe's. As a high school student, I thought that some day I might become a reporter, and I had crushes on several attractive girls who either didn't know I existed or didn't care I existed. . . . It occurred to me: What if I . . . had something special going for me, like jumping over buildings or throwing cars around or something like that? . . . Joe was a carbon copy of me." Shuster agreed: "I was mild-mannered, wore glasses, was very shy with women." In the artwork, Siegel said, Shuster "wasn't just drawing it, he was feeling it."

As soon as Siegel and Shuster reached into themselves, created from their own feelings, needs, ambitions, and lives, the miscellany of sources—comic strip heroes, movie idols, even Nietzsche's *Übermensch*—came together, not, as before, in a rather nondescript character who just happened to be called "the Superman," but in *the* Superman.

Gripped by the new idea late in 1934, Siegel stayed up all night writing new Superman stories. Clutching these, he rushed over to the Shuster family apartment early in the morning, and the two started to develop the character. Penniless, awkward, shy, living in a world that stacked the odds against them, the boys from Cleveland designed their hero, *their* super hero, a fantasy figure based on real life, their real lives, and embodying all that was necessary to climb above those lives and reach into something better.

Strong Ingredients

Their super hero would have superpowers, but not the sinister mental abilities of a Bill Dunn. Instead, Superman would be the ultimate strongman, who also possessed prodigious athletic and acrobatic ability. He could outfight, out jump, and outrun anyone, including the most diabolical and powerful of thugs. His enemies would be common criminals but, very soon, also crooked politicians, tyrants, and anyone who had injustice and evil in mind. Superman would, in effect, make himself indispensable to society.

Literature, folklore, and mythology are full of strongman heroes —think of Samson from the Old Testament or Hercules from Greek lore—but Siegel and Shuster kept thinking, and they built on this universal foundation a unique character. The costume came early in the process. Shuster said, "Let's give him a big *S* on his chest, and a cape, make him as colorful as we can and as distinctive as we can." This was not an original idea. Douglas Fairbanks's Robin Hood, a matinee favorite of the boys, was clearly identified by his form-fitting outfit, and Flash Gordon, a character that had debuted in newspaper strips earlier in the year, wore a distinctive tights outfit. But Shuster took these elements and made them unique: the colors were bright, and the *S* within its shield was not only graphically striking, it suggested at once a kind of noble or knightly crest as well as the badge of an ultimate—*interplanetary,* no less—policeman.

Interplanetary. Why did Siegel and Shuster design their super hero as a being from outer space? Why not a garden variety earthling? Interviewed in the 1980s, the boys were none too illuminating on this point. "It just happened that way," Siegel said, and Shuster lamely added: "We just thought it was a good idea."

The fact is that Siegel and Shuster thought of themselves as creating science fiction, and in 1934 science fiction usually involved something or someone from outer space. But whatever the conscious motives behind their decision to make Superman a strange visitor from another planet, the choice freighted this super hero with much of the stuff that has made him so appealing for so long.

If Superman was the ultimate strongman, athlete, and cop, his origin on the planet Krypton also made him the ultimate immigrant. That meant a lot to Americans, most of whom were two, three, or just one generation removed from an origin elsewhere and many of whom were immigrants themselves. All too typically, the American immigrant experience involved as much prejudice, oppression, and even persecution as it did empowerment, and, in Superman, Siegel and Shuster created an immigrant who possessed great power and used it against all who would prey upon the weak and disenfranchised. Even more immediately, Superman was not just an immigrant, he was a refugee, sole survivor of a planet torn apart by irresistible internal forces. By 1934, the rise of fascism and Naziism was already beginning to produce political exiles, adding to the hundreds of thousands who had, since 1776, sought in the United States freedom from foreign oppressors. Superman-as-immigrant must have struck a chord with Americans, but his outer space origins made him even more than a super immigrant. Many religions feature saviors of extraterrestrial origin, Christianity being the most familiar to many of us. Can that *S* on Superman's chest suggest Savior?

The story of Superman's origin has been subject over the years to several revisions. The earliest version portrays a nameless motorist discovering the "sleeping babe within" the crash-landed spaceship that had been launched from doomed Krypton; he turns the baby over to an orphanage, where Clark Kent grows into Superman. Later versions tell of a discovery by kindly, childless Jonathan and Martha Kent, who raise the rocket-borne baby as their own. All versions are variations on the "holy foundling" theme present in many mythologies and most familiar in the Judeo-Christian tradition as the story of Moses, a foundling set adrift in a basket and recovered among the bulrushes.

It's fun to poke around the awesome social-mythic-religious pedigree of Superman, but the important point to make about it is this: Siegel and Shuster had created a true super hero, a character of depth and genuine value, a figure that would not only give rise to thousands of very good stories, but a figure worthy of being accepted as a role model, an example of ethical and powerful conduct.

The Superman Within

Siegel and Shuster came close to creating in Superman a comic book deity. Good thing they didn't come *too* close, because as good as it is to be a god, there's one thing a god can never be: a hero.

Mere mortals inhabit one plane of existence, gods another, and never the twain shall meet. Most religions address this problem by providing beings who partake of both levels, who are godlike and human at the same time. Think of the Greek Prometheus, the Hindu Buddha, or the Christian Christ. Siegel and Shuster addressed their version of this problem by providing Superman with an alter ego, Clark Kent, the earthly incarnation of the otherworldly super hero. Kent was a reporter, the profession Siegel imagined himself one day pursuing. Kent wore glasses, just like Shuster. Mild mannered, he was awkward around women, especially Lois Lane, for whom he longed. This was something both young Siegel and Shuster identified with. If the character of Superman owes something to Douglas Fairbanks, as Siegel claimed it did, Shuster once remarked that "Clark Kent, I suppose, had a little bit of Harold Lloyd in him." Whereas Fairbanks was the cinema swashbuckler's swashbuckler, Lloyd was considered the comedian's comedian of the silent screen. Known as the "Glasses Comedian" because of his trademark big round horn rims, Lloyd dressed neither like a clown nor a Chaplinesque "Little Tramp," but always wore the slightly stiff suit and tie of the average young man. That he fit into the crowd made his zany daredevil physical comedy all the more hilarious.

Movie audiences may have variously fantasized about the likes of Douglas Fairbanks, but they identified with cinema's Harold Lloyds. Clark Kent was Siegel and Shuster's enduring link of self-identification with the super hero they had created, and he served a similar purpose for generations of comic book readers and film and TV viewers. Clark Kent humanized Superman as Jesus humanizes God or Buddha humanizes the Everlasting Om. But this did not mean that Clark Kent "brought Superman down" to a human level anymore than Christ "reduces" God to mere human terms. Instead, the character of Clark Kent brings us *up* closer to the level of Superman. The powerful message this *Daily Planet* reporter conveys is that a Superman may dwell within even the most mild mannered among us. Therein lies perhaps the brightest spark of Siegel and Shuster's genius. In his red cape and boots, blue tights, and yellow belt, Superman cuts a dazzling figure, but it is the ordinary suit and tie of Clark Kent that commands our attention over the long haul. Clark's suit, not Superman's costume, is the uniform *we* wear, and it is thrilling to contemplate that, within each of us, beneath our perfectly ordinary exterior, beats the heart of a Superman.

3

CODE OF A SUPER HERO

FASTER THAN A SPEEDING BULLET, MORE POWERFUL THAN A LOCOMO-TIVE, YADDA, YADDA, YADDA. It's easy to see why Superman has appealed to generations of kids. For them, the fascination with superspeed, the ability to fly, superstrength, superhearing, X-ray vision, and something approaching invulnerability is endless. Add to that such novelties as superbreath (Superman can stay underwater indefinitely by holding his breath, he can extinguish a massive fire by blowing it out, or can halt an advancing tidal wave by freezing it with a blast of breath) and superventriloquism (Superman can mimic anyone, broadcast his voice thousands of miles, yell at 1,000,000 decibels) and what child could resist?

But, let's face it, the ideal appeal of all those superpowers wears a little thin somewhere past puberty. The average reader of Superman comics is 21 years old. As a cultural icon, it's proof that Superman never loses his potency. It's like he's discovered some pop-culture Viagra. For instance, the first *Superman* movie, released in 1978, was a hit with adults, as were *Superman II* (1980), *Superman III* (1983), and *Superman IV* (1987). Back in 1966, it wasn't kids who were ponying up Broadway ticket prices for *It's a Bird, It's a Plane, It's*

Superman, a musical comedy produced and directed by no less than Harold Prince, who, with twenty Tony Award wins by 1999, holds the record. *The Adventures of Superman* TV series of the early 1950s was certainly aimed at the younger set, but *Lois and Clark: The New Adventures of Superman*, which premiered on ABC in 1993 and ran through 1996, was a sexy romantic adventure series, and *Smallville*, which premiered on the WB Network in 2001, is all about Clark Kent's teen years.

Even the superpowers of a Man of Steel can't support an audience this large, diverse, and durable. Packaged one way or another, Superman has ended up appealing to just about everyone of any age. We're all fans—some more than others, to be sure, but you'd be hard pressed to find a person who doesn't have at least some very positive associations with Superman.

What's going on here?

For kids, it's all about the superpowers. That's what gets you into Superman in the first place. But, as you grow up, you discover that Superman is much more than the sum of his superpowers. He is a super hero, with the accent on hero.

The Hero

Ask a child what a *hero* is, and you are likely to get a definition that fits Superman pretty well. As most kids see it, a hero is a man with great strength and exceptional abilities combined with courage. This childish or naive definition of *hero* is quite close to the meaning of the word conveyed in mythology and legend. The ancient Greek heroes, for instance, are men endowed with great courage and strength celebrated for their bold exploits. Furthermore, the legendary hero is almost always of divine ancestry—a parallel with Superman's extraterrestrial birth. It is no accident that the child's definition of hero should so closely resemble the hero of myth. The age of myth, after all, corresponds to a kind of childhood of human civilization.

Put the emphasis on Superman's superpowers, and the childish/mythic definition of *hero* works just fine for the Man of Steel. Yet it is not a complete definition. Superman is indeed a man of great strength and courage, whose origin is, in a sense, divine. But he is also much more.

Our Hero

Superman debuted in *Action Comics* #1, published in June 1938. This very first story begins with a highly compressed account of Superman's origin: "As a distant planet was destroyed by old age, a scientist placed his infant son within a hastily devised spaceship, launching it toward Earth!" A year later, in the summer of 1939, *Superman* #1, would fill in some of the names and details: "Just before the doomed planet, Krypton, exploded to fragments, a scientist placed his infant son within an

SUPERMAN

Debut: *Action Comics* #1, June 1938
Real Name: Kal-El

A refugee from Krypton, his doomed native world, the infant Kal-El was rocketed to Earth by his scientist father, Jor-El, and his wife, Lara. After landing near Smallville, Kansas, the rocket was discovered by Jonathan and Martha Kent, who rescued the infant, named him Clark, and raised him as their own son.

Born on a planet with a red sun, Clark grew into young manhood under Earth's yellow sun, which confers on him extraordinary powers, including great strength, super-senses, and the ability to fly. He is also nearly invulnerable, except to the radiation from kryptonite, a substance that reached Earth from his shattered native planet and that, under Earth's yellow sun, is lethal to any Kryptonian.

Jonathan and Martha Kent encouraged the boy to keep his powers and his origin secret, but after he graduated from high school, Clark spent seven years exploring the world in search of a worthy career and decided to become a super hero. Using materials from his spacecraft, Kal-El fashioned a costume reflecting his Kryptonian roots, which he wears when he is not "disguised" as Clark Kent. Deciding that he could best serve humankind by closely monitoring world events, he secured a job as reporter for Metropolis' *Daily Planet*. It was the paper's star reporter, Lois Lane, who, seeing the super hero in action and noting the Kryptonian "S" symbol emblazoned on his chest, conferred on Kal-El the name Superman.

Thus Superman began his dual life as a mild-mannered reporter and a foe of criminals, tyrants, and would-be destroyers of the world. Thus also he began to fall in love with Lois Lane, and the two eventually married.

experimental rocket ship, launching it toward Earth!" We next learn that "an elderly couple, the Kents" found the rocket, retrieved the baby inside, and turned him over to an orphanage. A short time later, the Kents returned to the orphanage.

"We—we couldn't get that sweet child out of our mind," Mr. Kent says. "We've come to adopt him if you'll permit us,"explains Mrs. Kent. The orphanage director replies: "I believe it can be arranged" while thinking to himself: "Whew! Thank goodness they're taking him away before he wrecks the asylum!"

The third panel of the story shows the diaper-clad refugee from Krypton hefting a large dresser above his head, a broken board having been shoved to the side. This is humorous, of course, but there is a serious point: We're all lucky that babies don't have superpowers. Lacking mature judgment and a developed moral sense, a superbaby would wreck everything in sight. That's precisely the problem with superpowers. Remarkable as they are, in and of themselves they are no more than tools, which can be used well or used poorly, constructively or destructively. As a craftsman needs good tools, a super hero needs nifty superpowers, but, in unskilled hands, even the best tools are useless or worse than useless, and in a person without moral judgment, superpowers can wreak havoc. In panel number 5, still on page 1 of the story, Siegel and Shuster address this issue. Mr. Kent lays a kindly hand on his adopted son's shoulder.

"Now listen to me, Clark! This great strength of yours—you've got to hide it from people or they'll be scared of you!" Mrs. Kent adds: "But when the proper time comes you must use it to assist humanity."

It is an important moment in the life of Superman. This panel provides an explanation for the necessity of disguise and also lays the foundation of Superman's career as a doer of good. Here, Mr. and Mrs. Kent focus their adopted son's attention on the needs of others. Disguise yourself, Mr. Kent says, so that you don't scare others. Use your powers to help others, counsels Mrs. Kent.

The next half-dozen panels quickly take us through Clark Kent's growth into adolescence and young adulthood. With him, we discover his superpowers: "As the lad grew older, he learned to his delight that he could hurdle skyscrapers . . . leap an eighth of a mile . . . raise tremendous weights . . . run faster than a streamline train—and nothing less than a bursting shell could penetrate his skin!" This proves a problem for young Clark's physician, who we see sputtering, "What th'—? This is the sixth hypodermic needle I've broken on your skin!"

The seventh panel shows Clark gazing down at the headstones of his adoptive parents, whose passing "greatly grieved" him "but . . . strengthened a determination that had been growing in his mind. Clark decided he must turn his titanic strength into channels that would benefit mankind. And so was created—SUPERMAN, champion of the oppressed, the physical marvel who had sworn to devote his existence to helping those in need!"

Thus, at the end of the second page of this very early Superman story, we are brought to what we might call the mature definition of *hero*. Both children and myth define a hero as a man with great strength and exceptional abilities combined with courage. The more mature and modern definition reinforces the aspect of courage, but adds nobility of purpose and a willingness to sacrifice self for others. To pull off a heroic deed, one must have some skills or powers, and the more skillful and more powerful the better, but more important is nobility and selflessness.

The 1939 *Superman* #1 now picks up the story first told in *Action Comics* #1. The young adult Superman goes on to rescue an unjustly convicted man from a lynch mob and then sets out to bring to justice the real murderer, a floozie named Bea Carroll, singer at the Hilow nightclub, who "rubbed out" one Jack Kennedy "for two-timing her." Working against the clock—for another woman, Evelyn Curry, has also been wrongly convicted of the murder and is facing imminent execution—Superman takes himself to the Hilow and waits for Bea in her dressing room. The scene is provocative: "Say! What are you doing in my room?" Bea asks. "Waiting for *you*, naturally!" Superman replies.

But there will be no romance.

"I thought you might be interested in learning I know that you killed Jack Kennedy!" Superman goes on to tell Bea that Sims, the man he saved from the lynch mob, "told me everything—how you shot Jack, then framed Evelyn!"

Now Bea, hands on hips: "You attract me! Couldn't we talk this over?"

Bea's charms prove ineffective on the Man of Steel. "You're wasting your time! I'm only interested in seeing that you get what's coming to you."

The stories of all maturely defined heroes, whether Ulysses, Superman, or even Jesus Christ, have in common the theme of temptation, which all mature heroes successfully resist. The point of this resistance is not self-denial in and of itself, but sacrifice for the benefit of others. For Superman, temptation comes early—on page 6 of *Action Comics* #1—and his successful resistance to it marks him, from the outset of his career, as a mature hero.

Superman continues his first adventure by carrying Bea off, not to some tryst, but to make a confession to the governor, who pardons the doomed Evelyn Curry just minutes before the warden is scheduled to pull the switch.

The salvation accomplished, Superman, now as Clark Kent, brings the exclusive story back to the (as-yet unnamed) editor of the *Daily Star* (it would not become the more familiar *Daily Planet* until *Action Comics* #22 in March 1940). This feat wins Kent a job as a reporter.

Well, he earned the job, and who would begrudge a *little* harmless profit from a good deed? However, Superman sought even this modest benefit not for himself but because (as he soliloquized), "If I get news dispatches promptly, I'll be in a better position to help people. *I've got to get that job!*"

Action Comics #1 continues with Superman stopping what today would be called an episode of domestic violence (but which Siegel and Shuster called "a wife-beating at 211 Court Ave"). This done, the bashful Clark Kent works up the courage to ask fellow reporter Lois Lane out on the town: "W-what do you say to a—er—date tonight, Lois?" The date goes sour, however, when gangster Butch Hatson cuts in on Clark and Lois as they dance. Of course, Superman could easily dispose of the interloper, but that would probably blow his cover.

"Clark! Are you going to stand for this?" a disgusted Lois exclaims.

"Be reasonable, Lois. Dance with the fellow and then we'll leave right away."

The result of these words is painfully humiliating. "You can stay and dance with him if you wish," Lois says, "but I'm leaving NOW!" And when the gangster interjects, "Yeah? You'll dance with me and like it!" Lois slaps him across the face. "Lois—Don't!" Clark exclaims, even as he thinks silently: "Good for you, Lois!"

The gangster now turns to Clark: "Fight . . . you weak-livered pole-cat!"

As the badman pushes his palm into Clark's face, the mild-mannered reporter can manage nothing more threatening than, "Really—I have no desire to do so!"

In the meantime, Lois, having donned her coat, storms out. Clark rushes out to her taxi, and, as she is about to drive away, she calls him a "spineless, unbearable *coward!*"

Now the humiliation is total. A comic book? This is downright painful to read. But that is the point. Superman is willing to suffer painful humiliation as well as sacrifice what he hopes will be a budding romance in order to preserve the disguise that puts him "in a better position to help people."

Superman/Kent does not take time to mope. Realizing that Butch Hatson won't take a slap in the face from any woman, he is seen next in his Superman costume, watching from a hill as Hatson and his thugs drive in pursuit of Lois's taxi. They overtake the cab, seize Lois, and drive off with her in their sedan. Superman blocks the road, the felonious vehicle bears down on him, he leaps over the onrushing car, then runs behind it, overtakes it, lifts it with one hand, shakes out the occupants, then smashes the car against some rocks. Apprehending the fleeing Butch Hatson, Superman suspends him by the seat of his pants from a telephone pole. This done, he takes Lois into his arms and transports her by leaps and bounds (for Superman does not actually fly until the early 1940s) back to the city. As for Clark Kent, the next morning, at the office, Lois treats him "colder than ever."

The rescue of Lois Lane, totally selfless, must have been very hard on poor Clark, but he wastes no time licking his wounds. Instead, he next embarks on a mission to stop a corrupt senator from bulldozing through Congress a dangerous piece of legislation: "The bill will be passed before its full implications are realized," Senator Barrow remarks to a fellow conspirator. "Before any remedial steps can be taken, our country will be embroiled with Europe." It is a story that will be continued in *Action Comics* #2.

You, Hero

Consider this very first installment of Superman. No doubt about it, the superpowers of a super hero are a lot of fun, yet the central theme here is of the disciplined use of those powers, which means self-sacrifice. Clearly, the superpowers drew a crowd of kids to *Action Comics*, but it is the discipline and self-sacrifice, the maturity of Superman, that make the Man of Steel an *enduring* hero, a character who still interests us after all these years.

Yet do these qualities make him a suitable role model?

The pat answer is Yes, of course. But, superpowers aside, the Superman of *Action Comics* #1 is a very tough act to follow. Maybe you just want to be more successful at your job, get ahead further and faster at the office. Is it the lesson of Superman that you have to give up everything up to do this?

If it were easy to imitate a hero, everyone would be a hero, and stories about heroes would be too common to hold our interest. The point is that heroism isn't easy, but hard, so hard that it's the exception, not the rule, it's newsworthy, worth our special attention. The example of the hero is not intended for literal-minded imitation, but for inspiration. The example of the mature hero does not teach acts of self-sacrifice, but the principle behind self-sacrifice. You can, in fact, be a hero without giving up everything, but the one thing you *must* give up is an exclusive focus on yourself.

Superman's code, the code of a super hero, is to serve others. Now, in the real world, *your* world, the world of your business, your clients, your bosses, your colleagues, your subordinates, this kind of self-sacrifice, action to benefit the collective enterprise, is the very thing that elevates you to the position of Office Superman. Put others first, in the context of your business, and you will become everyone's go-to guy. Become the go-to guy, and, be assured, you will be rewarded.

Learning the Code

Putting others first poses moral challenges, of course, but, intellectually, it seems pretty straightforward. For example, an opportunity comes your way. Instead of taking it for yourself, you give it to Joe in the next cubicle. Right?

Couldn't be further from right.

Focusing on what others want does not mean giving up your place in line. It means learning to get ahead by giving others what they need.

Consider the classic job interview question: "Why should I give you this job?" The most honest answer might well be, "Because I need the money," but that's far less likely to land you the job than something like, "Because I offer the skills you need." In the job interview situation, most of us know enough to be a hero or, at least, to present ourselves as one by telling the interviewer how we will help *him*.

Or consider another situation, the last time you bought a car, for instance. On that occasion, the salesperson could have said, "Buy this car so that I can pay my mortgage this month." Such a pitch might well reflect the salesperson's truest motive. But he didn't say anything of the kind, did he? Doubtless, he talked to you about safety, performance, economy, resale value, and so on—all the benefits the sale will bestow on you and none of the benefits it will give him.

This isn't rocket science. In fact, in many situations, we almost instinctively put the focus on what the other person needs, and we do this precisely to derive a benefit for ourselves. The difference between most of us and the hero is that the hero raises this instinct to a more conscious, consistent, and deliberate level. Those who aspire to be an Office Superman must learn to do likewise. Develop the habit of looking for ways to be so helpful that you make yourself indispensable.

You should not have to look very hard.

Jane in Accounting says to you, "Uh-oh. We've got a real problem."

Your first inclination is to duck and cover. Racing through your head is the thought *Why me?* Or, *Keep on walking, Jane.* Or, *No, Jane.* You've *got a real problem. I don't want any part of it.* Don't follow your first inclination. Instead, respond with: "How may I help?" Then let Jane lay out a course of action.

Learn to embrace problems as opportunities to excel, not as calamities from which to hide.

You pass by Ed's cubicle. He's holding his head and moaning. You're a naturally sympathetic guy, so your first inclination is to say something like, "Tough day, Ed?" But don't follow the first inclination. Instead, stop, look Ed in the eye, and say, "How may I help?"

Beth runs up to you. "I've got a customer here who is driving me crazy." Your first inclination is to say something like, "Well, it takes all kinds" and run the other way. Instead, make it, "How may I help?" And when Beth walks you over to her customer, turn to him, introduce yourself, and ask: "How may I help you?"

This question, expressed just this way—"How may I help?" or "How may I help you?"—is the key to the code of a super hero. A super hero helps. That is his nature.

But nothing is more comical than a super hero who offers unwanted help or the wrong help. Before you act the part of the mature hero, giving of yourself, ask others to give *you* guidance: *How* can I help? The question offers aid, but it also asks for help in the form of instruction. The question itself helps to remedy the situation at hand by forcing a degree of focus. Get an answer to this question, and you are well on your way to offering focused help, the kind of help that, in the end, will help you to achieve the status of Office Superman.

Do Well by Doing Good

In a good cause, self-sacrifice is, in the long run, no sacrifice at all. By benefitting the collective enterprise, whether it is the nation, humankind, your family, or your business, your sacrifice ultimately benefits you. Mature decisions typically involve short-term sacrifice for long-term gains. From the beginning, the Superman stories revolved around self-sacrifice as much as they did around the super hero's superpowers. The benefit of self-sacrifice to Superman? Longevity and eternal relevance. Superman remains the most durable of super heroes, the gold standard against which others are measured.

Superman proves that it is a very effective personal business strategy to do well by doing good. Look around you. Help your bosses. Help your colleagues. Help your subordinates. Help your customers and clients. Embrace their problems as your opportunities. Over time—and not very much time at that—your helpful approach will create an environment in which you are the go-to guy, the indispensable Office Superman. It is a reward not for the taking, but for the giving.

4

LOOK!
UP IN THE SKY

FACT: JERRY SIEGEL AND JOE SHUSTER CREATED SUPERMAN, NOT MOLEMAN, FERRETMAN, OR WORMMAN. There's a good reason for this. The boys from Cleveland were writing for an audience that wanted to look up in the sky and not down here on the ground, let alone beneath it.

As a species, human beings naturally gaze up at the sky, in contrast, say, to dogs, who just as naturally keep their eyes and noses close to the ground. Most religions and mythologies set the dwelling place of divinity not in the bowels of the Earth, but somewhere in the heavens, where spirits and angels soar. Generally speaking, the sky is equated with joy, hope, ambition, and aspiration, whereas the ground suggests stasis, stability, routine, and even despair. You're either "flying high" or "brought down low," "soaring" or "down in the dumps," "reaching new heights" or descending into the "valley of despair."

Little wonder, then, that, from the beginning, Superman was a hero of the air. It was only natural. Natural, too, was the ever loftier altitudes Superman attained over time. As previously mentioned, when he debuted in *Action Comics* #1 during June 1938, Superman was not capable of actual flight, but could "hurdle skyscrapers" and "leap an eighth of a mile." In *Superman* #4, from spring 1940, the Man of Steel "leaps into the stratosphere—and beyond," and by October of that same year (*Superman* #6), he "speeds thru the sky at such a terrific speed, his figure appears to blur." In April 1941 (*Superman* #9), Superman "streaks thru the clouds like a skyrocket gone wild" and covers "hundreds of miles in minutes." By August 1950 (*Superman* #65), he makes a round-trip journey to a planetoid five billion miles away in five seconds flat, achieving a speed greater than 10,000 times that of light. And this, we are told, isn't even his maximum flying speed. By May 1957 (*Superman* #113), he hurtles through outer space, covering light-years in "split seconds," and moves "out of our solar system . . . out of our island universe!"

In large part, the ongoing story of Superman has been a tale of higher and higher. It's what we like to hear, what we crave in our heroes, whether fictional or actual. All eyes are focused on the person who aims higher and then higher still.

And while the physics-minded among Superman fans might balk at the ability of the Man of Steel to exceed the speed of light, as a super hero, Superman is almost obliged to do just that. In his Special Theory of Relativity, Albert Einstein explained why light speed is a universal absolute, the great speed limit of the universe, which not even a super-scofflaw can violate. But people generally scorn limits and cannot abide even the thought of an absolute limit. Physics aside, human nature dictates that Superman be able to go faster than the speed of light—and still have speed to spare.

The JFK Factor

His status as an embodiment of the human urge to soar, to achieve ever loftier goals goes a long way toward explaining Superman's enduring appeal. But it isn't the whole story. As readers, we are often charmed and delighted by the off-handed ease with which Superman performs many of his feats, but how often can we witness— with sustained and undiluted interest—the Man of Steel effortlessly lift a car using just one hand? Superman would not be flying into his seventh decade if his life and career consisted of a string of stories devoid of conflict and struggle. Sure, many things are easy for Superman, but, just as his superpowers have grown, multiplied, and expanded with time, so have the challenges he confronts. Most of the time, the Man of Steel faces real dangers and wrestles with situations that involve risk and require a strenuous effort that pushes even the capacious envelope of his superpowers.

There must be hundreds of high schools in this country that share with the state of Kansas the familiar Latin motto, *Ad astra per aspera*—literally, *To the stars through difficulties,* or, more gracefully: *Through difficulties, to the stars.* It is an appealing motto, of a piece with the memorable speech President John F. Kennedy made to Congress on May 25, 1961, setting the national "goal, before this decade is out, of landing a man on the moon and returning him safely to the Earth." Kennedy declared: "No single space project in this period will be more impressive to mankind, or more important for the long-range exploration of space." He continued, in a candidly realistic vein, "and none will be so difficult or expensive to accomplish," but he did not present the difficulty and expense as negatives or disincentives. Instead, he concluded:

> We choose to go to the moon. We choose to go to the moon in this decade and do the other things, not because they are easy, but because they are hard, because that goal will serve to organize and measure the best of our energies and skills, because that challenge is one that we are willing to accept, one we are unwilling to postpone, and one which we intend to win, and the others, too.

This is vintage JFK, the idea of purposefully choosing to do something not because it is easy, but because it is hard. Did this position strike the American people as perverse? On the contrary, it was received as an inspiration. Kennedy explained his rationale by pointing out that such a difficult goal would "serve to organize and measure the best of our energies and skills." He understood the risk of a lofty goal. We might fall short of it. But he also understood something far more certain. Though we *might* fall short of a lofty goal, we will *certainly* fail to reach the heights if no such goal is set.

Demand great things of yourself, and you *might* fail to achieve them. Demand nothing great of yourself, and you will *certainly* fail to achieve greatness. The apparent security of the low road is an illusion. Choose the easy route, reject the arduous climb, and you will have failed even before you set out. The heights will remain forever out of your reach.

In the years since the thousand days of JFK's presidency a legion of revisionist historians has labored to expose the many failings of his administration. These scholars point out, often quite accurately, that Kennedy made precious little headway with a hostile Congress, that most of his key legislation either died aborning or had to wait for the sponsorship of his successor, Lyndon Johnson. Yet, after all these years, the magic of JFK remains undiminished. Whatever his failings, President Kennedy inspired us, and his memory continues to do so. He inspired us to aspire, and this legacy of inspiration has outlived him as well as the disappointments of his administration. Call it the JFK factor. It is an inexhaustible source of energy, a perpetual invitation to heroism.

Lofty Realism

No one was more stunned by JFK's "moon speech" than the staff of NASA and its small cadre of astronauts. The American space program was struggling at the time, and the goal of reaching the moon by the end of the decade seemed highly unrealistic to many, including the experts. Yet it *was* a goal, and, as scientists, engineers, and astronauts began to tackle the project, that goal, while extremely ambitious and difficult, began to seem increasingly feasible. In the end, of course, the landing of *Apollo 11* on July 20, 1969 proved the lofty goal to have been, in fact, realistic— achieved with a bit more than five months to spare before the decade expired.

In 1961, JFK's goal may well have seemed unrealistic. At the time, any number of criteria and assessments might have revealed it as unrealistic. And yet, because the goal was achieved, it must be seen to have been, by definition, realistic after all— regardless of all the evidence and indications along the way. As things turned out, it was one of history's greatest goals—not just because it was so audacious and ambitious, but because it was audacious and ambitious as well as realistic. As goals go, it was a masterpiece because it spectacularly balanced the greatest daring, the prospect of humankind's most fantastic adventure, with doable reality.

Balancing audacity with reality is the essence of the art of setting what, in Chapter 1, we called a *worthwhile goal*, one that is both lofty, a strenuous stretch, yet realistic: achievable. To veer too far toward the audacious invites failure, frustration, and discouragement, but to slip too far the other way, to set an insufficiently ambitious goal, puts a weighty cap on achievement.

Do You Need a Goal?

Few of us make it a regular practice to set goals. This is not the result of laziness or apathy. Even the hardest-working of us more often than not fails to set goals. Among many hard workers the thought is simply to work as hard as you can in the sincere belief that things will come out all right in the end.

But what's "the end"? The end of a particular project? The end of the day? The week? The month? The end of your career? And what does "all right" mean? Certainly doesn't sound like much, so why settle for it? In any case, this approach is not a rational plan for workplace success, but is, rather, a grim description of a dreary daily grind.

People as diverse as JFK and the football coach at the local high school understand that a goal functions to focus effort, to inspire effort, and to leverage effort. Set an inspiring and worthwhile yet realistic goal, and you should derive inspiration, sharpen your focus, and leverage your effort. In setting your goal, don't yield to the temptation to go easy on yourself. You may reason that there is no harm in setting the bar at a comfortably low level: "I can achieve this, and then anything above and beyond it is gravy." While it is possible to exceed a goal you set, it is not likely that you will do so, at least not significantly. Even if you do, this success will be in the nature of an accident, a result unplanned for. Is it rational to rely on accidents? Is it a good idea to stake your career on them? So, do you need a goal? Yes, you need a goal.

What Goal?

As discussed in Chapter 1, it is important to define your goal as precisely as possible. Quantify it: "I will increase my sales revenue from X dollars to XX dollars." Then build a time frame around it: "I will increase my sales revenue from X dollars to XX dollars within Y weeks."

You may find it helpful to break your goal down into the discrete steps necessary to achieve it. The *goal* is your desired destination, and *objectives* are the individual steps you must take to reach that destination. "To increase my sales revenue from X dollars to XX dollars within Y weeks means that I will have to identify Z more sales prospects this week and ZZ more within the next three weeks." Your goal may be to increase revenue to XX dollars, but your first objective is to identify Z more sales prospects.

Open Yourself to Challenge

There is no sure way to know if you are setting your goal high enough. The best you can do is to build a kind of floor under your goal, which should keep you from sinking too low. Do this by setting a goal that you are *not* fully confident about. That's right. Go for something you do *not* know for a fact that you can achieve. This will force you to stretch, to innovate, to take risks. True, you *may* fail. That is a possibility. However, if you set a goal you *know* you can achieve, you turn the possibility of failure into the certainty of failure. It is certain that you will fail to stretch and, therefore, fail to excel. Set a goal you know you can achieve, and you will neither innovate nor take risks. Instead, you will trudge along the well-worn path of business as usual. Most likely, the result will not be disaster, but, also most likely, it will be disappointment. No bang, just whimper.

Stretch, Don't Snap

Once you have set a goal that is seasoned with a vital pinch of doubt, step back. The idea is to make the goal hard, by no means a sure thing, but, just as important, by no means an impossibility, either. A difficult goal should excite you and, perhaps, scare you just a little bit. If, however, the goal you have set is simply overwhelming, it is too ambitious. An impossible goal is as bad as no goal at all because it will fail to focus your effort.

Blend Quality with Quantity

A goal worth going for must inspire you. This is an absolute requirement. A goal toward which you feel lukewarm or wholly indifferent is, in fact, no goal at all. You must move toward a goal; therefore, the goal you define must, by its nature, be attractive. It has to lure you, draw you toward itself. Although a hard goal may seem formidable, it is, in fact, a source of energy. It engages you the more you engage it.

To be inspirational, a goal need not be some airy idealistic fantasy. The nature of the goal should be such that progress toward it can be measured. That's why it is important to express your goal in some manageable, measurable quantity. Not, "I will become top salesman," but "I will increase my sales revenue from X dollars to XX dollars within Y weeks." The qualitative and quantitative dimensions of your goal are not mutually exclusive. On the contrary, they are measures of each other. The quantitative measure tells you where you are in relation to your goal at any given point in time, and the qualitative measure is the degree to which you feel inspired, energized, and gratified by your relation to the goal.

Superman never tires of the super hero business, and he's been at it nearly seventy years. Continue to set difficult, realistic, high-quality, and highly quantifiable goals for yourself, and you will not only move ahead—measurably—in your business life, but you will also remain energized and inspired by the journey.

5

ON BENDING STEEL IN YOUR BARE HANDS

AT THE START OF HIS CAREER, IN *ACTION COMICS* #1, SUPERMAN SET AN OVERALL GOAL FOR HIMSELF: to "turn his titanic strength into channels that would benefit mankind." The Office Superman sets a similar, albeit more modestly framed, goal each day he comes to work: *to achieve and demonstrate excellence.*

Just how are the two goals similar?

By achieving and demonstrating excellence, the Office Superman benefits himself, of course, but, more important, benefits the entire enterprise. Excellence is the most valuable commodity in any business. Conversely, Superman can benefit humankind only if he achieves and demonstrates excellence.

So the key quality the *Office* Superman shares with *the* Superman is excellence. Great! But what, exactly, is *excellence*?

Superman and the Office Superman alike achieve excellence when they satisfy the following five criteria:

1. They know what to do.
2. They know how to do it well.

3. They have the tools necessary to do what they do well.

4. They accurately assess what they have done.

5. They take responsibility for what they do and have done.

Know What to Do

"The world is faced by a menace such as it has never before encountered—a strange force, striking from an unseen source, spreads ruthless destruction. To halt the wave of terror, Superman, amazing champion of the helpless and oppressed, pits his own tremendous powers against those of the unknown menace!"

So begins, quite typically, *Superman* #13 (December 1941). Look closely at the language here: "a menace . . . never before encountered," "a strange force," "an unseen source," "ruthless destruction," "wave of terror." In terms of the story the paragraph introduces, these words and phrases are the liability side of the ledger. The liabilities at issue are nothing less than terror and destruction of unknown origin and nature.

Problems don't get any worse than this. "Ruthless destruction" is bad enough, but if its source has never been encountered before and is strange as well as unseen, who can possibly know what to do?

For the answer, move on to the asset side of the ledger: "amazing champion of the helpless and oppressed," "pits . . . tremendous powers against those of the unknown menace."

The language of the introduction to this story makes the situation compellingly clear: The world desperately needs somebody who knows what to do (liability). Superman knows what to do (asset).

Like the perpetually imperiled world of Superman, every workplace is filled with liabilities: the tasks that need doing, the projects that have to be completed, the problems that must be solved. The Office Superman offers the assets to cover these liabilities. He presents himself as the one who knows how to do the tasks, complete the projects, and solve the problems.

If you would present yourself this way, you must first ensure that you do, in fact, know what to do. This does not require genius or divine inspiration, but simply a commitment to learn everything there is to know about your job.

• Read or reread your job description.

• Obtain and read any company manuals relating to your position.

• Get a mentor—someone with more experience than you have. Ask questions. Watch. Learn.

Take nothing for granted. Let's suppose you work for a small maker of electronic components. Your job is filling orders. There are two kinds of orders, high priority and routine. You assume that high-priority orders must be filled first, so you move heaven and Earth to get them out the door no later than ten in the morning. To save time, you focus exclusively on the high-priority orders first, even though these often call for the same components as the routine orders. Since you fill the high-priority orders first without "wasting time" by also reviewing the routine orders, you usually have to make at least two trips to the stock room for the same items—one trip to fill the priority orders, and again, later, to fill the routine orders. Well, so be it. You've *got* to get those high-priority shipments out the door!

But you are making a mistake, each and every day. The fact is that the courier picks up high-priority shipments at 2:30. The orders you've rushed down to shipping sit idly on the dock for more than four hours.

You thought you knew what to do: give high priority to high-priority orders. But you did not bother to learn everything there was to learn. Had you known that even high-priority items aren't picked up until 2:30, you could have been saving time and effort by consolidating two trips to the stock room into one. This realization does not require inspired insight, inborn talent, or a special knack. It just requires learning your job thoroughly. That is the first responsibility of the Office Superman.

How do you know when you've learned your job thoroughly? When you can answer *yes* to these three questions:

    1. Do you know *when* you have to do what you do?

    2. Do you know *why* you have to do what you do?

    3. Do you know *how* what you do affects or is used by others?

Know How to Do It Well

Reading the earliest Superman stories is a real eye opener. In 1938, Superman's debut year, for example, he deals with a military torturer not by handing him over to international authorities, but by throwing him through the air—and to his death— as if "he were hurling a javelin." In a 1939 story, the Man of Steel attacks an aircraft carrying the arch-villain Ultra-Humanite and his gang by purposely thrusting himself into the propeller, thereby causing the craft to crash, killing everyone on board, except, as luck would have it, for the Ultra-Humanite. In a 1940 tale, Superman thinks nothing of electrocuting to death a subversive mastermind named J. F. Curtis. In 1941, the Man of Steel drowns a gaggle of human giants, kills gangster Joe Gatson by instantaneously hurling him into the path of the very bullet Gatson himself had fired, and pushes a Lex Luthor henchman out of a skyscraper window. In a memorable story of 1942, Superman electrocutes the Lightning Master, a scientist who has harnessed the power of lightning to carry out various acts of destruction.

Surprised? Modern fans of Superman are not comfortable seeing their super hero kill, even in a good cause. This is because, beginning about 1943, Superman changed his ways. He became committed to doing his job without needlessly sacrificing lives, and, ever since, Superman has resolved most crises without permanently hurting anyone, even the bad guys. From the beginning, from *Action Comics* #1 (June 1938), Superman knew what to do, but it took him until late in 1943 to begin to show that he had learned to do it *well*. In the case of the super hero business, this means getting the job done without undue bloodshed.

Talent and aptitude vary from one person to another, but it almost always takes study and practice, regardless of inborn gifts, to learn to do what you do well. Every job has a learning curve, even Superman's.

As for the Office Superman, he commits himself to climbing the learning curve as quickly and as productively as possible. He takes pride not in merely knowing what to do, but in knowing how to do it well.

Get the Necessary Tools

As some see it, Superman is all about the superpowers—flight, strength, speed, invulnerability, and the rest—but by the late 1940s, the creators of Superman were beginning to equip their hero with what would become a growing array of tools and super gadgets. Over the years, Superman has acquired any number of robots, including Kelex, his faithful servant housed at the Fortress of Solitude, and a fleet of robot fighters; a control hub of monitors, also housed in the Fortress, which allow Superman to maintain a vigil over the entire Earth; vast computer systems; a holographic encyclopedic universal library of knowledge; a special aquanaut suit; a super high-tech suit of armor known as the Warsuit; and a lot more.

If you want to be the Office Superman, you, too, will have to make sure that you get all the tools you need to do your job and do it well. This may be as simple a matter as determining what you need and then requisitioning it. However, in some organizations, and depending on the prevailing business climate, you may have to be prepared to justify an equipment request. Don't be bashful, but don't be self-centered, either. Prepare a memo that shows *not* how the new software or hardware item will "make your job easier," but how it will make you "more productive" or make your work product "more cost efficient." Sell the benefit *you* want as a benefit to *others* and, most of all, as a benefit to the enterprise as a whole.

You may discover that the tools you need go beyond a new computer or the latest accounting software. Maybe what you really need is more education or specialized training. If so, make it your business to find a way to acquire it. Many companies these days are very enthusiastic about developing the skills and expertise of their employees. Sell your firm on the benefits of educating you. The beauty of this kind of tool is that, unlike the new computer your company buys, you can take your education with you. It's completely portable and transferable to the next opportunity you may find, whether in another department or with another employer.

Accurately Assess What You Do and What You Have Done

By nature, Superman is a modest fellow who shuns the spotlight. In *Action Comics* #1, he is relieved to discover that newspaper stories don't mention him after his successful rescue of a woman wrongly condemned to the electric chair. Superman so craves seclusion that he even builds a Fortress of Solitude. The first reference to this is a "mountain retreat" the Man of Steel builds as early as 1942, but the full-blown Fortress of Solitude did not appear until 1958, when it was described as a great Arctic stronghold "deep in the core of a mountainside."

The Fortress of Solitude is about as remote from the public eye as it is possible to get, and yet no one is more famous than Superman. Throughout decades of stories, he has been buried in an avalanche of awards and honors. Stories from the 1940s mention radio programs devoted to him. In the 1950s it was television and movies. Several stories mention Superman as the subject of booklength biographies. The city of Metropolis presented him with its Outstanding Citizen Award in 1954 and the key to the city in 1965. In 1961, Superman was accorded honorary citizenship by "all the countries of the United Nations." Metropolis has erected several statues honoring Superman, and in 1949 members of the "Super-Saved Club" blasted a Mount Rushmore-like tribute to the Man of Steel out of the top of a lofty mountain peak. Buildings have been dedicated to Superman, including, according to the 1943 *Action Comics* #67, "the nation's largest army officers' training center." Indeed, the celebration of Superman is just about endless, perhaps the most impressive monument being the one described in *Superman* #155 (August 1962): The people of a distant world reshaped their very planet into a sculpture of Superman's head to honor him for having liberated them from the terrible dictator Drago.

Even if you are very good at your job, it's not all that likely you'll get a planet carved in your image. But it is important for you to accurately assess your performance and how others perceive your performance. You need to be as objective as possible in this assessment. How you yourself feel about what you do is important, but it is not enough. You need also to look at quantitative results: sales figures, volume of work produced in a given period, and so on. In addition, solicit feedback from subordinates, colleagues, bosses, and customers—whoever is affected by what you do. This can be tricky. On the one hand, you don't want to *provoke* criticism or complaints, but you also don't want to come across as if you're begging for praise. The best way to get objective feedback is to ask specific questions. Avoid asking, "How am I doing?" Instead, try something like this:

"John, does that new-format sales report I prepared give you more of the information you need?" And when you do get feedback, express gratitude for it, respond to it, and use it. "John, thanks. Your remarks on the new format are really helpful. I will add the additional data line you suggested."

Take Responsibility for What You Do

"Whenever Superman wants to get away from it all, he retires to his secret sanctuary, the Fortress of Solitude." According to *Action Comics* #261 (February 1960), it is "the most glamorous hideaway in the entire universe!" Superman calls it "the one place where I can relax and work undisturbed! No one suspects its existence, and no one can penetrate the solid rock out of which it is hewn!"

The Fortress is a dazzling sanctuary, which houses much of Superman's special equipment as well as his trophies, mementos, even his faithful dog, Krypto. Such a retreat would continually lure and tempt any mere mortal from the cares and responsibilities of the world. But not Superman. To be sure, he makes good use of this refuge, but he never uses it to retreat from his responsibilities.

Nothing you may do as Office Superman will count for much if you fail to take responsibility for what you do. Take pride in your work. Follow projects through to completion, even after they leave your hands. If you are assigned a task, asked a question, or presented with a problem, take ownership of it. This means that you cannot simply shed or abandon it, but that you must complete, answer, or resolve it.

Know what to do, know how to do it well, and, finally, *own* what you do. The foundation on which the Office Superman builds everything is commitment—responsibility to the enterprise and everyone associated with it.

Stand on Your Record

In his earliest days, Superman often had a public confidence problem. As a "strange visitor from another planet," he experienced some difficulty finding acceptance. For example, in *Action Comics* #6 (November 1938), he is described by police officials as a vigilante "mystery man," and, indeed, through stories as late as those that appeared in early 1942, the police regard him as a fugitive. About this time, however, and without explanation, it becomes clear that Superman works not against the cops or in spite of them, but in partnership with law enforcement. From mid 1942 on, he collaborates with the police, the FBI, and other forces of justice. Moreover, he is universally trusted by ordinary people.

Well, he earned that trust. He can stand on his record.

The Office Superman also builds a record he can stand on, but he does more than just stand on it. He actively uses it to promote himself.

Looking for a better job? Chances are, your very best prospect is not the firm on the other side of the street or the other side of the country, but the company you're working for right now.

Start Climbing

If you make sales, you're a good salesman. If you create customers, you're a *great* salesman. The great ones don't just take the money and run, they develop customer satisfaction, customer loyalty, and repeat business. They're in it for the long haul, and they understand that the *best* customers are *current* customers. They are the people you know all about, and who know all about you—and that is terrific, provided that you've done a great job of satisfying them. A positive history is the best advertisement.

So it is with career advancement as well. Often, your best opportunities are among the people who know you best. A high level of performance is the most effective advertisement.

But you can't rely on it. People often talk about "rising" in an organization. Usually, however, you don't *rise*. You have to *climb*. You do this by promoting yourself, by actively building a case that exhibits the consistent excellence of your achievements. Perhaps the most effective way to begin your climb is to identify and recruit a mentor, someone in the organization who will sponsor and guide you, and who will generally promote your ascension.

A mentor must be someone to whom you have access. This person must be in a field, area, or department that interests you and that suits your skills and training. The prospective mentor must, of course, be willing to work with you. Finally, and most important of all, the prospective mentor must be someone with the power to promote you. Very often, just as your best prospects for career growth are typically within your present firm, so the most promising candidate for mentor is your current boss.

It's Your Move

Learn from your mentor, and, as you learn, be aware that you are on continual display. Take advantage of this high visibility to demonstrate excellence. Assuming you perform at a consistently high level, you may approach your mentor-boss to discuss an increase in your responsibilities: a promotion.

Make *your* move, but make sure it is a move toward the other party in this discussion. Don't focus on your needs (more money, more money, more money!), but on what you can do for the firm, for the department, and, most of all, for the boss. Build the case for your advancement by showing just how you can make this person's life easier and more successful.

Get Specific, Stay Specific

You can apply a lot of adjectives to Superman: *strong, brave, clever, resourceful, loyal, honest, fast, selfless, powerful, heroic—super.* But some seven decades of Superman stories have not been built on adjectives. They consist of stories, the interaction of characters and actions. They consist of specifics rather than abstract words. Crashing through a solid steel door is far more compelling a description of Superman than is the word *powerful.* Raising a car above his head with one hand says a great deal more than the word *strong.*

Even if your boss has mentored you, you cannot depend on his intimate knowledge of your record. Before you sit down to discuss a promotion, be sure your conversation is amply supplied with a list of solid accomplishments. Steer clear of empty claims and puffed-up adjectives. Always show rather than tell. Wherever possible, use numbers to demonstrate results. Best of all is to express results in dollars—dollars you made for the firm and dollars you saved for it. Money is the language of business, and the Office Superman must speak that language fluently.

Build It Yourself

The familiar phrase "climbing the corporate ladder" gets the part about having to *climb* all right, but it also suggests that there is a *ladder* all ready and waiting for you. On this you cannot rely. Sometimes opportunities really do lie in wait, but, very often, they must be created.

Above all, the Office Superman is creative, and he is even prepared to create a new position where none currently exists. This is a significant challenge, but creating a position is also among the most exciting and fulfilling career moves you can make.

Step one is to learn, learn how your department or organization works and how it works in relation to other departments. Armed with this knowledge, imagine yourself as a consultant hired by your department or organization. In the imaginary role of consultant, report to yourself on how your department might be improved by the addition of such-and-such a position or the replacement of one position by another. Work out your recommendations, then decide what facts and figures you need to support them. Secure this data and then give your imagination free reign to create scenarios that demonstrate the benefits of the new position. Finally, combine these scenarios with your facts and figures and with data relating to your own performance in your current position. The goal is to show that you are the ideal candidate for the position you yourself have created.

When you pitch your boss on the new position, avoid presenting your proposal as a remedy for a deficiency your boss has somehow created or failed to address. Instead, put the emphasis on yourself as an asset to the department. It is best not to begin by stating the need for a brand-new position. Instead, simply explain how you see your new role. Let your boss draw the conclusion that this new role requires a new position.

Superman can perform a dazzling array of feats of strength, speed, and daring. The Office Superman likewise focuses on performance. He knows what to do and how to do it well. That's a lot, but it isn't enough. The Office Superman seeks nothing less than the positive transformation of his career, and if this requires transforming the reality in which he works, well, bring it on.

CHAPTER 6

ON CHANGING THE COURSE OF MIGHTY RIVERS

CLARK KENT–FOR HE WAS NOT YET SUPERMAN–LEARNED THE FIRST BIG LESSON OF HIS LIFE on the first page, fifth panel, of *Superman* #1.

"Now listen to me, Clark!" his foster father tells him. "This great strength of yours—you've got to hide it from people or they'll be scared of you."

Like most of us, just about from the beginning, Clark Kent learns the importance of fitting in, and, in a manner more dramatic than most of us adopt, he carries the lesson with him lifelong in his dual existence as the Man of Steel and the mild-mannered reporter.

And yet, we can hardly call Superman a conformist, who marches in lockstep with his contemporaries. Crime, tyranny, and corruption are all around him, and against these things, of course, he does not hesitate to fight. Nor does he ever really forsake his true identity. Although he walks among us as Clark Kent, he readily emerges as Superman whenever the need arises. When we stop to think about it, Clark (Superman) Kent should not fit in at all. In the deepest, most extreme sense, he is an alien, "strange visitor from another planet," yet he was raised as one of us, and he works hard not at being just one of us, but the very best of us, fighting for truth, justice, and the *American*—not the Kryptonian—way.

Mastery of the workplace, success in business, achieving the status of Office Superman hinges on how well you fit in and yet also on how spectacularly you stand out. In any enterprise, aliens alienate, but carbon-copy conformists rarely advance. Mousy timidity goes properly unrewarded, but showboats are typically torpedoed. The key is balance.

Anatomy of a Failed Superman

In *Action Comics* #254 (July 1959), Superman's arch foe, the mad scientist Lex Luthor, invents a "duplicator ray" with which he attempts to clone the Man of Steel. The result is a being named Bizarro, who, by his own description, is "not human . . . not creature . . . not even animal!" Animated from lifeless matter, Bizarro is "a grotesque imitation of Superman" (*Action Comics* #263, April 1960), endowed with Superman's strength and superpowers, and even a "dim copy" of Superman's memory. His skin is chalky white, and his face faceted, as if chiseled from rock. Whereas Superman always manages to keep his jet-black hair perfectly coifed, spit curl in place even in flight and fight, Bizarro's mop is perpetually matted and unkempt. If he has Superman's powers, he does not have Superman's mind, and, in fact, comes across as a dimwit. His ungrammatical speech ("Me have no friends . . .") serves to emphasize his slowness of intellect, which seems all the more pathetic precisely because it is married to superstrength.

If there is a single word to describe Bizarro as a failed duplicate of the Man of Steel, it is *unbalanced*. His chaotic and outlandish appearance, along with his inarticulate imbecility, make his superpowers grotesque phenomena rather than what they are in Superman, supreme wonders. For all his might, Superman is a figure of grace and intellect, whereas Bizarro, equally strong, is a super clod. Superman fits in *and* stands out—simultaneously. Lacking balance, Bizarro can never fit in, and, for him, standing out is not an opportunity to excel, but an occasion for ridicule.

Achieving Balance

Achieving balance in the workplace requires your attention to two broad areas:

1. How you put yourself across as a person
2. How you put yourself across as a *business* person

Because you can't put yourself across effectively in category number 2 without first doing so in number 1, we'll begin there.

The Non-Verbal You

Superman has telescopic, microscopic, and X-ray vision. When it comes to cutting himself the biggest slice of the electromagnetic spectrum, well, he's got us poor human beings, whose vision is restricted to the visible spectrum, beat. Nevertheless, we are intensely visual creatures. In the brain of each of us, far more of the cerebral cortex—the part devoted to higher mental activity—is dedicated to processing visual information than to any other single function. What this means is that, before you've said a word, before you can *tell* people who you are and what you are all about, they've already started sizing you up.

If you need quantitative proof of this, go back to the year 1971, when the psychologist Albert Mehrabian published his classic study of what makes some speakers more persuasive than others. He found that 55 percent of persuasion is the product of the speaker's facial expressions and body movements. Vocal qualities, including tone and pitch of voice as well as the pace of delivery, accounted for another 38 percent. The actual *words* the speaker used contributed no more than 7 percent to the persuasiveness of his speech.

If you want to be an Office Superman, make sure you can be sure of your nonverbal self.

Walk Tall—or Walk Taller

Forget Napoleon. Tall people have a built-in advantage when it comes to projecting an image of credibility and authority. Superman stands a respectable 6-foot-3, right up there with traditional Hollywood heroes like John Wayne, Gary Cooper, and, more recently, Russell Crowe. In the 1950s, Alan Ladd managed to become a leading man, but, at 5-foot-7, he had to stand on a box for those medium close-ups opposite Lana Turner.

Shallow? Quite. Unfair? Absolutely. But that doesn't change the underlying truth.

So start walking tall or walking taller. Avoid boxy-looking suits and all clothing with horizontally striped patterns. Don't wear baggy, loosely cut pants, and while you probably don't need to invest in "elevator shoes" or lifts, maybe you should think about buying shoes with slightly higher heels and somewhat thicker soles.

If you need proof that you *can* walk and stand taller, grab a Superman comic and find an illustration of Superman in one of his characteristic stances: hands on hips, chest out, eyes ahead, beaming with confidence. Now look at a picture of Clark Kent. He is rarely seen in a straight-on pose, but, rather, is typically depicted as leaning on a desk or bending, about to break into a run. While his body language does not obviously reinforce the meek, cringing persona he projects, his Clark Kent stance consistently seems shorter and less impressive than his Superman stance. And yet, as we know, Superman and Clark Kent are one and the same.

We'll talk more about clothes in Chapter 16, "Superman Suits Up," but even more important than *what* you wear, is *how* you walk. When your mother nagged you about slouching, you should have listened. Think about maintaining an erect posture, and, while you're working on walking upright, stride ahead as if you have a purpose.

Purpose is not, however, synonymous with *grim determination*. Walk straight, walk briskly, walk purposefully, but smile along the way. You need not freeze your face into a plastic grimace, but try to bring a *natural* smile to your visage by thinking of something that pleases you. Visualize a favorite person, memory, time, or place. And hold that thought.

Scowl, and the world may write you off before you say a word, but a smile is an invitation for everyone to deal with you.

Eye, Eye, Sir!

You'd be justified in thinking twice before you looked Superman in the eye. His X-ray vision may see through things, but his heat vision has been used, on occasion, as a weapon, to melt objects or set fires. Moreover, his piercing blue eyes, often described as unlike any eyes on Earth, convey an absolute honesty and truthfulness that some people may find more than a bit disconcerting. However, where mere mortals are concerned, the cardinal rule of effective body language is to make eye contact.

"Look me in the eye and say that," the stern father tells his mischievous son, and with good reason. We call liars "shifty" or "shifty-eyed," and dad knows that it's indeed hard for his son to lie to his father's face. Want to convey openness and honesty? Look others straight in the eye.

Although none of us has X-ray vision, our eyes are capable of another superpower: nothing less than the transmission of energy. Surely you've heard people talk about the "sparkle" in somebody's eye, as if that were something remarkable. In fact, we *all* have a sparkle in our eyes—eyes are naturally shiny—but it is rarely noticed, because so few people make full eye contact. Use that sparkle, and the effect can be electric, a transfer of your energetic enthusiasm to the other person.

Not surprisingly, Superman's personal presence is powerful. In many situations he encounters, he does not even have to use his superpowers. His mere presence suffices to resolve the situation.

Don't you wish you were perceived as so powerful? Maybe you can be.

Most of the time, eye-to-eye contact works all the magic you need. But, on occasion, the issue is less a matter of seeing eye to eye than avoiding a steamroller. To one degree or another, just about every workplace is charged with "office politics," which, more often than not, operates through coercion, domination, and, let's face it, out-and-out bullying. These unpleasant phenomena have one thing in common. They require both a victimizer and a victim. Obviously, it is to your advantage to opt out of the victim's role. You can start nonverbally. Instead of making eye contact in a confrontation with an office bully, set your gaze a touch higher. Don't look at the other person's eyes, but at his eyebrows. This sends the subtle, but unmistakable signal of your dominance. At the very least, it telegraphs the message that *you* are not one to be easily cowed.

In the Grip

Longtime fans of the Man of Steel divide the artistic and literary evolution of their super hero into three distinct periods: The Golden Age (from 1938 to 1961), the Silver Age (1962–1970s), and the Modern Age (1975–present). Each of these periods is characterized by a certain style of art and story. Today's Superman is spectacularly drawn, showing the influence of computer graphics, Japanese *anime* cartoons, and other aesthetic and pop-culture forces. Yet most fans, even those intensely enthusiastic about Superman's current incarnation, retain a special soft spot for the Golden Age, in which the art was simpler, more naive, innocent, and thoroughly charming.

The Golden Age of Superman corresponds to a time when people could utter the phrase "truth, justice, and the American way" without a trace of irony, camp, or kitsch. It was a time when fathers counseled their sons about the all-consuming importance of a shoeshine and a hearty handshake, as if these were the skeleton keys to commercial success.

Antiquated? Simple? Naive?

Think a minute. Can you recall in your business life a particularly memorable handshake? You may be surprised to find that, indeed, you can. The fact is that we remember touch even more vividly than we remember words.

Now, keep thinking. What made that memorable handshake memorable? Was it especially warm and powerful? Or was it colder and deader than an iced mackerel? Depending on your answer, you've identified either a highly positive or a highly negative memory. Positive or negative, a handshake makes an impression, and while that impression may not last lifelong or even to the end of the day, it will linger over whatever else occurs during the encounter the handshake initiated.

You're meeting a prospective client. You're armed with a kick-ass presentation, and you're eager to get into it. Impatient to get started, you return your prospect's greeting and offer your hand to accept his handshake. It's wintertime. You allow your prospect to grip your outstretched—and ice cold—hand. The merest trace of a grimace flashes across his lips. You think nothing of it and launch into your presentation, all the time unaware that, at some barely conscious level, the man on the other side of the desk is thinking not about your words but about your cold, dead hand. Will you make the sale? Well, the thoughtless handshake didn't help.

A handshake isn't magic, but it *is* human. At a powerful nonverbal level, it sets the context and tone for whatever follows it. Here's how to deliver a super handshake, one memorable for its warmth, sincerity, and openness:

Keep it dry. Nobody likes a clammy handshake. If necessary—and before you go into the meeting—dry your hands with a handkerchief or tissue.

Grasp the other person's hand fully. Be sure to get hold of the palm, not just the fingers.

Be moderate and considerate. Nobody likes a bone-crunching grip, and most people appreciate even less a dead fish. Convey positive, warm, controlled energy.

Make certain to hold onto the other person's hand a full second longer than what seems natural to you. Begin your verbal greeting *before* you let go. This literally *holds* the other person's attention as you exchange greetings.

Remember to make and maintain eye contact throughout the duration of the handshake. And whatever you do, *smile*.

Breathing Lessons

There's more to breathing than just staying alive. Superman, of course, uses his breath to accomplish great things—blowing storms away before they can do damage, putting out fires, even freezing an enemy or two. But anybody can discover and make use of some of the power of this most basic of activities called breathing.

We do not always "breathe easy." When excited or scared, the breath usually comes short and sharp. We speak of having to "catch our breath." Respiration is a sensitive barometer of emotion, and the big thing is that those around you can read this emotional indicator as readily as you can.

When anxious, our breath comes short, shallow, and rapid. This causes us to look and to sound nervous. It also contributes to the anxiety we already feel. Born of anxiety, short, rapid breathing intensifies anxiety.

Get control of your breathing, and you will automatically reduce your anxiety as well as the outward evidence of your anxiety. Give yourself a fighting chance by refraining from plunging headlong into any important meeting or communication. Out of sight of others, take a few deep breaths before speaking. When you feel yourself short of breath, force yourself to take a deep breath. Slow down. Then take another. You'll feel better, and you'll look better.

Put It Together

Once you become aware of the communicative power of body language, you can start putting together some of the more useful body language cues to help ensure that, wherever you are at the moment, you will fit in as well as stand out.

Nobody appreciates a display of nervous energy—fidgeting is contagious and makes everyone uncomfortable—but we all enjoy the feeling of relaxed energy.

Convey that feeling by eye contact and by opening your eyes wide. This expresses engagement with others as well as generally heightened interest in them. Sit still—not rigidly, but upright and without fidgeting. Smile and nod to communicate understanding and assent. An easy, natural nod is best. If you are seated, try leaning forward from time to time. This powerful posture expresses your intensity of interest and is a tactic that actively engages others.

Many people are self-conscious about their hands and may even confide that they don't know what to do with them. Well, why not *use* them?

Hand gestures are normal, natural, and human. Avoid flailing, and keep your hands away from your face and head—such gestures suggest nervousness, uncertainty, or outright deception—but do gesture with open hands, palm up, to suggest honesty and receptiveness to the needs and ideas of others.

Try "steepling." From time to time, put the fingertips of both hands together, steeple-fashion, to convey confidence.

Excited about somebody's suggestion or idea? Rub your hands together. It is a gesture that conveys positive expectancy. Just make sure you don't overdo it and end up looking like the black-caped villain of old-time melodrama. And whatever you do, don't confuse rubbing with wringing. Hand wringing conveys *extreme* anxiety and unhappiness.

Watch Your (Body) Language!

Non-verbal communication is powerful. Just be aware that the negative nonverbal messages we sometimes send may be even more compelling than the positive ones. Here are some things the Office Superman never does:

He never makes a tentative entrance, shuffling or sneaking into the room.

He never looks down and downcast, chin down and avoiding eye contact.

He never gives a bad handshake, whether the dead fish or the death grip.

He never fidgets.

He never sighs, which is an expression of despair that shatters the confidence of all who see and hear it.

He never yawns in public, because boredom is never a productive message.

He never scratches his head, because it suggests bewilderment.

He never bites his lip, which sends a strong signal of anxiety.

He never rubs the back of his head or neck, because these are indications of frustration and impatience.

He never narrows the eyes, because he knows that this suggests disagreement, resentment, or even outright anger.

He never squints, since this is the trademark of the clueless.

He never raises his eyebrows in disbelief, because this tells the other person that you do not trust him and what he is saying.

He never peers over the top of his glasses, because he is aware that this suggests disbelief plus contempt.

He never crosses his arms in front of his chest, because he does not want to appear defiant or closeminded.

He never rubs his eyes, ears, or the side of his nose, knowing that all these gestures telegraph doubt and self-doubt.

Take Note, Please

Two more chapters in this book will help you achieve the balance of an Office Superman. Check out Chapter 13, "Putting *Torquasm-Vo* to Work For You," to learn about creating, maintaining, and enhancing rapport through *verbal* communication skills, and Chapter 16, "Superman Suits Up," which offers advice on developing a look that's right for you in the context of your office.

Climbing Aboard

We've now considered the first component of creating a balance between fitting in and standing out: putting yourself across as a person. Now just a few choice words about putting yourself across as a *business* person.

Superman debuted in 1938. Batman made his first appearance just a year later, his creation clearly inspired by the immediate success of Superman. Ponder these two comic book super heroes for a moment. Superman is as vivid and positive a presence as his red-yellow-and-blue costume, whereas Batman is a darker presence, a quality conveyed by his dark-colored bat outfit and celebrated cowl mask. In a strictly literary sense, Batman is arguably an even more interesting character than Superman because, a man of mystery, sometimes even brooding, he is so much less transparent.

If Batman is more interesting as a figure of fiction, he has never achieved the degree of universal popularity Superman enjoys. Gotham will never honor Batman with the kind of monuments that Metropolis routinely dedicates to Superman. Both are pop culture celebrities, to be sure, but only Superman is a genuine icon.

At the core of the difference between these two super heroes is this: We never feel we fully know Batman's thoughts and intentions, and we are never absolutely sure just where he stands in relation to us, to society. In contrast to Superman, Batman is never fully "on board" the enterprise that we call society. The result is that, unlike Superman, Batman does not completely balance fitting in with standing out.

Make no mistake. Batman is a *very* successful super hero creation. His career is only a year behind that of Superman and, as with Superman, interest in his character shows no signs of flagging. As with the Man of Steel, the Caped Crusader has been the subject of comic books as well as television programming and more than one blockbuster feature film.

But who would you rather have on your side?

The Office Superman cannot afford to play it like Batman. There must be no doubt about his being "on board" the enterprise. As you might expect, a balancing act is called for here as well. Being on board does not mean mindlessly swallowing every project, program, and idea that comes your way. Being on board does not require you to become a yes man, anymore than being a congressman or senator calls for agreeing with everything others in the government do or ordain. There is plenty of room—and plenty of need—for intelligent debate and dissent. However, for a congressman or senator, dissent ends where the genuine interest of the nation begins. Senator Smith may disagree with 99 of his colleagues and still remain a patriot, as long as he is on board with the animating principles of the nation. Likewise, the Office Superman may dissent in particular cases and may offer alternatives to particular courses of action, but there must never be any doubt about his being on board with the underlying principles that drive the enterprise.

Dissent ends where the good of the company begins, and if you find yourself often at odds with the rest of the organization, you need to examine how you feel about the principles, the overall goals, of the enterprise. If you're on board with these, then do your best to help your colleagues see the light. If, however, you find that your difficulty is not about fitting in with your coworkers, but concerns the program of the organization itself, well, it may be time for this Office Superman to find a new office.

CHAPTER 7

HOW TO PLEASE PERRY WHITE

(DON'T CALL HIM CHIEF!)

PERRY WHITE

1938: SUPERMAN DEBUTS. He is the archetypal super hero. 1940: In *Superman* #7 (December 1940), Superman's creators introduce the archetypal boss. Known initially by his last name only, he becomes Perry White in *Superman* #10 (June 1941), but from the beginning he convincingly combines all the qualities of the classic boss. For generations of pre-teen and teen Superman devotees, Perry White would be a glimpse into the vocational future—*So, this is what a boss is like*—and a flash of intuition about the present—So this is *why my father hits the sauce when he comes home from the office.*

For better or worse, Perry White is *the* Boss, old school. Let's start with what is, from the collective point of view of Clark Kent, Lois Lane, and Jimmy Olsen—the employees—that "worse" part.

In his massively authoritative 1978 *The Great Superman Book*, Michael L. Fleisher begins his description of Perry White by quoting a single word from *Action Comics* #302 (July 1963): "gruff."

This one adjective may indeed best describe the editor-in-chief of the *Daily Planet*. It certainly goes with other words that have been attached to him in the pages of *Action Comics* and *Superman*: "hard-boiled," "irascible," "tough," and the like. It also aptly describes the portrayal of Perry White by actor John Hamilton on the *Adventures of Superman* TV series during the 1950s. When Hamilton's White wasn't barking at Clark or Lois, he was bellowing at Jimmy Olsen: "Don't call me Chief!" Which is exactly what forgetful Jimmy always called him.

But if *gruff* describes the "worse" side of the Perry White boss equation, it also implies the "better" side as well. The word *gruff* is roughly synonymous with *brusque* and *stern*, but it is in no way equivalent to *mean, nasty,* or *sadistic*. In fact, the connotation of *gruff* is of a superficial style, a kind of put-on, rather than a genuine personality trait. Perry White's infamous temper has been portrayed in innumerable Superman stories, including "The Remains of Krypton" (*Superman: Birthright* #6, March 2004), in which White scrawls a two-column list concerning Lois Lane.

Under the heading "KEEP HER (?)" he writes:

1. Best Writer
2. Good Interviewer
3. Three Pulitzer Nominations
4. Won't take "no" for an answer
5. No good place to hide her body

Under the column headed "FIRE" he writes:

1. No Boundaries
2. Despite inability to listen
3. ~~16~~ 17 lawsuits
4. Won't take "no" for an answer

No sooner does he finish the list than Jimmy Olsen pokes his head in the door to announce, "Chief? Receptionist says you have a call on line thr—" which predictably provokes White's famous bellow: "DON'T CALL ME CHIEF!" Jimmy leaves White's office, Lois asks him a question, and, finger in ear, Jimmy responds: "Head . . . roaring . . . can't . . . hear you. . . . Wait. Ears . . . clearing. . . ."

Surely we have all known people who come on gruff in order to hide a softer, more sentimental, and certainly more caring side of their personality. Perry White's gruff manner is part and parcel of his no-nonsense, straight-ahead dynamism. In his way, like Superman, he is a crusader for truth, justice, and the American way. He is, in fact, passionate about his newspaper work, which he regards as a mission. He is committed to producing top-quality journalism, which is not just careful, truthful, and penetrating, but also sensitive, sympathetic, and caring.

Less than Perfect, Less than Perry

Gruff Perry White is a tough boss and an intimidating presence, but he inspires the best in his employees. Some of us work for "nice" bosses, who are kind and considerate. Some of us work for nasty, insensitive boors, louts, and lummoxes. But we should all be so lucky to have Perry White as a boss. Gruff? Yes. Impatient? Very. Tough? As nails. But he challenges his reporters to produce their personal best, then to push the envelope beyond it, and, in this, he backs them 100 percent.

We should all be so lucky. But few of us are.

Current theories of management are all about redefining the role of the boss. These days, the ranks of upper-management are not supposed to be filled with task masters, but with "facilitators," people who make it possible for others to do their jobs and do them well. As the theory goes, the modern workplace is driven by knowledge resources rather than material resources. Traditionally, the boss held the keys to all the material resources, but, today, the principal resource, knowledge, is distributed widely among the workforce. Bosses are now expected to coordinate the collaboration among members of the enterprise rather than to push or pull them in the expectation of unquestioning obedience.

At least that's the theory.

In practice, even the most earnestly enlightened bosses still see themselves, at least after all the business school verbiage is elbowed aside, as the big cheese. Yet, unlike Perry White, who began his career in an era when bosses were *expected* to be the big cheese, today's managers are torn between theories of collaboration and a stubborn practical need to push, to pull, and generally to produce—in order to satisfy *their* bosses. The result is that most bosses fall far short of Perry White perfection. Their gruffness doesn't necessarily hide a heart of gold, and while they may work you hard, they don't always help you to be better than you think you are.

Wherever your boss or bosses fall on the leadership spectrum, it is your lot to deal with them and with their feelings, regardless of management theory. It is your job to manage your boss.

Create Respect

No one, not Clark Kent, not Lois Lane, not even the perpetually callow Jimmy Olsen, would make the mistake of blatantly buttering up—flattering—Perry White. He'd have none of *that*, thank you very much!

But now's the time to remember: Your boss *isn't* Perry White, and whoever first said "flattery will get you nowhere" obviously never tried it. Not that you can get by on flattery alone. Sucking up can't take the place of doing your job and doing it well. But make no mistake: instilling in your boss good feelings about himself or herself does indeed matter.

PERRY WHITE

Debut: *Superman* #7, November 1940
Full Name: Perry Jerome White

Perry White grew up in the notorious Suicide Slum neighborhood of Metropolis, where (according to some accounts) he enjoyed a friendship with young Lex Luthor.

Early incarnations of the Superman chronicles say little about Perry White's background, but the current story is that Perry started with the *Planet* as a copy boy at the tender age of ten. Having made his first fortune, Lex Luthor bought the paper when he was in his early twenties, sending Perry on assignment as a foreign correspondent. Luthor took the opportunity to seduce White's girlfriend, Alice Spencer. On his return from overseas, White married the pregnant Spencer, who gave birth to Luthor's natural son, whom she and Perry named Jerry. In the meantime, a consortium of financiers purchased the *Daily Planet* from Lex Luthor on condition that Perry White

be appointed managing editor. It is White who hired both Lois Lane and Clark Kent.

A man of great character, Perry White has endured many trials, including the death of his son, Jerry, and his own bout with lung cancer. For a brief interval, he taught journalism at Metropolis University, but soon returned to the *Planet*.

Begin by instilling in your boss good feelings about yourself. After all, he or she relies on you every day and may even have hired you to begin with. In any case, *you* represent a decision your boss has to live with. Best make him or her feel good about it. Toward this end, there is no substitute for top-flight performance, for always doing a job worthy of an Office Superman.

But there is more. Act in ways that demonstrate how good you feel about yourself and your work. When you speak to your boss, lower your voice. Deep voices convey more authority and confidence than high-pitched voices.

In the previous chapter, we mentioned the persuasive power of good breathing and how anxiety diminishes that power. Related to this is the effect of anxiety on your voice. The voice of fear is unmistakable. Thin, tight, quavering, high-pitched, it is totally unpersuasive. It is, however, almost completely useless to try fighting your anxiety. After all, "gruff" and "tough" bosses are genuinely intimidating. But you can learn how to deny anxiety expression through your voice by pushing your voice lower than normal and by slowing down in order to give each word its due weight. Pronounce each word carefully, and take time to breathe. You may still be scared, but you won't sound like it.

In speaking, you come across most authoritatively when you stand. If you've got something important to say to your boss, try to arrange things so that you speak standing up. This applies even if you are on the telephone. It's always a good idea to conduct the most important conversations on your feet.

Don't forget your body language. Your boss is senior to you in the company, but that is where the dominant-subordinate relationship ends. You are both adults, so put yourself across as an adult. Make eye contact. Use hand gestures to underscore verbal points, but keep your hands away from your face, especially your mouth. No hands in pockets, and if you're standing—a good idea!—don't shuffle your feet and don't rock from side to side.

Nick of Time

Jerry Siegel and Joe Shuster were movie fans, and they freely admitted that Superman owed a debt to the likes of Errol Flynn and Douglas Fairbanks. Super adventure comic books also owe something else to swashbuckler cinema: timing. Superman doesn't just rescue people, he saves them in the nick of time. That's one of the elements that makes any adventure thriller thrilling.

The Office Superman also strives for impeccable timing. He makes it his business to pick up on the rhythm of the workplace and the workday. He learns that there are advantageous and disadvantageous times for a conversation with the boss. And when he's figured this out, he exploits the good times and avoids the bad.

Each workplace is different, but, generally, Monday is not a great day to bring up issues that can be put off until Tuesday. Don't pin down your boss immediately before lunch or quitting time. Avoid bringing up potentially negative subjects just before a weekend or just before you know that your boss is going on vacation. Down time should never be brooding time. Don't try to shoehorn in a conversation when you know the boss doesn't have the time. Recruit time as your ally, not your adversary.

As for the conversation itself, get in tune with its natural rhythm of give and take. In talking with your boss, this often translates into the very essence of negotiation: asking *and* giving. When you approach your boss with a request, don't come on like a panhandler, as if you expect something for nothing. Approach him or her as a man of business, armed with a pledge to return fair value for fair value received.

If you want a raise, figure out a way to tell your boss how more money for you will benefit *her*. She already knows how it will benefit *you*. Have something to offer. Never walk into an important conversation empty-handed.

And that means not walking into it empty-headed, either. Plan what you have to say. You might want to draw up a written outline to use as a rehearsal script before you meet your boss. It is possible to become an overnight success. Just prepare overnight for success the next morning.

Start Pressing the Right Buttons

Now that you've thought about how to make your boss feel good about *you*, shift the focus to *him* or *her*. What does he or she need and want? What good (and true) news can you bring your boss? What issues—of importance to your boss—can you raise? What problems—of importance to your boss—can you solve?

Superman is about possibilities: What can be done. He is emphatically *not* about limits: What cannot be done. About possibilities we are always eager to hear. Limits, in contrast, are inherently much less interesting. Avoid peppering your conversation with limits, closed doors, and irreversible errors. Never sugar-coat or distort the truth, but do stretch your imagination to express yourself in the most positive, active terms possible. Never sweep problems under the rug, but do figure out ways to present them as opportunities.

Beyond Perry White

Perry White may be the archetypal boss, but most real-life bosses stray far from the archetype. Now, the happy fact is that most bosses much of the time actually behave in mainly reasonable ways. Issues of talent and competence aside, at the very least they want to do what's good for the enterprise, and, insofar as you are part of the enterprise, what they want to do is at least intended to be good for you, too.

Nevertheless, no boss is reasonable all of the time and even the best, subjected to enough pressure, fall into destructive patterns of behavior at least sometimes. In my experience with bosses, I've counted at least six destructive patterns.

1. The tyrant: You may not be familiar with the nineteenth-century author and member of the British Parliament, Lord Acton, but you've probably heard his most famous pearl of wisdom: "Power tends to corrupt and absolute power corrupts absolutely." The plain fact is that some folks find it almost impossible to be in charge without being a tyrant.

The tyrant operates in ways that cast his subordinates in the role of children—that is, little people who cannot make decisions and are therefore wholly dependent on the "parent." The tyrant speaks in monologues and thereby avoids dialogues. When he asks questions, it is not so much to gather information as it is to keep you feeling unstable, unconfident, and inferior. Routinely, the tyrant makes threats, sometimes outright, but more often couched in such phrases as "you'd better," "get on top of," "get on the ball," or "get on the stick."

Superman routinely confronts tyrants, and he always enjoys the upper hand because, for him, it's all an easy matter of perspective. They *think* they're powerful, but he *knows* he is.

Well, you may not feel more powerful than your boss, but you can put him or her into perspective. Resist the impulse to fear. Instead, think: What, exactly, can your boss do to you? Does this particular manager have the power to fire you? If so, has he or she fired a lot of other people? In most cases, most tyranny is just so much noise. Assess the reality.

The next step is to use the powers you truly do have. You have the capacity, for instance, to make your boss feel more important, which is precisely the way he or she wants to feel. You can do this by asking for advice (always an empowering request). You can do this by finding something to admire about the boss—some accomplishment or idea, for example—and offering a compliment on it. You can enlist even the tyrannical boss as your mentor by finding ways to maneuver him or her into investing time in you by instructing you.

2. The guiltmonger: The guiltmonger is the mirror image of the tyrannical boss. He won't hammer *you* down, but he will try to prove to you that you are tearing *him* down, usually by your unwillingness to "go the extra mile." The guiltmonger will never actually order you to put in extra hours, but he will wearily glance up from his desk at 5:30 and say something like, "Oh, no, don't stay late. You have more important things to do. My family is used to my working late."

It's hard to walk away from a conversation with a guiltmonger feeling good, but you can escape outright manipulation if you are able to separate your commitment to your job and career from your personal relationship to your boss. You also need to know the difference between the genuine demands that come with your job and the bogus emotional demands that come from your boss.

If an unreasonable demand is made on your time, offer a valid reason to refuse it: "I wish I could change my day off, but I have a medical appointment that would take months to reschedule." Unfortunately, your stock of legitimate excuses is not inexhaustible. As an alternative, try administering a dose of reality. Your boss starts with the guilt: "Oh, well, I'll just stay here and work on this report myself." Reply with reality: "Do you really have to? You know, I'll be available to do it tomorrow. I could rough out a draft by lunchtime, you could review it, and we'd go from there."

3. The blamer: From time to time, each of us is blamed for something that is not our fault. Resist the impulse simply to defend yourself. By all means, do defend yourself, but, in addition, offer to pitch in to correct the problem, even though you did not create it. Just because you are not to blame does not mean you cannot be part of a solution.

The situation is more difficult when you find yourself saddled with a boss who makes a habit of doling out blame. Take a deep breath to keep yourself from shouting your innocence. Then set about to determine the facts of the matter. Deny nothing until you have the full story. By gathering the facts, you will calm your boss by shifting his or her focus from personalities to events, and you will also gain an opportunity not only to demonstrate your blamelessness, but perhaps also to begin to resolve the problem.

After you have all the facts, direct your focus as well as that of your boss to the facts and away from yourself or other personalities. Often, *things* can be fixed. *People*, however, rarely can be.

Finally, the most potent superpower you can hurl against a blamer is your willingness to accept responsibility—but not blame. Make it clear that, although the situation in question is not your fault, you are prepared to accept it as your problem and will work to resolve it.

4. The dreamer: Some bosses are great believers in the power of inspiration, which, unfortunately, means that you may be directed to act on whatever idea recently drifted through the boss's consciousness, good, bad, or indifferent.

It begins: "On my way into the office this morning, I got a brainstorm . . ."

Naturally, you cannot and should not try to dodge every idea your boss comes up with, but if you are confronted by a harebrained "inspiration," you owe it to yourself, your company, and even to your boss to attempt to return her to reality. Never respond with cold water: "It'll never work!" This will only provoke hostile stubbornness. Indeed, it is always best to withhold voicing any judgment at all. If possible, respond only to the mechanics of your boss's instructions. For instance: "What kind of priority do you want me to give this?" Or: "Should I put such-and-such on hold and get to this right away?" Respond in a way that guides your boss's gaze back onto day-to-day reality. If your organization has some standard procedures in place for dealing with new ideas, concepts, and programs, trot them out. Get your boss involved in filling out forms or writing reports. This may give him or her time to think—and to rethink. If the idea survives this process, who knows, it may be a very good idea after all.

Yet another approach to a fleeting fancy is to play for time. "Can you give me some time to review this? I think I'll have lots of questions for you." In this way, you can take up the assignment without leaping onto the bandwagon.

5. The bumbler: Whereas the tyrant creates fear, the guiltmonger grief, the blamer resentment, and the dreamer useless work, the bumbler, an incompetent manager and leader, creates chronic chaos. Try to get a handle on the situation by taking extra steps with your boss to confirm his instructions and correct his errors. Avoid taking verbal instructions, if you can. Instead, make use of e-mail or even paper memos. Get whatever you can in writing. Above all, be *helpful*. Do your best to educate and assist your boss. It is to everyone's benefit that he succeed in the hard climb to competence.

6. The emotional volcano. Some bosses explode—routinely. The explosive boss is by definition both a poor manager and a poor communicator. When you find yourself in proximity to the blast, think it through. Just what is it that intimidates you about the boss's temper? No one likes being yelled at, but are there real consequences beyond the outburst of ill temper? If you truly believe that you are in danger of getting canned, start looking for another job—right now. But if the issue is mainly emotional, cope with it.

It is foolhardy to try to cork a volcano. Instead, let it erupt. Let the lava flow. Listen to the tirade, and try to maintain eye contact throughout, as if you are having a regular conversation. When the initial energy is spent and you can get a word in, offer a note of calm. This does *not* mean urging your boss to "calm down." Nothing is more aggravating to an angry man or woman than being dismissed in this manner. Instead, accept the emotion: "I can't blame you, for being angry, but . . ." And, after the "but," introduce some viable alternatives to raw emotion: ". . . but I need to talk this problem through. Would it be better for me to come back and discuss this later, or do you want to sit down and go over it now?"

Offer help. Offer alternatives. You should neither meekly submit to abuse nor participate in a shouting match. If two people yell, neither can hear.

On the Plus Side

Not all of us are privileged to have Perry White for a boss, but, whatever his or her flaws, every boss is a human being, and that, friends, is valid reason for hope.

Act on that hope by taking steps to bond with your boss. Just as you need to respond effectively to criticism and blame, so you need to respond effectively to praise. A lot of us have a hard time taking a compliment, but learning how to accept one graciously is a vital skill. Successfully acknowledging a compliment is an opportunity not only to savor a very pleasant moment, but to give your boss the pleasure of having bestowed recognition where it is deserved. When you accept a compliment with appropriate grace, your boss receives the highly satisfying feeling that she has acted well in placing confidence in you.

The rules for accepting a compliment are simple. First, say thanks: "Thanks!" Second, express pleasure: "I'm so happy you're pleased with the project!" Third, use the opportunity to express your high regard for your boss: "Coming from you, this really means something." Fourth, share the compliment with others who deserve it: "You know, Pete and Sarah were very helpful in the advice they offered." Even better: "Well, it was you who gave me the idea to try such and such."

Shameless Self-Promotion

Disguised as Clark Kent and maintaining a remote Fortress of Solitude, Superman can hardly be accused of showboating. But he is no shrinking violet, either, and he never ungraciously dodges recognition. On the contrary, he freely accepts honors and awards when they are bestowed on him. To do otherwise would be to rain on *everyone's* parade.

It behooves the Office Superman to be gracious, but also more aggressive, than the Man of Steel when it comes to self-promotion. In business, the most direct form of self-promotion is career advancement, either by securing a raise in salary or obtaining a promotion. These forms of self-promotion are negotiations, and, as with any negotiation, the best position to take is not adversarial, but helpful. *Help* the boss see the benefits—to himself and to the enterprise—of giving you the raise or the promotion you seek.

Let's start with the matter of a raise. The best thing you can do to help your boss in this negotiation is to answer the question:

Why do I need a raise?

Well, there are cars to be bought, mortgages to be paid, and children to educate. That's a perfectly valid answer, but it's not the one your boss needs, and it is always most compelling to focus on what your boss needs.

Prepare diligently for the salary discussion. Come to the discussion equipped with an oral resume that hits the highlights of the year's achievements. Supplement this with facts about what others, in similar jobs, are getting paid—assuming, of course, it's more than you're getting now.

It is a very good plan to do enough research to form a firm idea of how much more money you can reasonably expect. However, do not begin the discussion by stating a dollar amount. If the initial number is too high, you'll be embarrassed, but it will be far worse if you begin too low. While you can always negotiate downward, you cannot start low and negotiate up. Lowball yourself, and that's where you'll be stuck. The best negotiating tactic is to avoid being the first one to mention money. Instead, try to elicit a dollar offer from your boss. Get him or her to name a figure, and use it as the basis for further negotiation.

Talking to your boss about a promotion is similar to negotiating for a raise. As with a raise, your object is to persuade your boss that you are valuable, that she is getting good value for the good value she offers you. This is a *business deal* that you are negotiating, not a handout.

Always go into this negotiation armed with a menu of your accomplishments for the company. Focus your boss on this thought: If you accomplished so much in your current position, think how much more you can achieve in a position of greater scope and responsibility.

"What Would I Do Without You?"

Ponder Metropolis. While a sophisticated and diverse city, it is also besieged by crime, megalomaniacal businessmen, and more than its share of crooked politicians. What would Metropolis do without Superman?

It is not likely that your boss is faced with the multiple menaces that threaten to lay to waste Superman's adopted home. But, as a leader, your boss has plenty of problems to be solved and plenty of needs to be met. Your object is to become to him the Office Superman, to whom he poses the question: *What would I do without you?*

CHAPTER

8

A LEAGUE OF YOUR OWN

IF ANYONE IN THE ENTIRE UNIVERSE COULD MAKE IT ON THEIR OWN, 100 PERCENT SOLO, IT'S GOT TO BE SUPERMAN. Man of Steel, X-ray vision, the ability to fly, the whole invulnerability thing—you'd think he could just hang out the NO HELP WANTED sign and be done with it. But then, in March 1960, readers of *The Brave and the Bold* comic series suddenly saw the Man of Steel unite with an array of super heroes—in alphabetical order, Aquaman, Batman, the Flash, Green Lantern, J'onn J'onnz (the Martian Manhunter), and Wonder Woman—to defeat Starro the Conqueror, the mother of all extraterrestrial giant starfish. This super task force decided to dub itself the Justice League of America.

Readers liked the JLA, as they soon took to calling it, and it became a comic book staple, supplementing but, of course, never supplanting the solo Superman. Did the creative stewards of Superman at DC Comics have a thematic message in mind when they debuted the JLA? Maybe something like this: No man, not even Superman, is an island. It's possible. More likely, though, it just seemed like a good way to freshen up a number of super heroes and put them in a new context with new fictive possibilities. Besides, who hasn't posed such hypotheticals as "What if Superman and Batman teamed up?" It's natural and inevitable. Curiosity is all that's required. No thematic abstractions are necessary.

The fact is that people, super heroes included, are simply more interesting when they group together and team up. Generally speaking, people working together have more potential than a person working alone. By definition, business requires at least two people, call them a buyer and a seller, and most businesses require a lot more. In any case, being an Office Superman is never a solo act.

Small Talk, Big Results

Both Superman and his alter ego, Clark Kent, are men of action. Except within the confines of the Fortress of Solitude, Superman reveals himself only when there is something that desperately needs doing. As a reporter, Clark Kent spends less time in the office than he does out and about, getting the stories where the stories are. It's no wonder, then, that we rarely see Superman/Clark during a lull in the action. Maybe that's why the name is *Action Comics*, not *Lull-in-the-Action Comics*, but that also points out one big difference between the comics and real life. No matter what you do for a living, there are always plenty of lulls.

Lulls are, in fact, important to the business day. They are part of the rhythm of creativity. They provide space for a breath, and that in itself is important, but they also give you time to think, to review, and to revise. And there is another way to fill the lulls: with conversation, shooting the breeze, small talk.

Managers of the old school really hate small talk. They dismiss it as an activity for "clock watchers" and "goldbricks" (those are the words old-school managers like to use). And it's true, small talk can be a major waste of time. That, however, is also true of most business activities. For instance, suppose you put in hours of research on a project that ends up never getting off the ground. We accept the fact that some research leads to great things while some, probably most, dies at a dead end. Yet just because it does not offer a 100 percent guarantee of a productive outcome, we do not abandon research as a waste of time. Likewise, the fact that some small talk is productive and some is not is no reason to shun it altogether.

When it works, small talk heightens your visibility in a positive way, promotes team building and organizational morale, and increases your awareness of the needs and attitudes of those you work with. This is especially important, because the more you know about your colleagues, subordinates, and bosses, the more effectively you can communicate with them.

Think of the people you work with as your customers, individuals to whom you continually sell yourself, your ideas, your projects, your point of view, and your value. As any good salesman knows, a big part of selling is knowing your customers, identifying their needs, desires, and concerns, then addressing your sales appeal to these issues. How do you find out about your customers? By getting them to talk about themselves.

Small talk is conversation, nothing more, nothing less. Some people are naturally good at conversation, while others just aren't. As a rule, those who aren't kill conversation by failing to listen. They may be preoccupied or simply uninterested in what the other person has to say. Some conversation killers are just too shy or self-conscious to pay attention to what someone else is saying.

If you can avoid killing conversation, you're on your way to having good small talk, even if you aren't a "born" conversationalist. Begin by choosing the right time. If you're doing something else that's really important, don't interrupt yourself to start a conversation, and if someone wants to talk to you, reply gently that you'd love to talk, but you're up against a deadline or you're in the middle of a demanding problem. Offer a rain check: "Can I drop by your office for a chat after lunch?"

When you do find the right time and start a conversation, be sure to look at the other person. Don't let your eyes wander. Ask questions; they are the fuel of small talk. You don't have to pepper your partner with queries, but when the conversation flags, try something like, "And then what happened?" or, "What did you do next?"

Conversation is about give and take, which means restraining any urge you have to interrupt the speaker. Wait your turn, and when you do weigh in, try to be positive. Negativity of any kind usually stifles conversation, especially small talk, which is supposed to be light, breezy, and pleasurable. In this vein, avoid using small talk as an occasion for criticism. Criticism is serious, and is something best done in private. Never ambush your small talk partner.

Small talk must not be confused with gossip. Water-cooler gossip and rumor mongering are common in the workplace, but they undermine morale and the spirit of collaboration. Unlike genuine small talk, gossip and rumors tear down rather than build up.

It is also vital to resist any urge you may feel to demonstrate that you're smarter than the other person. The goal of small talk is not to show off, but to acquire information about those you work with. You already know what *you* know. Give the other person a chance to tell you what he or she knows.

Small talk is spontaneous, it just happens, but that doesn't mean you can't prepare for it. Keep yourself well-informed on current events. Read the newspaper daily and at least one good news magazine each month. Listen to the news as it is presented and discussed on Public Broadcasting Service television and radio or from other media sources that cover stories in depth. Stay well-informed about developments in your business or profession.

Preparation means nothing if you don't actually seize opportunities for small talk

CHAPTER 9

THERE'S SOMETHING ABOUT LOIS

EXCEPT FOR THE MAN OF STEEL HIMSELF, no one in some seven decades of Superman chronicles has claimed more comic book real estate than Lois Lane. She is the only supporting character in the vast Superman cast who was present from the very beginning, (*Action Comics* #1, June 1938). As a reporter for the *Daily Star* (*Action Comics* predecessor of the more familiar *Daily Planet*), Lois was a rarity in 1938, not only because she was a woman reporter, but because she was a woman with a career. Back then, the vast majority of women were housewives. True, many young women entered the work force in service and subordinate roles, as waitresses and secretaries, for example, but these were jobs, not careers, and they generally quit once they had found a husband. World War II changed this social scene somewhat, bringing women into the work force in unprecedented numbers, but, after the war, most returned to domestic lives, and it was not until the early 1960s that women began to pursue careers in large numbers.

Over the years, the portrayal of Lois Lane reflected this process of social change. Although Siegel and Shuster were ahead of the pack in their portrayal of Lois as a career woman in 1938, closer examination suggests they weren't quite so far in front as they appear to be at first glance. In her debut appearance, Lois puts off Clark's query, "Why is it you always avoid me at the office?" with, "Please Clark! I've been scribbling 'sob stories' all day long. Don't ask me to dish out another." This tips us off that the early Lois Lane was not a hard-hitting journalist, but a "sob sister" (the term is used in *Superman* #7, December 1940), one of a class of newspaper-women, popular in the 1930s and 1940s, who specialized in churning out trashy romantic tearjerkers for a female readership. Although Lois is a professional, Siegel and Shuster depict her with a limited horizon.

This changed a bit during the war years, when Lois was sometimes portrayed as a full-fledged war correspondent, but then, during this period and into the 1950s, she also does stints as a weather editor (a position at the bottom of the journalistic heap), head of the lost-and-found department, and staff cartoonist, as well as editor of the *Daily Planet's* Paris edition and, in the absence of Perry White, even acting editor in the Metropolis office. At times, during the 1950s, she is elevated to the status of "Clark Kent's rival reporter at the *Daily Planet*" (*Action Comics* #176, January 1953), only to be characterized as well as "the prettiest girl reporter in Metropolis" (*Action Comics* #195, August 1954).

It is only as the 1960s dissolved into the 1970s that Lois Lane was depicted as a reporter with a very solid reputation for executing daring and dangerous journalistic assignments. These earned her a shelf full of awards and honors, including a Pulitzer Prize. From this point on, no Superman writer dared call her a "girl reporter." Times had changed, and there could be no backsliding. Women had become reporters, not *girl* reporters, just as they had become doctors, lawyers, managers, and CEOs, all without the addition of gender-qualifying adjectives.

Lois Lane's evolution as a career woman did not end the romantic and sexual interest—and tension—between her and Clark Kent or Superman. If anything, it made them more acute, more complicated, and more interesting. Even back in 1938, office romances could probably get pretty messy, but as the playing field has leveled over the years, love, sex, and the workplace have become difficult issues with the very highest stakes. A generation or two ago, Clark could have safely made certain assumptions about "sob sister" Lois, including the assumption that the *Daily Planet* was nothing but a stepping stone en route to marriage. The days of such assumptions are long gone.

Risky Business

So let's cut to the chase. Can today's Office Superman afford to have an office romance?

There is an easy answer, and it is *No, he cannot.*

Easy, but not very realistic. Look at this way. A week consists of seven days, or 168 hours. Of this, 56 hours are devoted to sleep, leaving 110 hours. By law, you don't have to work more than 40 hours a week, but most people who do more than flip burgers for a living approach 60 hours a week. Throw in an hour a day for the commute, and you have 65 hours, leaving you with 45 more-or-less free hours each week. The obvious conclusion is that we spend most of our waking life at work. Now, who do we find at work? Since we're no longer living in 1938, we find men *and* women, and we find them, on average, in nearly equal quantities. Aside from the fact of their maleness and femaleness, this coed group has a lot in common: same employer, similar career interests, involvement in the same day-to-day issues. So is it any wonder that, in recent surveys, about 80 percent of employees report some sort of romantic or sexual experience with a coworker?

No, it is no wonder at all. In fact, the contemporary workplace is the most likely place for Americans to meet a romantic partner. In 1996, after a rocky office romance (lasting 58 years, if we say it began with *Action Comics* #1 in 1938), Lois Lane and Clark Kent provided corroborating evidence of this trend by finally tying the knot.

And yet, romance in the context of business is risky business. Most managers don't like to see their employees "involved" with one another because they feel office romance results in productivity loss and compromised professionalism. If employees focus on romance, they say, they can't be focused on work.

Common sense certainly prompts us to side with managers on this issue, but a number of studies and some "anecdotal data"—experiences individuals tell interviewers—suggest that office romance can actually increase productivity. Charles A. Pierce, a professor at Montana State University-Bozeman who specializes in organizational and industrial psychology, concluded that "employees often channel romantic energy to work tasks. They bring enthusiasm and energy to their work." He reported that "blanket policies" against office romances are "not based on research."

The idea that office romance can increase productivity may seem counterintuitive, but it really isn't so strange. Romance is romance. For all its potential heartaches, love and sex are generally pretty happy things, and if you're happy—feeling pretty good about yourself—you'll probably do a better job at work. This holds true whether the object of your affections is in the same office, at home, or working for another firm.

So, an office romance does not necessarily reduce productivity and may actually increase it. That still leaves the other common managerial objection: compromised professionalism.

The professional interacts with all employees—coworkers, subordinates, and bosses—fairly, attentively, and even-handedly, refraining from favoritism or bias as well as the *appearance* of favoritism or bias.

Can an office romance create favoritism or bias? The answer depends on the character of the two people involved in the romance. There is a risk, but it can be managed, provided that a willingness to manage it exists. The acid test is what happens to professional objectivity if the romance ends badly or if one of the partners becomes involved with someone else in the office. Green eyes do not go well with a gray flannel suit.

Despite the risks, professionalism is not *necessarily* compromised by romance, but perhaps the more serious concern is the *appearance* of favoritism or bias. In a recent panel discussion at the University of Massachusetts, some workers reported that office romance has what might be called an "all the world loves lovers" effect. The knowledge that two coworkers were happily engaged in a relationship served to lift the morale of the entire workplace. More commonly, however, panelists reported a noticeable negative response to office romances. One woman who had been involved in an office romance commented "that . . . coworkers weren't so open and sharing with me anymore. There were even some suggestions that my relationship . . . had more to do with career potential than sincere affection. Personally, I felt hurt. Professionally, I was frozen out of the information loop."

This *is* serious. You may possess the maturity and integrity of character to ensure that your personal feelings will not compromise your professionalism, but you cannot ensure that others will invariably perceive your fairness and objectivity. Superman's superpowers give him control over a great many things, but his double life often creates problems for his poor alter ego, Clark Kent. When trouble strikes, Clark, of course, must disappear in order to transform himself into Superman. Looking on, others—often it is none other than Lois Lane—see Clark apparently running from danger. Based on appearances, they naturally assume he is a coward, and although nothing could be further from the truth, Clark is powerless to change that perception. Reality notwithstanding, those involved in an office romance may well find themselves the helpless victims of perception.

Issues of perception are potentially most damaging when the romance involves a boss and a subordinate, but they are still critical when peers are involved romantically. If you and a colleague are "involved," others may feel that they no longer have full access to you. Resentment and suspicion may result.

The University of Massachusetts panel reported that women are less tolerant of office romance than men. Their feeling is that they, as women, are members of a class that has struggled to be taken seriously in the workplace, and that office romance undermines this struggle, making it harder for women to project a professional image.

LOIS LANE

Debut: *Action Comics* #1, June 1938
Full Name: Lois Joanne Lane

Born in a U.S. Army hospital outside of Wiesbaden, Germany, Lois Lane is the daughter of General Sam and Elinore Lane. While on a trip to Metropolis with her sister Lucy, fifteen-year-old Lois lied about her age and tried to secure a position at the *Daily Planet*. Managing editor Perry White told her to come back when she was older, but instead Lois carried off a daring infiltration of Lex Luthor's sinister LexCorp, obtained secret documents, escaped from temporary captivity, and turned the documents over to Perry White, who agreed to hire Lois on a part-time basis while she finished school.

Lois graduated from college at the top of her class, became a successful writer, and blossomed into the *Planet's* star reporter. Her biggest journalistic coup was becoming the first reporter to cover the exploits of Superman. Indeed, it was Lois, inspired by the "S"-shaped Kryptonian symbol on his costume, who gave the super hero his name.

Lois Lane dedicated a large part of her professional life to discovering the true identity of Superman, all the while carrying on a romance with Clark Kent, which culminated in an engagement, at which point Clark revealed his identity to her. After marriage, she has continued to work as the nation's top journalist, and has become, in the fullest sense, the partner of the Man of Steel and the sharer of the all-important secret of his dual identity.

Managing the Risks

All right, Office Superman, after reading this maybe you're ready to declare your intention *never* to mix business with pleasure. However, the fact of life is that you cannot predict if or when Cupid's arrow will strike. Romance may be the furthest thing from your mind when, just the same, you and a coworker fall in love. That is reality. Just be aware that all office romances have the potential for creating a hostile response from fellow workers. This being the case, do everything you can to maintain fairness, openness, and objectivity in dealing with everyone.

In 1997, editors at DC Comics collected the various individual stories leading up to and surrounding the marriage of Lois Lane and Clark (Superman) Kent in a trade paperback called *Superman: The Wedding and Beyond*. This slim volume makes highly revealing reading for anyone interested in the perils and pleasures of office romance and marriage between coworkers. Suffering from a strange diminution of his powers, Superman recounts for Wonder Woman some of the emotional highlights of his life. Among other things, he reveals the problems of being simultaneously "involved" and competitive in the office. "Lois dedicated herself to getting the lowdown on Superman," Superman recalls. "It took her years to forgive Clark Kent for beating her to it and writing the story first." *Years* to forgive him! Superman continues: "It's not that I wanted to ace her out of the story . . . but I did want to control what the public knew about Superman." Despite his feelings for Lois, Clark Kent felt that he could not compromise the identity of Superman. Not only did competition conflict with romance, but so did a larger view of ethics.

Nevertheless, Superman goes on, "over the years we got past that and I grew closer to Lois as Superman—and Clark. It was Clark she eventually agreed to marry, but I couldn't let her go into the marriage without telling her the truth." Here is another crux: secrets and marriage do not mix, especially when the partners work in the same office.

As it is, the road to marriage was a rough one for Lois and Clark, whose engagement, at one point, was broken off. Lois later explained: "Our relationship disintegrated because I thought his life as Superman was too demanding and unpredictable. Guess I was so afraid of losing my individuality, of becoming a subordinate Mrs. Superman . . . that I acted like a jerk and an idiot!" Lois Lane and Clark (Superman) Kent are extraordinary people, to be sure, but the problems they faced first as workplace lovers and then as married colleagues are all too typical.

For colleagues who are romantically involved or married, the professional and emotional hazards can be difficult to navigate successfully. But even more immediately dangerous is the workplace issue of sexual harassment.

The legal definition of sexual harassment, according to Title VII of the Civil

Rights Act of 1964, goes like this:

> . . . *[any] unwelcome sexual advances, requests for sexual favors, and other verbal and physical conduct of a sexual nature when submission to such conduct is made either explicitly or implicitly a term or condition of an individual's employment; submission to or rejection of such conduct by an individual is used as the basis for employment decisions affecting such individual; such conduct has the purpose or effect of unreasonably interfering with an individual's work performance or creating an intimidating, hostile, or offensive working environment.*

That's what the law calls sexual harassment. *You* can call it kryptonite.

Sexual harassment is not just sleazy and hurtful, it's against the law. Most of the time, it's pretty easy to avoid breaking the law. Don't steal, don't kill, and don't cheat on your income taxes. But while the law on sexual harassment is admirably clear in its definition, the interpretation leaves a lot of gray areas. It's easy to come up with examples of sexual harassment. Overt sexual advances, repeatedly asking for a date after being told no, making suggestive comments—all these constitute a violation of the law. But what, exactly, is a "suggestive comment"? Everyone would probably agree that "Want a little action tonight?" is suggestive, but how about "You look gorgeous"? And just what constitutes an "overt sexual advance"? Is it a hand on the shoulder? In fact, any physical contact or touching may be interpreted as an overt sexual advance, so anything other than a handshake is risky and should be avoided.

Sexual jokes, comments, and other suggestive language, even if they aren't directed at a particular person, may constitute a violation of Title VII, which protects individuals against being subject to "an intimidating, hostile, or offensive working environment." Same goes for exhibiting pornographic material or sexual graffiti—even if it's in your personal work area and you consider it a form of high art.

In Chapter 8, we talked about getting positive results from office "small talk." Better make sure the conversation doesn't drift to sexual matters, though, and these include talk about fantasies, preferences, activities, or body parts. Even certain gestures or facial expressions may be interpreted as obscene and therefore offensive, contributing to a hostile work environment.

Understand this: Sexual harassment is hardest on the victim. But it also has grave consequences for the accused offender, even if the offender was unconscious of his or her offense. It can damage or destroy careers.

Your Superpowers Are Useless . . .

All employees need to be aware of the risks of romance and sex in the workplace, but managers and supervisors bear the heaviest burdens. Most employees who complain about sexual harassment have legitimate reasons for doing so, yet it is also the case that some people lie, and even honest folks can honestly disagree on the nature of some word or act.

If you are in a management or supervisory position, protect yourself by avoiding intimate, overly familiar conversation with subordinates, by not touching them, and by ensuring that you use no language that can be interpreted as offensive.

Turn on your emotional radar. If you feel uncomfortable with a certain subordinate, don't put yourself in a situation where you are alone with him or her. Include a third party in any one-on-one conference. And here's what may be the really hard part. If you are a manager or supervisor, you'd better think carefully before you become romantically involved with a subordinate. You are exposing yourself to accusations of sexual harassment, and you are exposing both yourself and the other person involved to accusations of favoritism. At the very least, you run the risk of undermining your authority with other subordinates.

"Good For You, Lois!"

Superman will never be out of work as long as Lois Lane is around. She gets in a lot of trouble, and it's almost always up to the Man of Steel to come to the rescue. But that doesn't mean she's a woman who can't look out for herself. In her very first story, in *Action Comics* #1, she responds to the overtures of mobster Butch Matson in no uncertain terms. "You'll dance with me and like it!" he barks at Lois. Her reply is a sharp slap in the face. "Good for you, Lois!" Clark says to himself.

Decisions about office romance can be complicated, but there's at least one that's a no-brainer. When Lois Lane says no, that means *no*. All interpretation must stop with this monosyllable. *No* doesn't mean maybe, and it certainly doesn't "really mean" yes. Play fast and loose with the definition of this most simple of words, and you may find yourself in a situation that has escalated from harassment, mostly a civil matter and bad enough at that, to sexual assault, a case for the criminal courts.

The "American Way"

The full integration of women into the workplace is part of a new American revolution that has transformed offices from places of racial, ethnic, and cultural homogeneity to arenas of diversity. Back in the early 1950s, when the memorable phrase "Truth, justice, and the American way" became associated with Superman, the American way the writers doubtless had in mind was overwhelmingly white and male. Today, the American way looks far different, more colorful and varied in every way and, for this fact, stronger.

You can still find people who resist diversity in the workplace, but most readily realize that workplace diversity is not only right, because it reflects the make-up of our society, it's also good business, again precisely because it reflects the make-up of our society. To succeed in a diverse society, a business needs the multiple perspectives of a diverse work force.

JLA Revisted

In the last chapter, we saw that Superman and his creators grasped the benefits of diversity as early as 1960, when the Justice League of America debuted. Joining the Man of Steel were Aquaman, Batman, the Flash, Green Lantern, J'onn J'onnz (the Martian Manhunter), and Wonder Woman, each of whom offered special strengths that, combined, created a whole greater than the sum of its parts.

Aquaman is thoroughly at home in the ocean. He can breathe water and communicate telepathically with aquatic life. He brings a special ecological and environmental awareness to the super hero business.

Batman, very much a human being, imparts a somewhat dark and gritty point of view to the business of fighting crime and other perils.

After Wally West was hit by a combination of lightning and chemicals, he became the Flash, the Fastest Man Alive, a specialist in extreme speed.

The Green Lantern has had various alter egos, but the power of each comes from an emerald power ring, which allows the wearer to create virtually any object imaginable and also to shoot blasts of energy, to enable flight, to create defensive force shields, and so on. Sounds great, but, because of impurities in the ring, it is powerless against the color yellow. Like most of us, the Green Lantern can really use someone to watch his back.

J'onn J'onnz, known as the Martian Manhunter, possesses superstrength, the ability to fly, near-invulnerability, telepathic powers, and the capacity to change form and to achieve intangibility and invisibility. His only weakness is fire. Even a little flame can do him in.

In 1940, the company that would become DC Comics hired the eminent psychologist William Moulton Marston to serve on its board of consultants. Marston expressed concern that an all-male pantheon of super heroes presented young comic book readers with an unbalanced view of the world, and in 1941 Wonder Woman debuted, the first stories written by Marston himself under the pseudonym Charles Moulton. An Amazonian princess who leaves her native Paradise Island to fight for right in the male-dominated world at large, Wonder Woman possesses superstrength, stamina and agility, plus important accessories, including a magic lasso, an invisible airplane, and bullet-proof bracelets. In her early adventures with the Justice League, and as its only female member, she functioned as a kind of secretary—Ugh!—but, over the years, the JLA learned to make far more extensive and productive use of her powers.

Diversity: A Superpower

When they debuted the Justice League of America in 1960, the creative stewards at DC Comics exhibited an appreciation of what we might today call multiculturalism, the incorporation into an enterprise of people of diverse backgrounds and perspectives. The diverse enterprise is both more interesting and more powerful than a culturally monolithic organization. Successful leaders have long realized that if everyone thinks the same way, no one is really thinking.

In the American workplace, diversity has been made possible as well as mandated by law, beginning with the Civil Rights Act of 1964. But savvy business people, and that includes the Office Superman, aren't just obeying the law. They recognize that diversity is critical to the success of any enterprise. As the American context of business continues to become increasingly diverse, more women, more partners in two-income families, more employees who are caring for children or elderly parents, more physically disabled or disadvantaged workers, and more older workers will enter the workforce, as will more people of diverse racial, ethnic, and cultural backgrounds. Good thing, too, since a business community that reflects the realities of the community at large can better understand that larger community and thrive within it.

Tune Yourself Up

Before he embarks on any mission of importance, Superman prepares, often in the contemplative confines of his Fortress of Solitude. Before he can know what to do in a given situation, he knows that he must first know himself. As you enter the diversity of today's workplace, you may need to take a similar self-inventory.

Ask yourself how you feel about diversity. Can you readily look beyond gender? Color? Ethnicity? Disability? Or do you see these things instead of the person behind them? Are you comfortable with people who are different from you? Does prejudice ever influence your treatment of others?

It is important to know where you are coming from, so that you can, if necessary, adjust your course. Consider: If prejudice directed against you can make your corporate climb difficult or even impossible, the prejudices you may direct against others, purposely or without thinking, will also drag you down. The realities are these: During your career, you *will* work for or under the supervision of people of all kinds. More and more of your clients and customers will come from all sorts of backgrounds, as will the other people on whom your career depends, your colleagues and subordinates. Add to all this the force of law. Federal legislation protects the rights of minority workers, and lawsuits based on bias of various sorts have become a kind of industry unto itself.

But the bottom line is that while thriving in diversity is a necessity, it is hardly a *grim* necessity. Working well in a diverse environment brings increases in efficiency, productivity, and workplace harmony. It enhances your understanding of the people with whom you work, your customers and clients as well as your colleagues, subordinates, and bosses.

Inclusion Is the Key

Discrimination is about exclusion. Diversity is about inclusion. Instead of looking for ways to exclude this or that individual, the Office Superman finds ways to include more people in more opportunities and more aspects of the job.

By 2005, women will make up 48 percent of the workforce, and an ever-growing number of women will occupy the top management levels. Obviously, it is long past time to stop thinking of men as executives and women as secretaries. But women are sometimes excluded in subtler ways, sometimes by the way many of us use language. It doesn't take an Office Superman to recognize that such synonyms for *woman* as babe, baby, broad, chick, doll, gal, and sweety are sexist and offensive. But much sexist language is so ingrained in English that it seems perfectly natural and normal. Traditionally, English has used the masculine pronoun, *he*, to refer to men as well as women. The effect, on a more-or-less unconscious level, is to make women culturally invisible, as if they were second-class beings. Unfortunately, it's not always easy to avoid the generic *he*. Some folks have proposed such substitutes as *he/she, he or she, or even s/he.* All can be pretty awkward. The Office Superman looks for more inventive ways around the problem. To begin with, get rid of pronouns whenever possible. For instance, *He really understands his employees.* could become *Effective managers understand their employees.*

Man is also frequently used generically as a substitute for *human beings.* Try using *people* or *person* instead of *man*—unless, of course, you are referring to a male. Similarly, *artificial* is better than *manmade*, and *humankind* or *humanity* is preferable to *mankind.* Instead of talking about a *businessman* or *businesswoman*, take gender out of the picture altogether by being specific: *advertising executive* or *stockbroker.* Convert *chairman* to *chair*, *insurance man* to *insurance agent*, *mailman* to *letter carrier, salesman/saleswoman* to *salesperson* or *sales representative,* and *spokesman* to *representative.*

As a form of address, *Ms.*, which once seemed strange, has been common for so long that it sounds quite natural. Unless a woman requests a different form of address, use *Ms.* rather than *Miss* or *Mrs.*

Even Office Supermen sometimes stumble when it comes to the nonverbal aspects of relating to women in the workplace. Yes, courtesy still counts. Shake hands with a woman as you would with any business associate—firmly and warmly—and remember that neither a man nor a woman welcomes a knuckle-busting grip. It's still quite okay for a man to open or hold a door for a woman—or, indeed, for another man. It is also fine for a woman to open and hold a door for a man. Courtesy need not be gender specific.

Meet Maggie Sawyer

In "Bloodsport" (*Superman* #4, April 1987), Maggie Sawyer, a detective with the Metropolis P.D., is introduced. As we follow her in subsequent stories, we see her rise in the department to head the Special Crimes Unit and then to the rank of Inspector. Formerly married to Captain Jim Sawyer, with whom she had a daughter, Jamie, Maggie divorced and later began a lesbian relationship with Toby Raines, a reporter for a *Daily Planet* rival newspaper.

While the comics stretch our imaginations with fantastic tales and characters, they are, first and foremost, rooted in contemporary social reality. As the heated dialogue and strident debate over such issues as gay marriage attest, our society and our government have yet to come fully to terms with many aspects of sexual orientation. Where employment is concerned, however, there is no room for dispute. Discrimination on the basis of sexual orientation is illegal, and, diversity of sexual orientation is an open, visible feature of today's workplace just as it is of our larger reality.

Enabling the Disabled

We're born black, Hispanic, white, Asian, Native American, male, female, but any of us at any time can become a member of another minority: the disabled. Many people feel uncomfortable around the disabled. Fearing to cause pain or offense, they sometimes don't know how to act or what to say. The law—the Americans with Disabilities Act (ADA), passed in 1992—makes it a crime to discriminate against disabled persons in the workplace (and in other public places). But, the law aside, there are compelling human and business reasons to avoid discrimination, even when it is motivated by a desire to be kind and considerate.

The first step away from your own awkwardness is to focus on the person, not the disability. Don't ignore the person, and be careful to avoid referring to him or her in the third person. For example, if someone is pushing the person's wheelchair, don't direct questions to the helper: "Would he like to hang up his coat?"

When you are introduced to a disabled person, offer a normal greeting. Of course, you may need to make common-sense allowances for the disability. If a hand or arm is disabled, be prepared to shake the left hand—or not to shake hands at all. Speak up to a blind person: "Shall we shake hands?"

A wheelchair is an extension of personal space. Don't touch or handle it. When you approach a visually impaired person, alert him or her to your presence. A simple hello is often enough, but if the person doesn't return your greeting using your name, identify yourself. Resist the impulse to pet or otherwise interact with a seeing-eye dog—unless the owner explicitly invites you to do so. The dog is a working animal, not a pet.

In working with hearing-impaired people, be sure that you are clearly within sight before you make a greeting or begin a conversation. If the person has an impairment of speech, summon patience. Listen carefully, and do not interrupt. Resist the temptation to complete the person's sentences.

The Office Superman sees himself as a helper—but, he wonders, should he automatically offer help to a disabled coworker? Fortunately, there is a very simple answer to this question: Just ask.

If, for example, a coworker in a wheelchair encounters a steep ramp, don't start pushing. Instead, *ask*: "May I help?" If a visually disabled coworker seems to be having trouble negotiating a hallway, touch his or her shoulder, offer your arm, and *ask*: "May I direct you somewhere?"

Leap Stereotypes in a Single Bound

We all know that lead is the one element impervious to Superman's X-ray vision, but even the penetrating gaze of the Man of Steel can't see through stereotypes. They blind us all. And that is a tragic thing, since it's a lot easier to mistreat an abstraction than to abuse a real live person. On the flip side, it's hard to feel kindly toward a stereotype, but quite natural for most of us to get friendly with a fellow human being.

The Office Superman vaults over stereotypes by cleaving to the Golden Rule. He treats others as he would have them treat him. His attitude toward the differences he encounters is respectful rather than judgmental. He is as flexible as steel in Superman's hands, because he understands that rigid people create many unnecessary difficulties in dealing with people from different backgrounds.

The most important superpower required for thriving in the diverse workplace is the power of listening—and learning. When speaking or working with a person of an ethnic or racial origin that is different from yours, make no reference to it. Never put the other person in the position of speaking for his or her race or nation: "What do *you people* like to eat, anyway?" But if he or she wants to share some aspect of cultural or ethnic heritage, listen, learn, and enjoy the good conversation. Pick up on the cues. Mirza comes into the office wearing a piece of traditional jewelry from her country of origin. You greet her with, "What a beautiful necklace! Is that from your country?" And let the conversation begin.

This Is a Gift

The Office Superman doesn't merely accept diversity where he works. He is comfortable with it—a good thing, since workplace diversity is inevitable in a diverse society like ours and since the law backs it. Even more, the Office Superman thinks of diversity as a kind of gift. Diversity is good business. In the workplace, it represents the marketplace in which business must either thrive or falter. Above all, the Office Superman soon learns to stop thinking about "diversity" altogether. People, after all, are people, and that's the way he sees them.

10

WHAT DO I DO WITH JIMMY OLSEN?

THE *DAILY PLANET* IS EASY TO THINK OF AS A MODEL OFFICE. At the top is the archetypal boss, the Chief, Perry White. In the middle is a pair of colleagues, Clark Kent and Lois Lane. At the bottom is Jimmy Olsen, the apprentice or "cub reporter."

In truth, this is not quite how Jerry Siegel and Joe Shuster imagined it when Jimmy made his debut in December 1941. Back then he was described as an "office boy" and didn't even get a surname until April 1942, in *Superman* #15, when he was called Jimmy Olsen for the first time. Today's Superman fans think of Jimmy as a young man in his late teens or perhaps early twenties, but until 1944, he was depicted as a boy about ten years old, and then he appeared in early adolescence, age twelve or thirteen. By the early to mid 1950s, he was clearly older, he lived in an apartment on his own, and he was no longer an office boy but, officially, a cub reporter.

Those of us who spent a portion of childhood glued to the *Adventures of Superman* TV series summon up memories of Jack Larson's portrayal of Jimmy Olsen as the kid who lugs around a Speed Graphic flash-bulb-encumbered camera and gets into a lot of trouble, often in tandem with Lois Lane. The comic book chronicles portrayed him rather differently, however. He still got into plenty of jams, but he was also clearly under the wing of Clark Kent, who served as his mentor. Even as an office boy, Jimmy showed himself to be an apt apprentice. In "Man of Steel versus Man of Metal" (*World's Finest Comics* #6, Summer 1942), Jimmy gives Clark Kent an important news tip, to which Clark responds with positive reinforcement: "You're an observant lad!" In return, Jimmy salutes his mentor: "I hope to be a top-notch reporter like you someday." A testament to Clark Kent's effectiveness as a mentor—and Jimmy's aptness as a pupil—came in 1954, when, in "Jimmy Olsen . . . Editor!" (*Superman* #86), Jimmy enjoys 24 hours of success as editor during Metropolis's celebration of Boy's Day. "That boy will be a good newspaperman someday!" Clark remarks, and, indeed, just a year later, Jimmy is named editor of the *Daily Planet's* London edition, "The International Daily Planet" (*Action Comics* #203, April 1955). In more recent years, Jimmy Olsen has really come into his own and is typically depicted as a superb news photographer. Indeed, it is thanks to his lens that some of Superman's greatest moments have been captured for the public and posterity. In many of the stories of the *Superman: Birthright* series, which began in 2003, none other than Lois Lane is seen as one of Jimmy's most ardent champions. The approval of this uncompromising professional, who pulls no punches as a critic and who confers praise only sparingly, is testament to how valuable a member of the *Daily Planet* team Jimmy has become.

The Heart of Leadership

The relationship between Clark Kent and Jimmy Olsen goes straight to the heart of leadership. Asked to define leadership, many of us would talk about making decisions and giving orders, both of which are, in fact, important leadership functions. But they are peripheral to the principal function. The heart of leadership is mentoring, empowering others in the organization to assume increasing levels of responsibility—ultimately, to do your job someday. It is for this very reason that the notion of mentoring threatens some leaders, who worry that they may be raising a nest of vipers who will ultimately push them out of a job. But that's not the way it works. In a healthy organization, you mentor those you lead even as you are mentored by those who lead you. This puts everyone in a position to move up.

Of Credibility and Communication

Young as he is, Jimmy Olsen, from his very earliest adventures, has already made two important choices in his life. He has chosen Clark Kent as his mentor and Superman as his friend (he is even the proud possessor of a "special wristwatch," a gift from Superman that produces an "ultrasonic signal" to summon the Man of Steel to his aid). Though wise, the choices were not difficult, because both Clark and Superman had amply demonstrated credibility, the worthiness to be believed and to be believed in. This quality, indispensable to leadership, is built on three elements:

1. *Your knowledge of what you know and what you don't know.* Effective leaders project a credible image of confidence. The surest source of confidence and self-assurance comes from knowing your job, knowing your facts, and knowing the basis of your own decisions and opinions. Just as important is knowing—clearly—what you don't know, that is, understanding the limits of your knowledge.

2. *Your ability to persuade with your ears.* The most persuasive leaders are not those gifted with golden oratory, but with the ability to listen and to hear. They spend more time listening than speaking, and when they do speak, what they say is based on what they have heard and digested.

3. *The courage to shun defensiveness.* Effective leaders express themselves with self-assurance, but they also stop to listen to all responses, especially to criticism. They never try to shout down critics, but, instead, strive to learn from them. To those you lead, make it clear that you are open to all points of view.

Of Clarity

Among Superman's more novel earlier powers was a super voice, which could reach stratospheric decibel levels so that, if need be, he could make himself heard over thousands of miles. Leadership does not require so loud a voice, but it does demand clarity. Charisma, confidence, persuasion, all are important aspects of communicating credibility and, therefore, conveying a leadership image. But even more basic is the ability to communicate clear objectives and goals.

The necessary clarity begins with an understanding of the difference between objectives and goals. Simply put, goals are long-term achievement targets, whereas objectives are the immediate steps necessary to reach these long-term targets. Effective leaders always separate objectives from goals, deciding which objectives are necessary to achieve those goals, and then they communicate both objectives and goals to those they lead. It is always best to define objectives in unambiguous and quantifiable terms, using, for example, numbers of units produced or total sales for the month. In this way, fulfillment of the objective and, ultimately, progress toward the goal can be measured precisely.

When you communicate an objective to a subordinate, achieve clarity by communicating what's to be done, when it is to be done (the deadline), and all the relevant specifications, limits, budget constraints, and other requirements. Once this nitty-gritty has been conveyed, paint the big picture, the larger context of the objective:

JIMMY OLSEN

Debut: *Superman* #13, November 1941
Full Name: James Bartholomew Olsen

In the earliest accounts, Jimmy Olsen was portrayed as no more than ten years old when he first tried to join the staff of the newspaper later identified as the *Daily Planet.* In somewhat later accounts, he was depicted as a teenaged "cub reporter." Later still, he was primarily seen as a junior photographer. In the current Superman chronicles, Jimmy is depicted as a young *Daily Planet* photographer, in many ways still wet behind the ears, but nevertheless a truly promising photojournalist.

Jimmy's mother, Sarah Olsen, raised her son on her own after her husband, Jake, a covert military operative, disappeared. The youngster grew up in the Bakerline section of Metropolis and excelled in academics, but, always restless, longed for action. He found a position as an intern on the staff of the *Daily Planet,* then became a junior photographer. At the hands of the *Planet's* tyrannical publisher, Quentin Galloway, Jimmy endured constant humiliation and abuse, but was befriended and defended by Lois Lane, who took him under her wing. (In Golden Age and Silver Age Superman chronicles, Jimmy's mentor was not Lois, but Clark Kent, whom the youngster idolized as the model reporter.)

In company with Lois, Jimmy has covered many important stories. In the most recent version of the Superman chronicles, the pair became the first two people to be rescued by the Man of Steel when he made his first public appearance; they scored a journalistic coup by covering their own rescue. Jimmy also later documented in pictures Lex Luthor's nefarious behavior.

The *Daily Planet's* irascible editor-in-chief, Perry White, has been a stern but caring father figure for Jimmy, instilling in him the very highest ethical standards of journalism. Jimmy was also befriended by Superman, who gave him a special watch that can transmit a hypersonic signal whenever young Jimmy finds himself in a life-threatening jam—which has proven to be quite often.

the final goal. Nobody likes the feeling of working in a vacuum. People do a better job when they know how their piece of the work fits into the whole.

In "Never-Ending Battle," one of the stories collected in *Superman: No Limits*, Perry White makes himself clear in an exemplary exchange with Jimmy Olsen. Jimmy admits to having doctored a photo of Superman published in the *Daily Planet*. He digitally removed the wedding ring visible on the Man of Steel's finger. As he explains to Mr. White, "I just didn't want to be responsible for the troubles it might cause Superman . . . or his wife." Unfortunately, a non-altered copy of the photo ended up on the front page of the *Planet*'s rival, *The Star*.

Perry White has every right to be furious with Jimmy, and he begins with sarcasm: "So *you*, Jimmy Olsen—Mr. Crack Photojournalist—*you* decided there are some things the public does not need to know."

"Well, I . . . yeah," Jimmy stammers.

At this, Perry White uses Jimmy's misjudgment as an occasion to make vividly clear one of the *Planet*'s cardinal principles: ". . . a journalist's *one goal* should be to ferret out the truth. The truth is *our goal*—and our *greatest weapon*. We discard it at our own risk. We have to *trust* the truth . . . trust that the truth will take care of it itself." After laying this out, he goes on to explain why this principle is so important: "If we want to stay a free press, we can't *not* trust the truth." A good boss, a good mentor, always completes the picture by providing reasons for his instructions and directives.

Perry White concludes by reinforcing the personal relationship between himself and his subordinate. He begins sternly: "The point is, I'm disappointed in you, son." But then he empowers Jimmy with a demonstration of his continued confidence in him: "You're *better* than this . . ." He then takes a step to prevent another misjudgment in the future: "You should have brought this to me." Finally, however, he reinforces the theme of confidence: "I also know you learn from your mistakes." He reminds Jimmy that "all these newfangled digital capabilities" have conferred on Jimmy "a great power," and he warns: "Just don't blow it, kid." But then delivers the ultimate vote of confidence by sending him off on his next assignment: "Now *move your tail* or you're going to be late for that press conference you're covering with Lane!"

Choose Your Followers

Chances are you won't be able to handpick all the people in your organization who report to you, but you may be able to exercise choice over individuals to whom you delegate specific tasks. Delegating work is a key leadership function, and it is also vital to mentoring. The first step is to match the right person to a given task. Choosing the right person does not set you free from the responsibility of monitoring the progress of a project, but you won't have to be a micro-manager. Build in a schedule of meetings for the purpose of monitoring projects. Schedule these meetings as far apart as possible while still retaining the possibility of fixing any problems that come up. Avoid, if possible, unscheduled meetings, which imply that you are unhappy with your subordinate's performance.

Empowerment: The Office Superman's Greatest Superpower

The hardest part about delegating tasks is doing it in a way that empowers the apprentice without overwhelming him and thereby endangering the project as well as both you and your subordinate. Avoid the sink-or-swim approach. Instead, ease your subordinate into progressively greater levels of responsibility. If possible, give him or her the leeway to do at least some aspects of the task his or her own way. Encourage creativity, provided that you can monitor the creative process.

Choose the right tasks to delegate. Typically, it is best to start by delegating repetitive and routine tasks. This not only frees you up, but provides an opportunity for the delegate to gain experience and practice.

Don't jump ship. To the degree possible, be available to provide help, but don't be too quick to offer assistance. If the apprentice asks you to prescribe a course of action, restrain yourself from responding with *the* answer. Instead, review with the delegate the various possibilities, leaving as much of the actual decision making to him or her.

Confident leaders don't rush to bail out a floundering apprentice. Often, they will add another junior member to the team and delegate that person to provide help.

Lighting the Fire

Delegating tasks and monitoring their progress are essential leadership processes, but the Office Superman adds another dimension as well. He takes on the responsibility of sustaining those he leads by projecting consistent enthusiasm. This does not mean walking around with a smile plastered across your face or refusing to acknowledge challenges, problems, and difficulties that arise. It is about conveying constant interest in the project at hand and excited anticipation over the results your apprentices are about to produce.

In *Superman: Birthright* #4 (December 2003), Lois Lane grabs Jimmy Olsen to give him the opportunity to get the first photograph of Superman in action. She pulls him into a helicopter—something about which he's none too excited.

"Up *there*?" he shrieks. "*Are you insane?*"

But Lois is undeterred.

"Galloway was *right*, kid. I *need* a big story. Besides, you *wanted* to be a reporter . . .!

And relax. Military family! I've been flying birds like this since I was *nine!*"

As they nearly crash on takeoff ("Whoops. Throttle's *this* one. Sorry."), Jimmy moans, "So wrong . . . *so* wrong . . .," but Lois keeps pumping the enthusiasm: "No, no. 'Front page . . . front *page* . . .' Buckle up and get that camera ready!"

Convey enthusiasm by talking with your subordinates regularly. Invite and suggest new approaches to stubborn problems. When the going gets tough, express empathy and offer consultation. Stoke the fires of enthusiasm by regularly sharing information and observations with those you lead. Be generous with praise for positive achievements, ideas, and attitudes. As need be, refocus the direction of your subordinates. Nothing kills enthusiasm faster than the futile spinning of wheels.

Focusing and refocusing are accomplished by providing continuous feedback. Superman is a super hero not just because he has superpowers, but because he applies them intelligently: to solve problems rather than to attempt to "solve" people. He does not criticize. He acts. As an effective leader, the Office Superman always directs attention to actions and the results of actions. He avoids putting personalities under a magnifying glass.

Useful feedback addresses only issues that can be corrected. This requires that the feedback be specific. Instead of making blanket statements or wholesale judgments, cite specific actions and discuss them in detail, using whenever possible such objective data as quantities, costs, time, sales figures, and so on. This kind of critical feedback is not only useful, because it is unambiguous and defines real issues, it also avoids attacking people. Nevertheless, it can still hurt. Therefore, the best tactic is to remain supportive, balancing criticism with praise. A good approach is to emphasize what can be done better next time rather than dwell on what was done poorly this time. You may not be satisfied with *this* particular result at *this* particular time, but it is important to convey your confidence in the delegate's ability to create satisfaction—ultimately.

Good criticism motivates rather than inhibits. It is important to approach the task of criticism as a mentor, not as a cop or a judge. Deliver feedback, including critical feedback, in a timely manner, but always think before you pounce. First and foremost, be certain of the need to criticize. Does this result really require improvement? Be certain that the "cure" of criticism is not worse than the disease. Perhaps correcting a particular problem is not worth the risk to a vulnerable ego.

Even though you are the leader, always ask permission to criticize. Instead of approaching the subordinate with something like, "We have to talk about how you're handling so-and-so," begin with "We have a problem with so-and-so. May I speak with you about it now?" Don't worry, you won't be turned down, and framing your feedback in this way will avoid putting delegate on the defensive. A defensive response to criticism is rarely productive. A subordinate focused on defending himself cannot focus on what may be truly useful in the feedback you're delivering.

Finesse

Superman, the Man of Steel, stronger than anybody. A bloke like this could be one big, brutal lummox. But, of course, the Superman we've known all these years is a graceful gentleman. Take a lesson from his grace and good manners. Resist the temptation to wield authority like a bludgeon. Be sensitive and discreet. Never criticize a subordinate in front of others. In *Superman: Birthright* #4 (December 2003), Quentin Galloway, publisher of the *Daily Planet*, reveals himself as the Boss from Hell by dumping a wastebasket on Jimmy Olsen's head: "Now, you will wear this wastebasket on *your head* so you can hear the gentle reinforcing echo as you say one hundred times, 'Mr. Galloway asked me for *strawberry*, not berry-*banana*.' Ready, Jack?"

"Umm . . .," says a cowering Jimmy, "it's 'Jim,' actually."

"Your name is whatever I put on your too-generous paycheck, you lout!"

Enter Lois Lane: "His *name* is *Jimmy Olsen*. . . . Jimmy. Not 'Lout," not 'Twit.' You think you're a *big shot*? *Publicly humiliating* an *employee* because *you're* in a bad mood about *frogurt* is *small* and it is *petty*."

Not only should you avoid inverting a wastebasket on the head of a subordinate, you should deliver any necessary criticism in appropriate privacy. It is also a good idea to avoid criticism first thing in the morning or at quitting time. Critical feedback is a dispiriting way to start the day, and it is certainly a bad idea to give somebody something to stew about on their way home.

Above all, criticize only what can be changed. If you criticize a subordinate for something over which he or she has little or no control, the result will be frustration, confusion, and resentment. In a similar vein, don't overwhelm your delegate with multiple issues. Address one problem at a time instead of dropping a cluster bomb of issues.

Praise Be

In *Superman* #13 (December 1941), the Man of Steel goes up against a green-suited Robin Hood-turned-terrorist who calls himself the Archer: "Victims are given the choice of paying a heavy fee or perishing before the unique criminal's deadly accuracy with the bow and arrow!" Eager for the story, Perry White thunders to Jimmy Olsen: "Where in blazes are Lois Lane and Clark Kent?" Jimmy replies that "They're not to be found anywhere, Mr. White," and then he offers: "I'll be glad to cover the story for you."

"*You'll* cover it?" White exclaims.

"I—I'd like to become a real reporter—like Clark Kent, and if you'd only give me a chance . . ."

"Hmm . . . You'd probably do a better job than Clark, at that. Tell you what I'll do, kid. Come back again in five or ten years . . . and I may give you a break . . ."

It's hard to blame Perry White for not taking young Jimmy seriously. Remember, as he was depicted before 1944, Jimmy Olsen was perhaps no more than ten years old. But in his sarcastic response to the would-be cub reporter, White reveals himself as very much an old-line manager. His approach to his subordinate is akin to the spare-the-rod-spoil-the-child school of parenting. *Praise an employee for doing his job? It'll spoil 'em. Isn't the opportunity to earn a living praise enough?*

Well, the idea of praise and reward is hardly cutting-edge management theory. It's a lot older than Perry White, even, and it is, in fact, part of ancient history. The Office Superman taps into this tradition and is always generous with praise for subordinates who create excellence.

Look at the last panel of "The Archer." As it turns out, Jimmy Olsen did get to write the story.

"Tell me, Jimmy," says his mentor Clark Kent, "how does it feel to get your first by-line?"

This simple statement is a superb example of positive reinforcement. It is not laden with lavish and empty adjectives, but instead focuses directly on the achiever by asking *him* how *his* accomplishment feels. Also of note is the specificity of the praise. Effective praise from a boss and mentor cites the achievement precisely. Clark doesn't say "How does it feel to have done a good job?" but specifically mentions "your first by-line."

The Office Superman goes out of his way to praise staffers for their contributions to the collective enterprise and he always includes the specifics, the same level of specifics he would include in criticism.

Praise is so important that, if you are the leader of a group of three or more people, you should consider establishing a program of regular reinforcement meetings, totally positive and upbeat occasions at which refreshments are served and stories are swapped. At such a meeting, greet your group with kind words. Share the specifics of what you are praising, and put the emphasis on results.

Stirring the Pot

The praise Clark Kent delivers to Jimmy Olsen—"How does it feel to get your first by-line?"—can be used only once, for the simple reason that a person gets a "first by-line" only once in a career. That's a limitation of praise. Like criticism, it requires a specific occasion. In the motivational arsenal, praise and criticism represent the extremes. They are important, but so is what gets said between them.

The Office Superman endeavors to be positively motivating in everything he says at all times. He takes every opportunity to express optimism. This does not mean that he blithely ignores problems or exaggerates good results while he neglects warning signals. Optimism is not about calling poor results good. It is *not* about misleading or lying. The optimistic vision sees everything in the best *possible* light—with the emphasis on "possible."

The Office Superman develops the good habit of looking for truthfully positive messages to deliver. Your department's productivity is up 5 percent. You had aimed for 10 percent. You could complain about having "fallen behind by 50 percent" or, with equal truth, you could emphasize what has been achieved—a 5 percent increase—and then say that the achievement will "now inspire us all to go on to another 5 percent."

Look for what *can be done,* not what didn't get done or what went wrong. Optimism focuses on presence, not absence or lack. It is about what you have now and where you can take it.

Develop an optimistic vocabulary. There is no need to sugarcoat the truth, but find ways to use positive terms when you might otherwise be tempted to speak in negatives. For instance, you might choose to call a *problem a challenge.* In some cases, you might describe it even more positively, as an *opportunity*. Criticism can legitimately be called *feedback*, and a *cost* may be termed an *investment*. You might term your subordinate's lack *of a particular skill* an *opportunity for professional development*.

When you speak to those you lead, speak the language of enthusiasm.

A long, hard project is nearing completion. "Well, folks, we're almost done" is one way of putting it, but why not add a dash of excitement with a phrase like on the verge of completion or on the threshold of completion?

Your work group has come out on top in sales this month. Put it to your staffers this way: "We annihilated the competition!"

Facts Above All

Optimistic and enthusiastic language are great ongoing motivators, but nothing is more inspiring than information, and, conversely, nothing kills inspiration more quickly than the sickly sensation of wandering in the dark that comes in the absence of information.

When he leads, the Office Superman is crystal clear in all directives and instructions. He sets clear objectives and goals, and he makes schedules and evaluation criteria unambiguous. Whenever possible, he quantifies his instructions: "We need to survey *eight* vendors by *September 6*."

"I Hope to Be a Top-Notch Reporter Like *You* Some Day!"

For young Jimmy Olsen, Clark Kent is a role model. He represents the career Jimmy longs for. He sets the pattern for Jimmy's professional behavior. In the context of the chronicles of Superman, the relationship between Jimmy Olsen and Clark Kent is a charming sidebar—charming, but not out of the ordinary. The fact is that subordinates in any organization typically model their conduct and performance on those who supervise them, and they do this for better or for worse. If you lead any number of people, you *are* a role model. You have no choice about it. What you *can* choose, however, is the kind of role model to present: good, bad, or indifferent.

Both Superman and his arch-rival Lex Luthor are powerful beings. The chief difference between them is moral, of course, but it is not so much that Superman is "good" and Lex Luthor "evil" as it is that Superman acts out of a strong moral sense whereas Lex Luthor acts without regard to morality in an ongoing and amoral effort to gratify his many appetites, ambitions, and desires. Both occupy leadership positions, but only Superman understands that leadership does not just mean giving orders, but leading by example. Whereas Luthor behaves just as he wishes, Superman behaves according to strong moral values. Superman is a powerful role model because, always and in everything he does, he presents himself as a role model.

The Office Superman takes care that his directives, coaching, and mentoring are never contradicted by his actions. If you tell your staff to deal with customers honestly, be certain that you yourself make no dishonest sales. If you stress the value of character, avoid exhibiting cynicism, irony, or sarcasm. If you expect your staff to work hard, be sure they see *you* working hard.

Clark Kent is sometimes Superman and Superman sometimes Clark Kent. The Office Superman, however, must always come across as who he is, without disguise or ambiguity. To keep the organization motivated, he conducts himself as a model of motivation from the very moment he comes through the office doors each and every morning.

C H A P T E R

11

PEOPLE OF METROPOLIS

YOU KNOW THE SCENE. BUSINESS TRIP. AIRPORT. BETWEEN FLIGHTS. Hard plastic seats, and the same "news feature" playing over and over again on the plasma screens overhead. The guy next to you strikes up a conversation.

"What business you in?"

Hardly a stumper, the answer comes quickly, automatically. After all, you *know* what you do for a living.

The thing is, the answer's actually even simpler than you know, because, although there are tens of thousands of different job descriptions in the civilized world, there is only a single correct answer to the question.

"What business you in?"

"I'm in the people business."

Whether you sell shoes, trade stocks, fill out tax forms, write computer code, or perform brain surgery, you are in the people business. Nothing you do for a living gets done without people. Everyone who comes within the sphere of your business is your customer, whether you are selling that person a car or an idea, and whether that person is a total stranger or a colleague in your own firm.

Ask a good salesman to tell you the measure of sales success, and he will reply "revenue produced" or "units sold." Ask a *great* salesman the same question, and he will tell you: "customers satisfied."

A sale is an event, but a satisfied customer is a relationship. It endures and grows over time, producing in the process not a single event, but many: repeat sales from this customer and, through favorable word of mouth, sales from other customers. To create customer satisfaction is to build around yourself a world, an environment receptive to you and whatever it is that you sell.

Consider: Everyone with whom you do business or want to do business is your customer. When you sell Miss Smith her car, you move heaven and Earth to assure her satisfaction with the short-term buying experience as well as the long-term ownership experience. But you also structure a deal that satisfies your internal customers, the sales manager and the finance manager. All three individuals are equally your customers, and in order to prosper you must create satisfaction in all three. Your business, after all, is people—not selling cars, but creating satisfaction and creating it all around.

"Now Listen to Me, Clark!"

Undoubtedly, fathers have been teaching sons about business since one Neanderthal decided to trade his club for another Neanderthal's wooly mammoth robe instead of cracking the club over his head and just taking what he wanted. In panel 5 of *Superman* #1, back in 1939, Clark Kent's adoptive father gives his boy this piece of business advice: "Now listen to me, Clark! This great strength of yours—you've got to hide it from people or they'll be scared of you!"

The counsel does not concern how to use or profit from his "great strength"; Mrs. Kent pipes in with that just after her husband speaks: "But when the proper time comes, you must use it to assist humanity." Instead, Mr. Kent tells his boy how to break into the *people* business. He advises well, focusing his child from the very beginning on what those around him need and want. This focus on others is the ideal orientation for the man of business, the Office Superman.

You come into the world of commerce with something to sell. It might be cars. It might be your talent. It might be nothing more (or less) than your willingness to work. Whatever the "product," your job is to create a vital connection between your merchandise and the people around you. That vital connection is their *need* to own it, to buy it from you.

Several panels (and years) after his father gives him his first piece of business advice, Clark Kent walks into the office of the man we'll later know as Perry White, editor-in-chief of the paper later called the *Daily Planet.*

"I know I haven't had any experience, sir, but still I think I'd make a good reporter," Clark pleads, hat literally in hand.

The response is predictable—"Sorry, fella! Can't use you!"—and it is a sad fact that Clark Kent's first foray into the people business is a miserable failure. His focus is entirely on himself and what he wants. Of the seventeen words he speaks to Perry White, four are the first-person pronoun. As for what he offers, it is nothing at all: the absence of experience and a deficiency of confidence. "I think I'd make a good reporter" is not the same as "I know I'd make a great reporter."

But Clark learns from this rejection. He is highly motivated to get the job; being a reporter will allow him to "get news dispatches promptly" so that "I'll be in a better position to help people." Accordingly, he makes it his business to find out what Perry White needs. Tearing off his business suit and revealing the Superman outfit beneath it, he "launches himself up along the side of the building in a great leap" and perches on a ledge outside the editor's office.

"*What's that?*" he hears Perry White shouting into the telephone. "A mob attacking the county jail? *Cover that story!*"

Now Superman/Clark Kent knows how to satisfy his customer: "Hm-m! Sounds like my big chance to impress the editor!" With that, as we summarized in Chapter 3, "Code of a Super Hero," Superman rescues an unjustly convicted man from lynching, saves an unjustly convicted woman from the electric chair, hauls off the real murderer to justice, and, of course, grabs the whole juicy scoop for Perry White. Once again, the editor's response is predictable: "You're O.K., Kent! Report to work tomorrow!"

Performance and Promise

As Clark Kent/Superman proves, when it comes to selling, there is no substitute for performance. And on an ongoing basis, day to day, performance is precisely what the Office Superman strives to deliver. But performance isn't enough. In the movies of Hollywood's "Golden Age," the films Siegel and Shuster knew, loved, and were inspired by, young hopefuls were always proving themselves by getting the proverbial Big Break that puts them in position to hit the inevitable home run. In real life, the Big Break doesn't always come to you, and performance, even great performance, doesn't always get recognized and rewarded. Your achievement needs to be sold with the promise of even greater performance to come. While it is critically important to demonstrate that you can give your customer—whether that "customer" is a boss or a client—what he wants, it is even more important to sell him on the *idea* that you can keep giving him what he wants, day to day and every day. This will shape his perception of you over the long haul, and will give you a leg up on the corporate ladder.

Climbing Toward the Sale

Think of everything you do at work as a sales transaction. It doesn't matter whether you're selling a widget to a new account or, to your boss, the idea of putting you in charge of the Big Project. The process of the transaction can be broken down into four steps, which old-time sales professionals were once taught by heart. Together, the steps have a distinctly operatic name: AIDA.

The first *A* in this acronym stands for *attention*. The first step in any sale, whether to an external or an internal customer, is to get the prospect's attention. The most effective way of doing this is to identify a need your prospect has. Recall Clark Kent's initial misfire when he lamely pleads for a job. Whatever else Perry White may need, it most certainly is not some novice in eyeglasses begging for work. Rebuffed, Clark—as Superman—eavesdrops on his prospect, identifies a need, then understands that by addressing this need he will at last command the editor's attention.

Your boss is courting a prospective client. You want to sell him on the idea of putting you on this new account. You could approach your boss with a plea: "This would mean *everything* to my career!" But—surprise, surprise—*your* career is not number one on your boss's list of needs. So, instead, you get your boss's *attention* by addressing what *he* needs: "Mr. Klein, I've worked up some portfolio concepts for the Kellerman account. Would you like to go over them now?"

You now have your prospect's attention. Notice that the hook has two parts: a statement directly relating to the prospect's need—"I've worked up some portfolio concepts for the Kellerman account"—and a question that enables you and your prospect to move directly from the *attention* phase to the *I* of the AIDA process.

Getting attention will not by itself make the sale. You now need to develop *attention* into *interest*. This is done by showing your prospect how *you* can satisfy the need you've identified. In this case, you outline, briefly but comprehensively, your ideas concerning the all-important Kellerman account. As you do this, you keep your prospect engaged in the process by asking questions: "This seems like an especially cost-effective approach to me. What do you think, Mr. Klein?"

Selling is an act of persuasion, and persuasion is all about transforming an "I" and a "you" into a "we." Asking questions changes monologue into dialogue, "I am talking to you" becomes "We are talking."

Interest both broadens and builds on *attention*, but there is another step on the climb toward closing the sale. This is the point at which you must make the "merchandise" irresistibly appealing. This is the point at which *interest* must become *desire*, the *D* in the AIDA acronym.

The transition from interest to desire is made by showing your prospect the benefits—to him—of owning what you are selling.

To your question, "What do you think, Mr. Klein?" your boss replies positively: "It might just work."

This is the fulcrum on which you lift his desire.

"I think so, too, Mr. Klien. Not only would this approach be cost-effective, we could implement it with the resources we have on hand and it would be ongoing. Kellerman would have the incentive to deal with us exclusively for the entire term of the project. We'd be cost-efficient *and* we could project out at least four quarters' worth of high-end business. Maybe even more."

Who wouldn't desire all this? Now, onto the closing step. We have desire. What has to be done in order to realize this desire? Here is the culmination of AIDA: *action*. A successful sales transaction does not conclude until all four steps have been climbed. Attention is good. Interest is nice. Desire is great. But, in the end, only *action* counts.

Complete your sales presentation by proposing a course of action. In selling an actual piece of merchandise, this requires as little as a statement of price. For higher-ticket items, the *action* phase typically calls for a discussion of "easy finance terms." But even if you are selling an idea and not a physical product, your task at closing is to tell your prospect how to act on the *desire* you have developed in him. The object is to propose a concrete action that will unambiguously and finally close the sale.

Make it as easy and clear-cut as possible: "Mr. Klein, let me put this into a formal proposal that we can present to the Kellerman people."

Thinking Beyond the Sale

AIDA is an effective systematic approach to selling ideas as well as merchandise, but, taken by itself, it is incomplete and inefficient. Too many hardcore sales-oriented firms drill into their employees the single notion that nothing but nothing is more important than *The* Sale.

This is a mistake. While the sale is very important, it is less important than the customer. Remind yourself: All business is people business. Focusing narrowly on The Sale leads to a one-shot approach that is incompatible with a people business. Events come and go. People stick around.

Instead of making the sale, focus on creating in the customer a feeling of trust and confidence. This transforms the sales *event* into a sales *process*. A one-shot deal becomes a sustainable business relationship.

The Metropolis Factor

Ask even the most casual Superman fan the name of the Man of Steel's home city and before your question is even off your lips, you'll get the answer. Superman debuted in 1938, and his city was identified for the first time by name—Metropolis—late the following year, in *Action Comics* #16 (September 1939). From that time on, it's been hard to think about our super hero without also summoning to mind his resident burg.

It's not that Superman never acts outside of the city limits. He travels to the far ends of the Earth when necessary. But his strongest relationships are all centered in Metropolis. Here he is best known, and here he is most honored. If the Man of Steel is in the super hero business, the people of Metropolis are his best customers.

Many of us find ourselves in work situations where the pressures of business produce a mania for prospecting, as if the assumption were that the only good customers are new customers and the even better ones are the customers you don't yet have. Just because this is a pervasive point of view doesn't make it a productive one. The truth is that your best customers are your current customers, and your best prospecting tool is the word of mouth of current customers. Customers are a key asset. Develop the asset. Develop relationships. Develop trust. The payoff is an ongoing and self-expanding program of sales.

This philosophy of business applies to external and to internal customers alike. Satisfy both classes of customer, and you build continuity into your career. Within the company, the positive relationship you develop with your immediate boss will percolate upward through successive layers of management and, soon, everyone in your particular "Metropolis" will know who you are and what you can do.

Communities

For the Office Superman, "Metropolis" has three layers, or rings. The innermost ring is your neighborhood—the office itself, in which subordinates, peers, and bosses are all "internal" customers, people with whom you deal every day, selling your ideas, offering your value for value they give you in return.

Beyond this inner ring is a larger neighborhood, which is occupied by your external customers, the people with whom your firm does business or wishes to do business. To these customers, actual merchandise is sold.

Then there is the outermost ring of your Metropolis. This region is the community at large, and it includes internal and external customers as well as people who may never buy any merchandise from your firm.

To its employees and to other firms, a business is a business. To this outermost ring, the community in which the business resides, your firm is a neighbor and a citizen. The Office Superman never forgets this larger community, and he looks for ways to promote good corporate citizenship within it.

Look for ways in which your firm can productively participate in community affairs, for instance by working to raise funds for charitable and community-oriented causes. Make it your business to become aware of worthwhile programs that will promote a positive image for your firm. Bring these to the attention of your bosses. Keep your focus on what's good for the company *and* for the community. Here is a classic opportunity for you to do well by doing good, to be recognized as both a business leader and a community leader.

The Office Superman does not merely fit into his personal three-ring Metropolis. He takes a hand in creating the communities in which he works and lives. By creating satisfaction among internal and external customers, he builds his success within his firm. By reaching beyond these two communities to the community at large, he promotes the prosperity of his firm as well as that of the greater context in which the firm either thrives or fails. At each level, the Office Superman seeks to create excellence, the environments that make success possible, probable, and even inevitable.

C H A P T E R

12

USING YOUR X-RAY VISION

IN 1895, THE GERMAN PHYSICIST WILHELM CONRAD RÖNTGEN was performing experiments on the phenomenon of fluorescence using a cathode-ray tube when he discovered that his device generated a stream of radiation that did more than make certain objects glow. It effectively rendered all sorts of opaque materials—wood, paper, aluminum, the flesh of his wife's hand—transparent! Because this new form of radiation didn't seem to behave like light, it was a profound mystery, and Röntgen assigned to it the label mathematicians and scientists always assign to any unknown quantity: *X*.

Almost immediately, X-rays were put to work in the field of medicine and, a little later, in industry. Here was a tool that could be used to peer into the inner workings of a human being or of a mechanical structure without cutting into the one or disassembling the other. In the early 1940s, when Superman began regularly making use of his own X-ray vision, the phenomenon of X-rays was well understood and was long familiar to just about anyone who went to the doctor. By the late 1940s, even venues as commonplace as the neighborhood shoe store often featured a fluoroscope machine, which provided real-

- Does your colleague approach hurriedly? Slowly? Reluctantly? With hesitation? With long strides? With short strides?
- Does he walk tall—back straight, head up? Or does he cringe a bit?
- Does he look at you as he approaches? Or are his eyes averted?
- Are his arms at his sides? Or are his hands in his pockets? Behind his back? Covering his mouth? Is he running a nervous hand through his hair?
- Is he smiling? Frowning? Grimacing? Biting his lip?

An entrance is a declaration. In announcing an individual's presence, it proclaims who he is. It won't tell you how the negotiation is going to turn out, but it will provide clues to the other person's state of mind and attitude. It will provide insight into how the other person feels as he or she enters your space. It will allow you to gauge the other's level of self-confidence and his receptivity (or lack thereof) to what you are about to propose.

Everyone knows that a really good poker player can see through the others at the table as if he shared with the Man of Steel a pair of X-ray eyes. But there's nothing supernatural about it. Experienced poker players look for what they call "tells," visual signs that suggest what kind of hand the other player holds.

Tells aren't just found around a card table. When someone makes an entrance, look for these:

- *Shuffling gait. Looks hesitant.* No rocket science here. If a person looks hesitant, he is. He'd rather not be approaching you.
- *Broad, quick stride. Looks purposeful.* He's eager to begin the meeting and feels confident of an outcome favorable to himself.
- *Rubs forehead or the back of his neck as he approaches.* This suggests anxiety and is strongly suggestive of confusion or possibly even something to hide.
- *Eyes meet yours, broad smile.* He's happy to see you and open to the impending discussion.
- *Arms thrust into pockets or folded across the chest.* These are signs of resistance and suggest a determination to hold onto what he's got, to resist change, to resist meaningful negotiation.
- *Looks at the ground instead of ahead or at you.* This is a sign of nervousness, anxiety, even fear. This person wants reassurance.

You can also make assumptions based on the person's behavior once he enters your space, your office, or your cubicle. For instance, does he take ownership of the space, sitting down without being invited? Or does he wait to be asked? If you don't immediately invite him to sit, does he ask—"Mind if I sit?"—or does he stand, awkwardly, waiting for your permission? These things say less about manners than they do about attitude.

Contact!

If there is a first communion in a business encounter, it is the handshake. This gesture transmits, either consciously or unconsciously, valuable information concerning how the other person feels about you and about the business at issue. How do you "read" a handshake? Just ask yourself how it makes you feel.

- A warm, firm handshake suggests a person willing, even eager to talk and deal with you.
- A limp, dead-fish handshake suggests either a lack of enthusiasm or the presence of hesitancy, timidity, or shyness.
- A clammy, cold handshake is a strong indicator that the other person is nervous, even scared.
- A vice-grip, knuckle twister signals aggression and a desire to intimidate.

It is easy to dismiss the handshake as a perfunctory business greeting, but we do so at our peril. Give as much attention to the handshake and how it makes you feel as you devote to anything the other person says.

Buy Signals and Signs of Resistance

You're making a sale or negotiating a position. The person you're talking to is mostly listening, not saying a great deal. How do you know whether you're getting warmer or colder? Non-verbal cues make an excellent thermometer. Experienced sales professionals look for what they call "buy signals" from their prospect.

- *The other person leans forward in his chair.* A buy signal. He likes what you are saying or, at the very least, he is open and intrigued.
- *Eyes widen.* A buy signal.
- *Rubs hands together.* A buy signal, which suggests eager anticipation.
- *Smiles naturally and broadly.* A buy signal.
- *Nods more or less vigorously.* A buy signal.

The opposite of buy signals are signs of resistance. When you see these, it may be time to change direction or to ask outright, "Am I leaving something unanswered?" or, "Do you have a question about any of this?"

Look out for these:

- *While sitting, shifts feet. Moves legs nervously.* A sign of resistance, indicating a desire to get up and leave.
- *Rubs forehead or back of neck.* A sign of resistance, suggesting frustration or confusion.
- *Puts hand to face or mouth.* A sign of resistance, suggesting anxiety.
- *Shakes head no.* A sign of resistance.
- *Winces.* A sign of resistance.
- *Folds arms across chest.* An especially strong sign of resistance.

A Matter of Style

Face it. You don't have X-ray vision and you never will. That's reserved for Superman. But you could fake it, if you wanted to. All you need to know is what's inside the objects you're looking at *before* you look at them. For example, you could look at a wind-up clock and tell people that your X-ray vision reveals a multitude of gears and springs inside. Then, turning your gaze on a pumpkin, you report no gears or springs, but an abundance of pulp and seeds. It's an easy trick, provided you know what to expect inside everything you look at. The fact is that, because of your experience in and of the world, you *do* know what's inside a great many things. This being the case, you could counterfeit X-ray vision pretty easily.

You can do something like this with people, too. No, you can't look through them, and you can't really collect a whole life history on the basis of a handshake. But you can use your experience with people as well as the experience others have had to predict what's "inside" those you deal with in day-to-day business.

It's all a matter of style.

Open up a Superman comic, and you can expect the Man of Steel to behave in certain ways in a given situation. Same goes with most of the other "regular" Superman cast. Whereas, whatever else he does, Superman can be counted on for bold action despite all dangers, Clark will behave with a degree of reticence. Present Lois Lane with a challenge, and she will never back down. Give Jimmy Olsen an opportunity, and he will demonstrate a boyish and buoyant desire to please. Put Perry White near one of his reporters, and he will vent his famously irascible temper, only to moderate the outburst with expressions of confidence and encouragement and a noble statement of sound journalistic principles. Lex Luthor, who became an increasingly complex character over the years, can nevertheless be counted on to act from impulses and motives of massive egotism. None of this means that all Superman characters are utterly predictable. A good storyteller introduces twists, kinks, and unexpected variations in his characters' style. A good storyteller will, from time to time, upset expectation. But, for the most part, he will make his characters act and react consistently, that is, "in character." That's why a figure like Bizarro is so intriguing. Confected by super-villain Lex Luthor in *Action Comics* #254 (July 1959), Bizarro is a kind of failed Superman clone who incorporates many physical features of Superman yet inverts most of his attributes in—well—distinctly bizarre, typically backward, ways. Bizarro violates expectation, but the point is that for a reader to understand Bizarro, he must be fully familiar with the character of Superman. He must know what to expect.

Superman stories work—and Bizarro tales tantalize and delight us—precisely because character is predictable. In living, breathing people, as opposed to fictional folk, character is usually called personality, but it, too, is more or less predictable. When personality operates in such narrowly defined situations as a business trans-action, it usually becomes more rather than less predictable. In this more predictable form, we might call personality *style*.

Keeping it Simple

As of the early twenty-first century, the world contains some 6,500,000,000 people, each different, each unique. Or, at least, sort of.

Although no two people are exactly the same, human behavior, especially in a given situation, can be grouped together and classified into distinct styles. Thus, instead of trying to pick one of 6,500,000,000 approaches to working with col-leagues, subordinates, or bosses, you can choose from as few as four.

In a productive work context—a business, an office—most people most of the time function according to one of the following styles.

Cautious: This is the style of a highly conscientious person. She learns the rules, and she follows them. Highly organized, she finds a place for everything and puts everything in its place. Her conversation is careful and guarded. She may speak slowly and even with reluctance, because she always thinks carefully before she speaks. Imagine a circle. If impulsiveness is at 0 degrees, the cautious-style individual is located at 180.

The cautious person is detail-oriented and demands a high degree of quality and detail from everyone else. She likes receiving reports. She likes detailed plans. She wants everything in writing. She is happiest when working alone, because she knows that while others may or may not fail her, she can always depend on herself.

Persuasive: If the cautious person strikes her coworkers as reserved, maybe even uptight, the persuasive person seems free-and-easy and fun to be with. Conversationally, he is a self-starter. Beaming, bubbly, and energetic, he is an out-going optimist who loves to work with others and likes to be influential in a group.

Dominant: The person who exhibits this high-octane style makes quick, typically impulsive decisions. He is a take-charge guy, who moves quickly into action—with or without a fully developed plan. Bold and aggressive, he is a leader, the first one to leap into the action—often without looking. In conversation, he gets right to the point. In an argument, he goes for the jugular. In contrast to the persuasive person, he spends little time trying to influence or persuade others. He just tells them what to do.

Supportive: People who have a supportive style go out of their way to fit in, coop-erate, and avoid conflict. They do as they are told and they rarely argue. They are good listeners and seem to have inexhaustible patience, except under extreme pressure. Supportive people are empathetic, readily appreciating the perspective of others. Undemanding, warm, genial, they are the folks most people call "nice."

Are *dominant*-style people always dependably dominant? *Supportive*-style people always reliably supportive? No. Sometimes *cautious*-style people are as bold and daring as dominant people. In some cases, *persuasive*-style individuals become shy and withdrawn. Yet, usually and in most business situations, people exhibit one of the four styles—persuasive, dominant, cautious, or supportive—with considerable consistency. And once you have successfully "read" a person's style, you are armed with some super information.

The Persuasive Style

If you think of the people you deal with day to day as your "customers," it is natural to take the next step, which is to work with them in ways that create satisfaction. Business people want to satisfy their customers. Customer satisfaction is the goal of a successful business.

To satisfy a customer requires understanding what he or she needs and wants. The person who approaches business with a persuasive style needs and wants attention. Friendly and informal, he wants genial informality in return. He is a schmoozer who likes to tell stories and therefore needs a receptive audience. He likes to feel good and is grateful for humor. He is generally optimistic and so is greatly distressed by cynicism, skepticism, and, most of all, pessimism.

The persuasive person needs to win others to his point of view. As a result, he craves recognition of his achievements, and, conversely, he takes rejection and criticism quite hard.

While you increase the probability of working productively with a persuasive person by recognizing his needs and acting to satisfy them, you don't want to fall into the trap of reinforcing the potentially negative aspects of this style. Be aware that the persuasive person will promote and oversell his ideas or point of view. Typically, he will ignore or gloss over problems, whether actual or potential. Optimistic by inclination, he is, in fact, very often overly optimistic. When you work with a persuasive-style person, you may need to compensate as much as encourage. Just be careful to focus all criticism on issues and not his personality.

The Dominant Style

Just because you find yourself working with a dominant-style person does not mean that you must or should assume a passive or submissive role. Quite the contrary. The dominant person does not necessarily expect or require others simply to take orders and obey, but she does appreciate working with people who are direct and get straight to the point. Schmoozing, so much a part of the persuasive style, has no place in the repertoire of the dominant person. She wants the focus on ends—results—and she wants to find and take the shortest possible route to the final product.

If you want to satisfy a dominant-style individual, keep your communication short and to the point. No small talk, please. Avoid digressing from the agenda at hand; stick to the point. Establish yourself as an equal by demonstrating competence and independence. However, whenever you can, let the dominant person initiate key actions.

In dealing with dominant-style people, be prepared for bluntness and for straightforward demands. This individual may seem unfriendly or even impolite, because she usually shows little empathy or interest in how others respond to her actions. Don't try to "correct" this. It's her style. But, for the same reason, don't be put off by it, either. It's *her* style. Work *with* it.

The Cautious Style

The chief danger in dealing with cautious-style people is altogether overlooking them. Quiet, methodical, and unassuming, they are all too often invisible. However, as people who value accuracy, precision, and attention to detail, they are highly valuable to any enterprise or project.

Like the dominant-style person, the cautious person has little interest in small talk and socializing. In contrast to the dominant person, however, he has no desire to rush to conclusions and end results. In dealing with him, allow him time to prepare, to make plans, and to ask questions about existing plans. Be sure that all expectations and objectives are clearly expressed in detail before embarking on any project. Don't skip over any steps. Assure this person that you can be relied upon, and, most of all, emphasize your commitment to achieving and maintaining a high standard of quality in any project on which you collaborate.

Innovation can make the cautious-style person uncomfortable, so try to use and to emphasize precedent, the tried-and-true, whenever possible. Avoid blanket statements, sweeping generalizations, and vagueness in general. Lack of clarity creates anxiety and frustration in the cautious person. Explain yourself fully and in detail. Assure the cautious person that time will be provided for quality control and for double checking each step of the work you do.

The Supportive Style

As the label for this style implies, supportive people are easy, even delightful to work with—*most* of the time. But in a crunch or a crisis, they may appear suddenly to cave in. That is, the supportive person is so anxious to avoid creating difficulty or aggravating a problem that she will avoid facing difficult issues and will avoid arguing with others, even if those others are wrong or are making a mistake. If the situation becomes truly critical, the supportive person, having suppressed her objections, may be overcome with emotion and lash out at others. This, of course, is the last thing you need in a genuine crisis.

Don't abuse the supportive person. The best approach is to be cooperative, agreeable, courteous, and appreciative. The supportive-style person responds very well to clarity and to a systematic approach. Stability is important to her, so avoid introducing unnecessary changes or innovation for the sake of innovation. Provide as much information as possible and express appreciation freely and frequently.

Avoid applying pressure to this person. The supportive-style individual is eager to please, but she does not respond well to high-pressure situations and often finds special difficulty with short deadlines.

Look! Up in the Sky!

Superman's many visual superpowers have one thing in common. It is Superman's willingness to look beyond himself and to see the needs of others.

It is a willingness the Office Superman must also possess. Anything short of this is, as far as business success goes, pathological nearsightedness—truly defective vision. To set your course for the stars, focus on others. Then fly accordingly.

PUTTING *TORQUASM-VO* TO WORK FOR YOU

"THE SUPERMAN" WAS THE NAME OF A CHARACTER JERRY SIEGEL WROTE AND JOE SHUSTER DREW BACK IN 1932. As you recall from Chapter 2, "Backstory," "The Superman" was very different from *the* Superman we all now know. For one thing, he was evil. For another, his superpowers were exclusively mental. As Superman finally emerged in 1938's *Action Comics* #1, the character revealed that Siegel and Shuster had learned two important lessons about how to create a super hero that would sustain more than passing interest in readers. They learned that he had to be dedicated to good rather than evil, and they learned that his superpowers had to be physical rather than mental, if only because it was a lot harder to illustrate internal, invisible powers than external, spectacularly visible ones.

Yet some mental superpowers soon returned to Superman. In *Superman* #4, for example, which was published in Spring 1940, Clark Kent was depicted with the unique mind-over-matter ability to "temporarily halt the beating of his heart." This mental trick would be used several times over the years, whenever Clark found himself in a situation where he wanted to play dead.

Throughout the 1940s and into the 1950s, various additional mental powers were added to Superman's attributes, including a superphotographic memory, a computer-like ability to make instant calculations and process data, an ability to store and retrieve encyclopedic volumes of knowledge, and various forms of telepathy. Most interesting of all was superhypnotism. In January 1941, Clark hypnotized Lois Lane to cure her of amnesia *(Action Comics* #32) and, in February 1941, he used it again, this time to induce amnesia, so that he could rescue Lois from a fire without revealing his dual identity *(Action Comics* #33). The hypnotic ante was raised in August 1941 when Clark Kent simultaneously hypnotized an entire tribe of South American Indians who held him captive *(Superman* #11).

Superhypnotism appeared in various forms and in various Superman adventures throughout the 1940s and 1950s, apparently culminating in "The Game of Secret Identities," a story from May 1965 *(World's Finest Comics* #149), in which Superman superhypnotized himself, actually altering his brain-wave patterns through "super mental control."

But there was much more mental power in store. Indeed, by the 1990s, Superman was, in some ways, coming full circle. In a story called "Home" *(Superman: The Man of Steel* #96, December 1999), Clark Kent/Superman encountered Kem-L, a Kryptonian ancestor, who engaged the Man of Steel not in a physical battle but a desperate contest in the mental realm of *torquasm-vo*.

Torquasm-vo is a technique born of the ancient Kryptonian mental discipline and martial art known as *torquasm-rao*. Using the fragmentary Kryptonian archives he has managed to uncover, Superman studied *torquasm-rao*, which calls for finding the inner Theta state of total mental balance. *Torquasm-vo* is a technique of achieving the total relaxation of body in order to hyper-extend the mind into this state of Theta. The exercise of the technique requires a tremendous mental effort, which leaves even Superman drained, especially because he is still very much immersed in the process of researching Kryptonian culture, including the subtleties of *torquasm-rao* and *torquasm-vo*.

When he does reach Theta, Superman can use astral projection to broadcast his consciousness outside of his body, enabling him either to communicate with others who are also in a Theta state or to confront enemies on the psionic, or extrasensory level. *Torquasm-vo* allows Superman to project his persona to a mental realm in which he can employ a kind of facsimile of his physical superpowers to fight adversaries in this mental arena. *Torquasm-vo* is thus a powerful faculty, although it has profound limitations. The Man of Steel cannot travel great distances away from his body, nor can he remain outside of his physical self for more than about an hour without risking exhaustion and total collapse. Worse, he may find himself unable to return to his physical self on his own, and thus he may be forever marooned in the psionic realm.

With his discovery of *torquasm-rao* and *torquasm-vo*, Superman came "home," not only in the sense of experiencing an adventure that was tightly bound up in his Kryptonian roots, but also in that he returned to the prehistory of his very creation as a comic book character: the mental realm of "The Reign of the Superman" of 1932.

Back to Basics

Torquasm-rao and *torquasm-vo* returned Superman to the root of it all. In like manner, the Office Superman can greatly benefit his career by getting back to certain basics, exercising his mind and imagination to create a business environment that is favorable to his professional growth and advancement.

Here is a variation on a theme introduced earlier. Recall the last time you purchased something from a really effective salesperson. What clinched the sale? Among the dozens of things the salesperson probably did right, almost certainly he or she did one thing and did it well: The focus was on *you*, on your needs, your concerns, your questions.

The world's most successful salesmen are afflicted by the same problems and pressures we all face: mortgages, credit card bills, car payments, college tuition, you name it. These may motivate him to close one sale after another, yet while his own needs unquestionably drive him, he makes sure that he always looks at the world not from his own point of view, but from his customer's perspective. His business is to understand the customer's wants, needs, doubts, and fears. This identification with another person is called empathy, and it is the *torquasm-vo* of the Office Superman, an ancient mental art that has stood in good stead countless generations of business people.

Enabling Empathy

Empathy is an exercise of the imagination in which you consciously look at a situation from the other person's point of view. But empathy works best when both you *and* the others you deal with can readily assume one another's point of view. It's a kind of transmigration of souls, or, at least, a talent for walking a mile in each other's shoes. In any case, this minor miracle of communication does not require magic, but it does call for *rapport*.

Rapport is a relationship of mutual trust and emotional affinity. It may build slowly, over a period of years, as it does, for example, between Clark Kent and Lois

Lane. In the earliest stories, Lois consistently spurns Clark, and the two don't develop true rapport until the stories of the early 1950s. But, sometimes, rapport is established instantly and spontaneously. Some people just "hit it off" with one another. From the beginning, for instance, Clark Kent and Jimmy Olsen develop the strong bond of mentor and protégé.

In the office, you can neither afford to wait years for rapport to develop nor hope that the chance of a moment will produce rapport in a flash. Fortunately, there are ways to promote and accelerate the development of rapport within the workplace.

Our perception of reality is largely shaped by language, and so it makes sense that language should provide a shortcut to rapport. It's simple, really. Make it your business to use the first-person plural pronoun whenever possible: *we, us,* and *our.* Make it your goal to move each conversation from an *I* speaking to a *you* to a discussion between *us.*

Here's how it can work:

"Accounting takes forever to process my expense vouchers," one of your coworkers complains to you.

You could respond this way: "*You've* got a real problem there."

Sounds decent enough—but, in fact, this response lacks empathy and, therefore, is a rapport wrecker rather than a rapport builder.

Change it to this: "*We've* got a real problem here." Now you've taken a big step toward rapport. The change in pronoun demonstrates empathy, an ownership stake in the other person's problem.

Disabling Empathy

We will devote an entire chapter—Chapter 19, to be precise—to "Dealing with Mr. Mxyzptlk," that is, to the subject of recovering from mistakes, blunders, and other disasters. But please take a moment to consider that little character right here and now. He is the comical imp from the Fifth Dimension whose principal function in life is to annoy and generally bedevil Superman. He is not evil, just impish, embodying the essence of mischief, a kind of self-appointed monkey wrench thrown into the workings of the universe.

What makes him do it? There is no easy answer. After all, Mr. Mxyzptlk is an element of chaos, and how can one break down an element? But an early description of Mxyzptlk in a story called "Dimensions of Danger!" (*Superman* #33, April 1945) provides a tantalizing and telling clue. In this story, he is characterized as vain and conceited. "Elfishly egotistical" is the key phrase.

Whatever else he is, and whatever else he represents, Mr. Mxyzptlk is the supreme egotist, a kind of wholly self-centered infant endowed with superpowers.

We might think of him as the rapport wrecker par excellence, because nothing destroys rapport more swiftly and surely than egotism, the unwillingness or failure to see beyond yourself.

Selfish, nasty habits tear down good feelings. These include using offensive or inappropriate language in the office, habitually arriving late to appointments or meetings, and slovenly or inappropriate dress or grooming. Failing to greet others is a blatant demonstration of bad manners, which means that it is also a pathological exhibition of ego. Even worse is failing to *listen* to others. Meaningful communication always runs two ways. In contrast, a mere monologue is a demonstration of rapport-wrecking egotism and has little positive value as genuine communication.

Helping Hands

The business of help—it's Superman's stock in trade. For Metropolis, and even all humankind, he is the ultimate source of aid. As such, Superman is a highly effective model for the Office Superman, whose secret of success is presenting himself as the indispensable problem solver and limitless source of help, the go-to guy of the workplace.

Offering help when help is needed creates rapport rapidly, but an even faster recipe for whipping up rapport is not to *offer* help, but to *ask* for it. Few things make people feel better about themselves than being asked for advice or help, and when they feel better about themselves, they like you, too. The request for help is empowering, and the Office Superman is never shy about asking.

He does not, however, ask aimlessly. Before seeking advice or assistance, identify the people who can provide what you seek. Know who does what jobs. Assess who in the office commands influence and enjoys respect. Determine just who is in the loop. Who makes the important decisions? Who is the leader? *These* are the individuals to get to know as sources of information and aid.

Planning for Rapport

A small, select minority of series television shows strike a chord and build a following that keeps them going for years. In the 1970s and into the early 1980s, it seemed that *M*A*S*H* would go on forever. In the 1980s, it was *Cheers*. In the 1990s, there was *Seinfeld*. These and shows like them played for a very long time, but, except for reruns, they're off the air now. What made them quit? The fans were still there. They surely didn't succumb to a deficiency of ratings.

What, then, finally killed them?

Fatigue. Not on the part of the audience, but among those responsible for creating the shows week after week after week. There comes a point in the life of even a very successful television series when the possibilities for new situations, new stories, above all, for *new surprises,* seem suddenly to shrink. At that point, the show and everyone associated with it are, in a word, exhausted.

That's one of the things that makes Superman so amazing. The stories have been flowing, without let-up, since 1938, and they show no sign of flagging. The Superman chronicles are a lot like life itself, with the possibilities of fresh spontaneity seemingly infinite.

And *that* is precisely the problem with life—at least as it relates to business. Life is spontaneous, difficult to control, hard to manage. The Office Superman relishes spontaneity and the myriad possibilities each new day offers, but he also devises ways to make spontaneity more manageable and, therefore, more certainly productive.

Think of a workday as a series of equations. Equations consist of known and unknown variables. The fewer unknowns, the easier it is to solve the equation. It is, therefore, to your advantage to find ways to reduce the quantity of unknowns in each workday.

Begin with the variable that is yourself. Before you start the day, jot down a short list of objectives and issues for that day. These can be objectives you want to accomplish as well as issues or problems you believe you need to confront. Next, review the list item by item. Determine your position relative to each item: How do you feel about the item? What outcome do you want from each item? What do you need to do to deal successfully with the item? What do you need from others in order to deal with it?

Here's a sample list:

1. Estimate costs for Smith project.
2. Speak to boss about idea for the Jones account.
3. Talk to Edna about expediting shipments to Acme.

Having jotted these down, our Office Superman reviews each item:

1. *Estimate costs for Smith project.* I'll need to talk to Pat to get figures. I need for her to make this a priority. If I can get these costs estimated today, I can get them to my customer before the competition reaches him. Important!

2. *Speak to boss about idea for the Jones account.* Boss is giving me a lot of resistance lately. I think this is a good idea, but I'm not sure. Got to get more hard data on the demographics of the proposed territory.

3. *Acme is pounding on me about shipping delays.* This makes me look bad and makes the company look bad, too. This issue must be resolved, pronto. The problem: How can I motivate Edna?

Now you can go off to work with a good idea not only of your objectives for the day, but of what they mean to you and what you have to do to achieve them. The day has suddenly become less spontaneous. You realize, for instance, that talking to your boss about your new idea needs to be put on hold, pending more data. Objective number 3 is certainly pressing, but number 1 needs your attention first. So, now you have your day's priorities mapped out, together with a plan of what needs to be done and who needs to be talked to. The equation that is your workday now appears with fewer and fewer unknown variables.

Taking Control

In his Golden Age phase, his earliest years, Superman was all about transforming the physical world by physical means—bending steel in his bare hands and changing the course of mighty rivers, that kind of thing. In his most recent incarnation, however, Superman has evolved into a more intellectual realm. *Torquasm-vo* is part of the new world of Superman, and it is about changing the world by purely mental means.

It is a most appealing idea, the notion of shaping reality with nothing but your mind. But if this seems fantastic, it is nevertheless no mere fantasy. The Office Superman always does the "physical" work necessary to achieve excellence. He produces the product, he makes the sales, he does whatever needs doing. But he also creates productive change by using his mind and by influencing the minds of others. He shapes the environment in which he works, just as he shapes the day in which he works. It is a brand of *torquasm-vo* that requires no Kryptonian pedigree, just a willingness to see beyond yourself and plan beyond the next hour.

CHAPTER 14

ON TRUTH, JUSTICE, and KEEPING YOUR CAPE CLEAN

THE YEAR WAS 333 B.C. Alexander the Great, marching through Anatolia (today's Turkey), entered Gordium, capital of Phrygia. He was taken to the chariot of Gordius, ancient founder of the city. The yoke of this chariot was lashed to the pole with a knot of extraordinary intricacy, its end completely hidden. Tradition, Alexander was told, held that this knot could be undone only by the man destined to conquer Asia.

Quite a problem for a would-be master of the continent. However, without a moment's hesitation, Alexander drew his sword and brought its edge down upon and then clean through the Gordian Knot.

Was Alexander the Great history's first super hero? Like Superman in so many adventures, Alexander was confronted with quite literally a knotty problem, apparently beyond the ability of mortal men to solve. Like Superman, he solved it in a single, bold, superdecisive stroke.

But here the similarity ends. Alexander was a brilliant general, a tireless commander, and a leader without fear. Yet his motivation was a single-minded desire for conquest, and, what is more (at least as semi-legendary history tells it), he was motivated by a lust for conquest for the sake of conquest alone. Just before his death, it is written, young Alexander wept, not for the misery he had caused untold thousands, but because there were no worlds left to conquer.

In contrast to Alexander the Great, Superman is a selfless hero, all of whose actions proceed from a profoundly ethical core. Now, *ethics* is a word to which innumerable volumes have been devoted over long ages. Let's cut the Gordian Knot represented by this vast literature with a very simple definition: *Ethics consists of determining what is right and what is wrong, and then doing what is right.*

The Core of the Core

Ethics is at the core of the Superman chronicles. This much seems too self-evident even to discuss. From the very beginning, Superman dedicates himself to serving truth, justice, and whatever is right, as well as to defending the weak against the tyranny and terror of the strong. About the validity of this life mission he never has doubt—although he sometimes questions his ability to carry out the mission.

In Chapter 7, we quoted Lord Acton's famous aphorism: "Power tends to corrupt and absolute power corrupts absolutely." Superman stands in glorious contradiction to Acton. That is part of the great dramatic appeal of the chronicles. We read Superman's adventures, knowing full well that, if he so chose, the Man of Steel's superpowers could give him anything the world has to offer. He could become a master thief or a supreme tyrant. He could become the world's richest man, if he wanted to, without even having to take a particularly immoral, let alone evil course. In "Hank Garvin, Man of Steel!" (*Superman* #73, December 1951), he transforms an ordinary coal mine into a diamond mine by hitting the walls of the mine with his fists. "Diamonds," he observes drily, "are simply bits of coal subjected to tremendous pressure over thousands of years! My fists speed things up a bit!" But Superman performs this feat for the benefit of others, not his own enrichment.

The entire career of Superman could illustrate the Gospel: "For what shall it profit a man, if he shall gain the whole world, and lose his own soul?" Ethics is the soul of Superman, which he will not exchange for any object of material gain.

Ethics is the soul of Superman, the quality at his very core. But what is at the core of this core?

Recall *Superman* #1, near the start of it all, and Jonathan Kent's advice to his foster son: "This great strength of yours—you've got to hide it from people or they'll be scared of you!" In terms of plot, this furnishes the reason for putting Superman in disguise and setting him out on the course of a double life. Makes for an inherently interesting plot line, which, of course, has proven to be incredibly durable over seven decades and counting. But in terms of ethics, it's a lie. The Superman story, the whole epic chronicle, begins, almost, with fatherly advice to lie—to lie to everyone all the time.

Real World Ethics

Dedicated to absolute good, Superman verges on sainthood. And that would be a real problem for his readers. Imperfect people are fascinating. Perfect saints are, well, dull. After all, who among us can truly identify with the moral perfection represented by saintliness? That's where the theme of the dual identity comes in. It introduces moral ambiguity and ambivalence, tinging an otherwise black-and-white outlook on the world with shades of gray. The theme removes Superman's ethics from the realm of saintly absolutes and firmly plants it here in the real world.

Justifying the dual identity—the Big Lie at the core of Superman—has occupied a good many comic book pages over the years, suggesting, quite rightly, that Jonathan Kent's simplistic fears about scaring people did not provide a sufficient moral rationale for a lifelong deception. So, for example, in "The Artificial Superman" (*World's Finest Comics* #57, April 1952), Clark's adoptive father expresses his fear that criminals might try to exploit his boy's "superpowers for evil purposes" if they knew who he was. That's a pretty good excuse for perpetuating the lie. Clark Kent himself worries that dropping the dual-identity would expose his foster parents to danger from vengeful gangsters in "The Story of Superman's Life." (*Superman* #146, July 1961).

There were also attempts to justify the deception on more tactical and strategic grounds. In "The Man They Wouldn't Believe," the narrator observes that "Disguised as Clark Kent, the Man of Tomorrow finds it possible, secretly, to ferret out crimes that need solving, and injustices that cry out to be righted" (*Action Comics* #61, June 1943). The disguise puts the element of surprise on Superman's side. In "The Truth Mirror" (*Action Comics* #269, October 1960), Superman worries that if Lois Lane ever accidentally "reveals my secret to the world, my undercover role as Clark Kent will be ruined. I'll no longer be able to investigate criminals as 'meek' Clark Kent so that they can later be captured by Superman!" Indeed, should his current cover ever be blown, Superman is clearly resolved to create a whole new lie, even if it "take[s] me years to set up a new identity!"

Over the decades, Superman's writers have toyed with various imaginary, hypothetical, and even hallucinatory scenarios in which Superman's identity is revealed. These are always tantalizing to readers, but perhaps the most brilliant is "When There Was No Clark Kent," published in *Superman* #127 (February 1959). In this story, eyewitnesses report Clark Kent killed in an explosion. Emotionally drained by years of living a double life, Superman seizes the opportunity to shed his alter ego once and for all and live openly as the Man of Steel. He takes up residence as Jimmy Olsen's roommate, only to find himself plagued by incessant phone calls, rubber neckers, admirers, hangers on, and a multitude of people seeking favors. This is crippling enough, but there is worse. Knowing where Superman lives, gangsters plot to lure him into a kryptonite ambush.

Before the final panel of "When There Was No Clark Kent," Superman concludes that the emotional strain of leading a double life is a relatively small price to pay for the benefits conferred by disguise. He concocts a semi-plausible explanation for how Clark Kent survived the explosion that had apparently killed him, and, with Clark resurrected, Superman resumes the grand deception.

Paying the Price

The many justifications for Superman's disguise are typical of real world ethics, which are usually based on the proposition that, in given circumstances, a good end justifies even morally questionable means.

We've all been there, of course. Who doesn't tell a "little white lie" now and then?

Ted comes to the office wearing a bright yellow houndstooth jacket and a polka-dot necktie.

"Like my new suit?" he asks. "Designer label. Cost me a fortune."

What can you say? The man looks like a clown, but why go out of your way to hurt his feelings? Maybe "Hey, Ted, I like really like it" is the best answer. It *is* a lie, but it is a lie motivated from a desire to avoid inflicting pain on a coworker. Surely, this is a case where the means (a lie) justifies the end (not hurting someone).

But is even a white lie, like this one, ethical? In the short run it does spare Ted's feelings, to be sure, and it also allows you to avoid the unpleasant task of criticizing someone's sartorial sense. Besides all this, where's the real harm in this white lie?

In the short term, there is no harm. But look beyond. By reinforcing Ted's bad taste, you may be setting him up for a fall down the line. Seeing him in this suit—and perhaps, later, in more suits just like it—what will his bosses, coworkers, and clients think of Ted? How will it affect his career? Moreover, Ted, like you, represents the company you both work for. Do you want a guy dressed like this fronting the organization on which your career depends? Looked at from the dual perspective of the short term and the long, most ethical questions become both more urgent and more difficult to resolve.

Even as Superman's writers took pains over the years to justify their hero's Big Lie as a case of means justifying ends, they also vividly portrayed the price of the ongoing deception. Lovelorn Clark Kent lives in a state of perpetual frustration because he is unable to reveal to Lois Lane his true identity.

In "The Man They Wouldn't Believe" (*Action Comics* #61, June 1943), Clark becomes so alarmed over what he thinks is Lois's plan to marry the playboy criminal Craig Shaw that he can no longer tolerate keeping his secret. "Somehow," Clark reasons, "I must win Lois for myself. But how? By proposing as Clark Kent?" That, he knows, will not work. "She despises Clark's meek character, and would turn him down. There's only one thing I can do! Reveal my secret to Lois!"

Clark perches in front of Lois Lane's apartment, awaiting her return from a date with Craig Shaw. She finally approaches.

"There's something I must tell you!"

The suspense builds as the pair ascends in an elevator to the roof of her building.

"Better prepare yourself, Lois. What I have to say will shock and amaze you."

But Lois remains calm as they arrive at the rooftop. "What did you want to tell me, Clark?"

"Just this! I'm not the quiet frightened little chap you believe I am. Far from it! The truth is—I AM SUPERMAN!"

And in a great moment of anticlimax, Lois bursts into laughter. Clark is unable to convince her of the truth he has labored so long to hide. When words fail, he suddenly leaps off the roof to demonstrate his invulnerability—only to land in a truckload of mattresses that happens to be passing by. He then takes a pistol, aims, and shoots himself—only to discover that it had been loaded with blanks. Worst of all, Clark has chosen to make his revelation on, of all days, April 1, and Lois naturally assumes that she is the butt of an April Fool's prank.

It's just as well that Lois doesn't believe Clark, because, as it turns out, she actually has no intention of marrying Craig Shaw, and, with that immediate pressure removed, Clark returns to the secret of his dual identity.

Yet Clark "Superman" Kent's means-justify-ends ethics also inflicts pain on others, not just himself. In a story called "The Six Lives of Lois Lane" (*Action Comics* #198, November 1954), for instance, the deception actually drives Lois crazy. She accidentally sees Superman changing into his Clark Kent identity, a sight so profoundly shocking to her that she falls prey to psychotic delusions of grandeur. Her discovery of the costume change occurs while she is deeply immersed in writing a series of *Daily Planet* articles on the "Great Women of History." This turns out to be bad timing, as far as her emotional health is concerned, because she suddenly believes herself to be, by turns, Florence Nightingale, Betsy Ross, Barbara Frietschie, Annie Oakley, Madame Curie, and Columbus's Queen Isabella.

Even in a very good cause, a "Big Lie" probably cannot be told forever. Untruth creates imbalance, and all systems—society as a whole or a particular business organization—always tend toward equilibrium. Sooner or later, the truth will out. After decades of deception, the creators of Superman had their super hero reveal all to Lois Lane because Clark "Superman" Kent believed that the disclosure, at long last, was a precondition of marriage with Lois.

In a sense, then, the balance of truth was restored to the Superman saga. However, fiction, unlike life, thrives on tension. Imbalance is the force that drives the plot of virtually every story, and the feeling created by the resolution at the end of most stories is a release of tension and a restoration of balance. Although Lois and Clark were married in 1996, the Big Lie still figures in the Superman chronicles. Now, Lois, sharing Superman's secret, participates in the perpetuation of the great deception.

As the issue of Superman's Big Lie demonstrates, ethics often involves judgments of relative values rather than absolute principles. Superman reveals his secret to his wife, because he believes that marriage cannot be founded on a lie, even a lie told with a noble purpose. But he continues to lie to just about everyone else in the world. That the ethical dilemma at the heart of the Superman chronicles is never resolved in simple black-and-white terms keeps the issue of ethics very much alive and lively in the Superman saga and gives us all something to think about.

Ethics Isn't Always Easy

Whatever other wisdom the chronicles of Superman may impart, they teach over and over again that ethics is not always easy. To carry out his ethical mission, Superman not only risks many physical dangers, he makes deep emotional sacrifices. Even so, he falls short of ethical perfection, precisely because he must adopt the ends-justify-means dual identity. The stresses and strains of this ambiguity serve to keep the theme of ethics front and center throughout the chronicles.

If ethics is not an easy matter for the Man of Steel, the Office Superman must also expect to face tough ethical decisions from time to time.

Honest Abe Lincoln once proclaimed honesty to be the best policy. Hard to argue against that, at least in the abstract, but in actual business we often encounter situations in which honesty seems like anything but the best policy.

Let's say a client asks you to quote him a price on a certain job. You estimate the time required to complete the work at four hours and price the job accordingly. The client agrees to the price. You do the job, but find that you have completed it in three hours. Do you adjust the price downward accordingly? Or do you bill the client for the sum he has agreed on?

If you adhere to the policy of honesty in this case, you'll be out 25 percent of the revenue you contracted for. If, on the other hand, you don't let on that the job took less time, you'll make the full four-hour revenue, and no one (except you) will know that the job was actually completed in three.

In the short run, honesty in this case will cost you money. It is a fact of business that, in the short run, sound ethics may negatively impact your bottom line. But no business survives, let alone thrives, on a single transaction. To thrive, a business must be conducted for the long run. Treat a customer ethically now, even at some immediate cost to yourself, and your ethical behavior is likely to pay off because of the fine reputation you will build over time.

Making the Right Decision

Sometimes it is an easy matter to discern right from wrong, but because any business decision typically involves weighing benefit and cost in relation to more than a few people, deciding ethical questions is often quite challenging.

As with making any important business decision, ethical matters call for careful thought. The pressures of the moment may push you toward a quick response made from motives of expediency or short-term gain. Also, many situations involving ethical issues are emotionally charged, tempting you to act out of anger or because doing such-and-such would just *feel* right. However, truly ethical action always considers the long term, and it weighs in the balance the interests of all concerned. You must think about how a decision will affect bosses, subordinates, peers, customers, shareholders, and the community.

An ethically sound decision must be an adequate and appropriate response to the present situation, but it must also harmonize with long-term goals, company policies, and other clearly understood principles of ethical conduct. An ethical decision *may* sacrifice short-term objectives in the interest of long-term goals and enduring principles, but no ethical decision will realize short-term gains at the expense of moral principles and long-term goals.

All good business decisions are built on reliable data and sound facts. This includes ethical decisions. Do not act until you are satisfied that you have all the relevant facts. By definition, an ethical decision is an equitable decision. An equitable decision can be made only when you have full, reliable information from everyone who will be affected by what you decide.

Be certain that you consider all available options. Make a list of possible actions, then choose from among them. You may find it helpful, for each option you list, to imagine the potential consequences for each individual who will be affected by the decision.

Thinking through the decision in a thorough and orderly manner has a good chance of producing a clear choice among the available options. If, however, you emerge still undecided, follow the Golden Rule. Ask yourself how you would want to be treated in this situation, then fashion your action accordingly. Remember, too, that you don't have to go it alone. Seek advice from people you respect.

Try on Another Pair of Shoes

Before acting on whatever ethical decision you make, put yourself in another pair of shoes. Look at the proposed action from a variety of perspectives. If it seems to you that others are likely to find the proposed solution unacceptable, rethink it and revise it.

Assess Collateral Damage

The Hippocratic Oath that was traditionally sworn by newly minted physicians has as its number-one provision, "First, do no harm." Take a lesson from the oath. Before you act on an ethical decision, ask yourself who, if anyone, might be hurt by the action. An ethically sound decision may create some pain, but it should do far more good than harm.

You Can Run, But You Can't Hide

Once you implement a decision concerning an ethical issue, take ownership of its consequences. Don't try to walk away. Follow up on the decision. Monitor its effects. Very few decision are irreversible or absolute. By monitoring the results of your decision, you can modify it, if necessary, to correct any problems or unexpected results that emerge.

The Circle of Character

Ethical action and ethical decisions are among the many valuable products you create for those with whom you work. Like any product a business produces, they become the property of others, who enjoy their benefits. What remains indisputably yours, however, is a quality called *character*. You carry it with you from position to position, job to job, place to place. It is an asset highly valued by employers and clients alike.

Character is really a collection of qualities, including trustworthiness, integrity, loyalty, fairness, and accountability.

Trustworthiness translates as reliability. It means that employers and clients can depend on you to meet your obligations and make good on whatever you promise.

Integrity is a quality of wholeness or wholeheartedness. People with integrity act from conviction, not from mere momentary convenience.

Loyalty is an allegiance to everyone who has an interest in your business: subordinates, coworkers, bosses, clients, investors, and the community in which you all live and work.

Fairness is the ability and willingness to make decisions based on information gathered impartially and evaluated without bias. Fair decisions are equitable in that they apply to everyone. They are also proportionate, imposing only reasonable, temperate, and truly constructive correctives.

Accountability is the acid text of character. It is the willingness and resolve to take responsibility for your actions.

Consistently ethical decisions are difficult—perhaps impossible —to make in the absence of character, and yet it is by means of consistently ethical decisions that character is both developed and demonstrated. The definition of character is therefore circular, as is the definition of ethical behavior.

As the character of Superman is defined by his actions, so his character is responsible for producing those actions. The same holds true for the Office Superman, whose ethical character, admired and valued by everyone with whom he works, is both defined and created by his consistently ethical actions.

15

MIND YOUR MILD MANNERS

IT'S NOT A MAJOR THEME IN THE CHRONICLES OF SUPERMAN, BUT IT IS A PERSISTENT ONE. Over the years, about twenty human or non-human facsimiles of Superman have emerged in the pages of the comics. The first was a thug known only as Miggs, in "Clark Kent, Star Reporter," *Superman* #36 (October, 1945). Next came an unidentified member of the Rockdust Bandits in "Sheriff Clark Kent," *World's Finest Comics* #30 (October 1947), and then there was ironworker Joe Poleski, a dead ringer in "Clark Kent's Twin," *Superman* #67 (December 1950). Another lookalike was the reporter Jack Wilde in "The Secrets of Superman," *Action Comics* #171 (August 1952), who was followed the next year by organized crime killer Dasher Drape in "Clark Kent, Gangster," *World's Finest Comics* #63 (April, 1953) and, the year after that, by naval aviator Guy Vandevier in "Clark Kent's New Mother and Father," *Action Comics* #189 (February 1954). From Krypton came the super-villain Mala in "The Outlaws from Krypton," *Action Comics* #194 (July 1954), certainly an unwanted visitor from another planet, but then, in "The Four Superman Medals" in *Action Comics* #207 (August 1955), Superman made deliberate use of an amnesiac citizen of Metropolis, who happened to be a lookalike, to attend an awards dinner at which both Superman and Clark Kent were to be guests.

In "Superman—Substitute Teacher" (*Superman* #100, September 1955), a Metropolis sub named Mr. Cranston was the lookalike, and as if he weren't a sufficiently average average Joe, Harry Winters, identified only as an "average American," found himself acting the part of Superman after he wore a Superman costume to a masquerade party in "The Make-Believe Superman," (*Superman* #127, February 1959). More exotic doubles have included Kell Orr, the son of Zoll Orr. As Zoll Orr, a scientist from the planet Xenon, was a dead ringer for Superman's birth father, Jor-El, so Kell Orr was a Superman lookalike in "The Second Superman," (*Superman* #119, February 1958). Metallo, a fascinating character who prefigured television's Bionic Man by decades, was a biomechanical reconstruction (a "human robot") of John Corben, a ruthless criminal/journalist, who had been severely injured in an automobile accident. Bearing a human brain but a mechanical heart and an "indestructible" all-metal body, Metallo impersonated Superman in "The Menace of Metallo" (*Action Comics* #252, May 1959). Another exotic impersonator, Hyper-Man, strange visitor from the planet Oceania, appeared in June 1960 as "The 'Superman' from Outer Space" (*Action Comics* #265). There was also Van-Zee, actually a "distant superkinsman" of Superman, who lives in Kandor, Krypton's capital city. Kandor survived the destruction of the planet because, before the cataclysm, it had been reduced to microscopic dimensions by the evil Brainiac, who bottled it, then stole it. It was subsequently recovered by Superman. Van-Zee, an exact double for the Man of Steel, served as Superman's ally in a number of stories in "Superman in Kandor," Parts I-III, (*Superman* #158, January 1963). Another Kandorian, Vol-Don, became a member of the Look-Alike Squad, an organization of Kandorian citizens who were doubles for Superman's closest friends, including Jimmy Olsen, Perry White—and Clark Kent. Vol-Don was the Kent look-alike, which meant, of course, that he was a de facto Superman look-alike as well in "Superman's Kryptonese Curse," (*Superman* #177, May 1965).

Another Superman ally, Batman, ran into a look-alike who was also a name-alike—an entity called Superman—during a visit to an extradimensional parallel world in "The Batman Nobody Remembered" (*World's Finest Comics* #136, September 1963). Rather closer to home, the real Superman recruited one Manuel Baeza, of the "tiny South American republic" of El Salmado, to serve as a lookalike in "The Great Superman Impersonation" (*Action Comics* #306, November 1963).

A number of criminals have used plastic surgery to transform themselves into look-alikes, including the gangster Blacky Barton in "The Death of Superman" (*Superman* #118, January 1958), the evil Kandorian scientist Zak-Kul in "The Shrinking Superman" (*Action Comics* #245, October 1958), Lex Luthor's henchman

Gypo in "Voyage to Dimension X" (*Action Comics* #271, December 1960), and Ned Barnes, a former Superman admirer who joined the Mob in "The Man Who Stole Superman's Secret Life" (*Superman* #169, May 1964).

Super-Menace appeared on the scene as "an unearthly force manifested into human form" created when the rocket ship that carried the infant Superman from the doomed planet Krypton sideswiped a space ship from another universe, thereby activating one of the space ship's "weird scientific devices," which created the duplicate. In three stories published in *Superman* #137 (May 1960), "The Super-Brat from Krypton," "The Young Super-Bully," and "Superman vs. Super-Menace," the duplicate did deadly battle with the Man of Steel.

As if all these duplicates and look-alikes weren't enough, Superman himself created Adam Newman, an android double, who appeared in two stories, "Clark Kent's Incredible Delusion" and "The End of a Hero" (*Superman* #140, October 1960).

The persistent fascination with the many Superman look-alikes lies in this: no matter how closely they resemble Superman, the doubles are not, finally, *the* Man of Steel. They are not genuine, and that fact is just enough to make the whole world seem strange and alien. This theme is latent in all the look-alike adventures, but it comes to the fore in the most famous pseudo-Superman, Bizarro, the entity Lex Luthor creates as a "grotesque, imperfect" Superman double.

Unlike the rest of the legion of doubles, Bizarro would never really be mistaken for Superman. As already mentioned in Chapter 12, "Using Your X-Ray Vision," he has chalk-white flesh and his face is faceted, as if chiseled from stone. He speaks in peculiarly ungrammatical English ("Me prove it!"), and possesses dim, highly imperfect memories of Superman's life, so he is far from fitting neatly into the Superman mold.

Most of the Superman duplicates are distinctly evil or at least menacing. Bizarro, however, is merely pathetic. He is not malicious, but a clod, and his cloddishness serves to underscore, by contrast, Superman's balanced grace, his "magnificent symmetry" ("The Wrecker," *Superman* #54, October 1948) as "the finest physical specimen on Earth" ("Superman Joins the Army," *Superman* #133, November 1959). The "wrongness" of Bizarro sets off and highlights the "rightness" of Superman.

The Ugly Superman

Far less well known than Bizarro is another Superman look-alike, who appeared, only once, in "The Ugly Superman" (*Superman's Girl Friend Lois Lane* #8, April 1959).

The story goes like this: One afternoon, Perry White assigns Lois Lane to do a *Daily Planet* piece on wrestling. After watching two bouts, Lois draws the painfully obvious conclusion that pro wrestling is not a sport, but an entertaining fraud.

BIZARRO

Debut: *Action Comics* #254, July 1959

In his July 1959 debut, Bizarro was described as a grotesquely imperfect duplicate of Superman, conjured from inanimate matter by Lex Luthor using a "duplicator ray" of his own invention. As science caught up with the comics, Bizarro was described (in *The Man of Steel* #5, October 1986) as the product of Lex Luthor's very imperfect attempt to replicate Kryptonian DNA. Luthor commissioned his top scientist, Dr. Teng, to scan Superman's genetic structure and use it to clone another Superman, who would take orders only from himself, Lex Luthor.

In the post-1986 Superman chronicles, Bizarro, a monstrously imperfect clone, nearly destroyed Metropolis, which was ultimately saved by Superman. Later, this creature allowed himself to be destroyed in a rain of disintegrating particles that had the beneficial side-effect of restoring sight to Lois Lane's blind sister, Lucy.

Some months after the destruction of Bizarro #1, Luthor created Bizarro #2, who, like his predecessor, emerged massively imperfect. The new being created a Bizarro Metropolis out of junk and garbage in an effort to please Lois Lane, with whom he fell in love (and whom, in his ungrammatical English, he called "Lo-iz"). After taking Lois to his strange city, he died in her arms, the victim of "cellular degeneration."

Bizarro #1 was later revived by the villain known as the Joker. Imbued with the reality-altering powers of the fifth-dimensional Mr. Mxyzptlk, this new incarnation of Bizarro sought to create an inverted Earth in which evil would replace good and a host of strange villains would assume control of the Justice League of America. Although Superman subsequently defeated the Joker and brought this scheme to an end, Bizarro survived and was later captured by General Zod (tyrannical ruler of the war-torn European country of Pokolistan), who amused himself by torturing this imperfect facsimile of his hated enemy, Superman. Later freed from captivity, Bizarro has tangled with Superman on numerous occasions.

However, in bout three, a short, stocky wrestler with a comically brutal face, impresses the reporter by demonstrating genuine prowess, tying his opponent into a pretzel before pushing him *through* the canvas of the ring. Intrigued, Lois interviews "The Ugly Superman"—as he bills himself—in his dressing room.

In the course of the interview, Lois takes pity on the desperately homely wrestler— "Poor man! He's dying for praise and approval! I'll give him a break! It's like kindness to dumb animals!"—and tells him she was "*thrilled*" by his performance in the ring. This is all the Ugly Superman needs to hear. The next day, he calls for Lois at the *Daily Planet* office and insists on a date.

"Don't fight it, honey! It's bigger than both of us! I brung you two tickets to the opera!"

When Lois protests that she and Clark Kent have an assignment to review a play that evening, the Ugly Superman deals Clark a severe beating. Like a good TV wrestler, Clark, "to hide the fact that he is really Superman . . . pretends the blows affect him." Not wanting to see Kent beaten to a pulp, Lois pleads, "P-please stop beating him! I'll go out with you! I'll do anything!"

As Clark Kent shadows the couple on their date, we watch the Ugly Superman take Lois to his "favorite eatin' joint," Harry's Hash House, for "the 60-cent special dinner." After all, "Nothin's too good for my gal!" Once seated, he devours a chicken, which he eats, whole, using only his hands and teeth. Later, at the opera, he puts his feet up on the rail of the box seat he shares with Lois and loudly chows down on peanuts and popcorn.

"He's embarrassing me!" Lois says to herself. "A pig at the trough has more manners!"

This panel is the thematic center of "The Ugly Superman" story. All of Superman's many doubles fall far short of the Man of Steel, but Bizarro and the Ugly Superman come up the shortest. Bizarro's grotesque physical presence contrasts with and thereby serves to underscore Superman's physical perfection. As for the Ugly Superman, his gross bad manners contrast with Superman's courtly behavior and make us realize just how naturally courteous and polite the Man of Steel is. Unlike Bizarro, Superman possesses physical grace. Unlike the Ugly Superman, the real Superman possesses social grace.

The Definition of Etiquette

Doubtless, there are any number of ways Superman could rescue Lois Lane from the companionship of the crude wrestler, but he devises a plan he believes will cause Lois the least amount of embarrassment. Disguising himself as an "old, bearded wrestler called . . . er . . *Methuselah*," Superman decides to show up the Ugly Superman in a contest of strength, so that "he'll be too deflated to bother [Lois] any more." This he sets about doing in a series of contests that end with Superman thrusting the imposter through a brick wall. While the Ugly Superman admits that "since you proved I ain't the strongest man in the world, I ain't good enough for Lois Lane," the real Superman, always the gentleman, quickly repairs the hole in the wall.

If any of his many doubles and imitators could somehow really become Superman, the world would be in for disaster. Superman is a super hero because his superpowers are balanced by lofty ethics, peerless physical grace, and supremely good manners. Take away any of these elements, and you've created a monster. Without the ethics, you have an evil monster. Without the physical rightness, you have a grotesque monster. Without the manners, you have the Ugly Superman: a big, strong oaf.

Etiquette is about rightness. It is the creation and maintenance of an environment in which everyone feels sufficiently comfortable and sufficiently valued to excel. It is also the creation and maintenance of an environment in which everyone sees and appreciates *your* graceful competence in all things. Think of etiquette as a demonstration of what the French call *savoir faire*, literally knowing how things are done.

The Office Superman regards etiquette in business as the ingredient that balances all of his other powers. It's a fine thing to be regarded as a first-rate accountant, but it is far greater to be seen as a warm, courteous, considerate human being who is also a first-rate accountant. Without manners, you may be a number cruncher—and valued as such, no less, no more. But having mastered good business etiquette, you are the indispensable member of the team who, incidentally, can crunch numbers with the best of them.

Remember Rapport

In Chapter 13, "Putting *Torquasm-Vo* to Work for You," we talked a good deal about the importance of rapport in the workplace. Effective business etiquette is essential to building and maintaining rapport, a relationship of trust and emotional affinity. Fortunately, the elements most basic to business etiquette are so simple that they don't need to be *learned* so much as *practiced*.

Where Superman might resort to his Fortress of Solitude to invent a secret Rapport Ray, you already own the equivalent of such a device. Nothing produces rapport more rapidly than a smile. Think of a smile as a standing invitation, showing those around you that you are open to contact, conversation, and cooperation. If you want to intensify the effect of this, your own personal "Rapport Ray," add a wave, as you walk into the office in the morning or pass a colleague in the hall.

A smile and a wave can be used almost anywhere, anytime. A handshake is used more selectively, but while it is true that you can't go around politician-fashion, shaking every hand you encounter, do take advantage of every situation that does call for a handshake. Remember the rules: Smile, maintain eye contact, and deliver a full, firm grip with a dry, warm hand, avoiding both the limp dead fish and the childish bonecruncher grip.

Whenever you meet, talk with, or even pass anyone in the office, make and maintain eye contact. When you walk through the hall, keep your head up. Looking down or otherwise averting your gaze is a habit destructive to rapport.

Offer a kind word beyond "Good morning." The greatest kindness is a compliment for some real achievement: "Good morning, Mary. That report yesterday was really helpful to me." As discussed in Chapter 13, it is also a great idea to find an *appropriate* time for a little small talk. Moderate schmoozing, without intruding or interrupting, is a strong rapport builder.

Don't hesitate to commit a courteous act or two. Some men have the idea that, these days, it's bad manners or maybe even against the law to open or hold a door for a woman. That's silly. Show courtesy to everyone, regardless of gender. If you are in a position to open a door, do so, just as a woman should open the door for you if she reaches it first. Similarly, offer to help a fellow worker—male or female—as he or she struggles through the corridor loaded down with a stack of papers. Act kindly at every opportunity.

A Question of Value

In the previous chapter, we talked about how Superman's dual identity intriguingly relates to the theme of ethics. The double life as Clark Kent and Superman serves another purpose as well. It shows us, in a dramatic way, what Superman does when he isn't on the job as a super hero. Through all these years, one of the most endearing aspects of the Superman chronicles is that the characters, including the Man of Steel, clearly have lives outside of work. Even when Superman isn't living in his Clinton Street Metropolis apartment as Clark Kent, he spends downtime in his arctic Fortress of Solitude, a place devoted not only to laboratories, invention, and monitoring the condition of the world, but also to Superman's leisure, his memorabilia and hobbies.

The Office Superman sees his bosses, colleagues, and subordinates as whole people, not just 9-to-5 accountants, salesmen, file clerks, and order processors. He recognizes that, like himself, they have lives beyond the office, and he understands that effective business etiquette honors the full value of those he works with.

If this sounds idealistic or hifalutin, it's really very much down to Earth. Follow this rule: In the office, treat everyone as you would in your home. It's that simple.

No one in the office is invisible, and no one should be treated as if they were. Everyone deserves a greeting, a smile, a wave, and, whenever possible, a kind word that shows how you value them.

"Ed," you greet the young man who distributes the office mail, "how's that night class going?"

In leisure hours at home, you often entertain guests. During working hours at the office, you also "entertain" guests. These may include clients, vendors, colleagues, subordinates, and bosses. Treat them with the cordial courtesy you would accord any welcome visitor. Greet your guest. If she is a colleague you see every day, try a simple "Hi, Cheryl. Come in. Make yourself at home." With clients, vendors, or colleagues you don't regularly work with, add a handshake. Always come out from behind your desk to greet your visitor.

The goal of hospitality has always been to make strangers feel less strange. If your guest is an outsider or a new employee, do not fail to make all necessary introductions. Here are some guidelines to follow:

- When introducing your boss to others, use her full name if you are on a first-name basis with her. Use only the last name if you address your boss as *Mr.* or *Ms.*
- Outside of the business context, it remains customary to introduce men to women: "Jane Doe, this is Tom Smith." In business, however, introduce the person of lesser rank to the person of greater rank, regardless of gender: "Mr. Boss, this is Susan Subordinate."
- One person ranks above all others when introductions are made: the client. Introduce all others to him or her: "Ms. Client, this is our manager, Mr. Boss."

As you would at home, attend to the needs, convenience, and comfort of your guest. If refreshments such as tea and coffee are available, offer them. If a pen and paper are required, supply them. At the end of the meeting, offer your thanks and a kind word: "Ed, it's always great talking with you." Or: "Great meeting! I look forward to working with you on this." If your guest is someone you don't work with on a day-to-day or routine basis, a handshake is an appropriate parting salute. If you have an office with a door, get up from your desk and show your guest out, and always escort outside visitors all the way to the exit or elevator.

When you are a guest in someone's office, behave as you would if you were a guest in that person's home. Be punctual in arriving and never overstay your welcome. Your host may definitively conclude the meeting, in which case it is, of course, time for you to leave. Even if he doesn't tell you that the meeting is at an end, your host may indicate his desire to conclude it by asking you a leading question: "Have we covered everything?" Or he may use body language, such as arranging papers on his desk or glancing at an appointment calendar. Pick up on the cues and make moves to depart. If you believe that you need more time, suggest rescheduling rather than extending the present stay. Value your host by acknowledging the value of his time: "Tom, I know you have a number of other people to see today. I'd like to revisit this matter later. Can we continue the discussion tomorrow at the same time?"

One big difference between entertaining guests at home and in the office is that, at home, you can usually focus all of your attention on your guest. In the office, however, interruptions come with the territory. As far as you can, schedule appointments to avoid interruptions. If at all possible, let your incoming phone calls go into voice mail, and if another visitor comes to your door, politely deflect her: "Alice, I'm in a meeting. Can I come by your office, say in half an hour?"

Sometimes, in the course of a meeting, we suddenly remember a phone call that just *has* to be made. Resist the temptation to interrupt and pick up the phone. Few violations of business etiquette are more egregious than interruptions initiated *by* the host. Suck it up. Hold the thought. Make the call *after* your guest leaves.

In an imperfect world, some interruptions are unavoidable. In these cases, always apologize and briefly explain the pressing need to interrupt.

Higher Values

To say that Superman never balks at going the extra mile is an understatement. He'll go the extra light-year, if need be. For the Office Superman, however, the extra mile will do.

Make it your business to learn something about the special days in the lives of your colleagues, subordinates, and bosses. Consider being the person in the office who organizes company or department birthday celebrations. Disrupting the work day several times a month to celebrate this or that birthday among a large group of employees is neither productive nor practical, but everyone's got to eat lunch. You could circulate an e-mail organizing a group trip to the local eatery. The birthday honoree gets treated, of course.

Births among your colleagues' families call for celebration, and everyone feels good about welcoming a new life into the world. Why not be the person who organizes a collection for the purchase of a modest baby gift?

If it's fun to share and celebrate good times, it is also important to recognize loss. When you hear that a colleague has had a death in the family, go out of your way to visit him when he returns to work. Empathize—without smothering the person in sentiment. "Jack, I'm so very sorry about your loss. You know, I met your father only the one time, but that was enough to make it clear that he was a wonderful person."

Navigating the New Office Geography

Four walls, a door, and maybe even a window were once architectural basics any white-collar guy could pretty much take for granted. Those days passed with the original Golden Age and Silver Age of adventure comics. Today, even personnel at fairly high levels get planted in a cubicle, which is a rectangle without doors, windows, or even solid walls.

Office etiquette dictates the following concerning the dreaded cube:

- Deal with it. This is the way of the modern office. Stop complaining.
- Your cubicle is your office. Treat it as such.
- Their cubicles are your colleagues' offices. Treat them as such. Respect the privacy of the cubicle as if it really were private. Pretend it has a door. Never barge in. Always ask permission to enter.
- Never enter a colleague's cubicle if the occupant is not present—except to deliver something or leave a note; and then it is quickly in and quickly out. Don't loiter in someone else's unoccupied cubicle.
- If you are scheduled to meet in a colleague's cubicle, wait outside until the person shows up.
- When visiting another's cube, ask permission before rearranging any furniture: "Do you mind if I move this chair?"
- When you leave, be sure your trash leaves with you. Clean up after yourself.
- Ask permission before you put anything—such as a coffee cup—on a person's desk.
- The fact that there's no lock on the cubicle door—and, for that matter, no door—is not a license to steal. Never borrow stuff—e.g., the calculator, the stapler—without permission. Always return whatever you borrow.
- Don't snoop or even appear to be snooping.

Electronic Etiquette

Superman doesn't always communicate face to face. When you possess the power of superventriloquism and can throw your voice millions of miles or dispense with vocalization altogether and use telepathy, a one-on-one conversation isn't always required. In business, of course, a great deal of communication—for many of us, *most* communication—likewise does not involve the physical proximity of the talkers. But the fact that you can't see the person you're communicating with, that you can't shake his hand and look him in the eye, is no excuse for abandoning solid business etiquette.

On the telephone, speak to be understood and understood fully and clearly. Most of us talk too fast on the phone. Slow down to give each word its full value. Don't mumble or slur your words, and do speak directly into the mouthpiece. When you answer the phone, don't start talking until you have the receiver to your ear and the mouthpiece in front of your mouth. A greeting that begins in midvowel can be very irritating.

These are the basics of effective telephone etiquette. Now for the advanced course:

- Stand up when you talk. This may feel strange at first, but your voice has more depth, resonance, and authority when you stand. Pavarotti never delivered an aria sitting down.
- Smile, even if you don't have a picture phone. Although you are unseen, a smile can be *heard* in your voice.
- Avoid speaker phones. They make most callers uncomfortable and suggest a lack of privacy. Use the speaker only when absolutely necessary, and always inform the person on the other end of the line that he or she is "on speaker."
- When you answer the phone, "Hello" isn't much of an answer. Always identify yourself and your company or department: "Good morning, Accounting, John Doe speaking."
- Whenever it is appropriate, conclude your answering greeting with: "How may I help you?" The phrase "May I help you?" invites nothing more than a *yes*, but preface this with a "how," and you prompt the caller to state his business, saving both of you time and one more possibility for misunderstanding.

Try to avoid putting a caller on hold, but sometimes this is unavoidable. No caller likes it, so it helps to ask permission. Say "May I put you on hold?" instead of "I'm putting you on hold." A request empowers; a command takes power away. It is also helpful to give the caller an estimate of his hold time: "I'll be back in just a moment."

If you are aware that you will have to put a caller on hold for an extended time, offer to call back: "Mr. Smith, I don't want to keep you on hold for what may be several minutes. Why don't you give me your number, and I'll call you back in fifteen minutes." Just remember to honor your promise to call.

Receptionists, secretaries, and executive assistants typically serve not as conduits to their bosses, but as gatekeepers and screeners to "protect" them from "intrusions." Even Superman might have trouble breaking through the phalanx surrounding some managers and CEOs, but the Office Superman has a few courteous tricks to navigate through the flak catchers.

When making a call, the object is to avoid triggering the screener's first defense, which is the "Who's calling?" question:

"May I speak to Perry White?"

"Who's calling?"

"John Doe."

"I'm sorry, Mr. Doe. Mr. White is in a meeting . . ."

Instead, announce yourself first thing: "Hello, this is John Doe from Doe, Ray, and Me, for Perry White." This tells the person who answers that you have a right to speak to Perry White and it increases your odds of getting the call through.

These days, more and more business communication takes place via e-mail. It is best to think of e-mail as face-to-face communication without the actual face. For most e-mails, a conversational tone is best, but don't get sloppy. Check your spelling and punctuation, and never send e-mail messages in all-capital letters. This is the digital equivalent of shouting, and it is most rude.

Read over your message before sending it. Make corrections and adjustments as necessary. Once you hit the "send" key, that message is irretrievably out of your hands.

The fax machine requires a special approach. The Office Superman never sends anyone an unsolicited fax, except in rare instances of genuine urgency. Unsolicited faxes tie up the recipient's fax line and consume paper and toner. Courts have even held that unsolicited "spam" faxes are illegal.

Always include a transmittal sheet that states the total number of pages, the date, who the fax is intended for, and who sent it, including your voice phone and fax number. Most important, be aware that, in most companies, fax machines are shared by several users and the machine itself is situated in a hallway or other semi-public area. Never send sensitive material without first alerting the intended recipient by phone.

Savvy Socializing

An invitation to a party or a dinner is usually a most welcome thing. An invitation to a business social event after a hard day at the office may be less than welcome, but, welcome or not, regard it as a command performance.

What's the worst error in business etiquette you can make? Not accepting the invitation. Office party? Go. Sales conference cocktail party? Go. Dinner with vendors or clients? Go. Go. Go.

Only one kind of behavior is appropriate at business social occasions. Call it alert relaxation. Appear both alert *and* comfortable, and you will show those around you that you are interested in them and what they have to say, yet you are also confident and relaxed with them. Projecting this attitude will tend to make others comfortable as well. Just don't relinquish your edge entirely. A business social occasion is, by definition, always more business than social. You *are* being watched, and you *are* being judged.

Begin by dressing appropriately for the occasion. For most events directly related to business, regular business attire is fine, but for dinner, you may want to ratchet it up a notch or two. "Black tie" events require formal wear, of course, whereas sporting events, company picnics, and the like call for neat and clean casual attire.

Keep social conversation positive. This is not the time to complain about issues at work, market conditions, or the like. It is never appropriate to grouse about personal issues, such as salary. Indeed, many employers regard discussing your salary with others as sufficient "cause for dismissal"! In any case, it is very bad manners. Always try to enjoy yourself, but, more important, always act as if you are enjoying yourself.

Ensure that you arrive at social events on time or very slightly early, but never late. In any business-related context, there is no such thing as being "fashionably late." If you are greeted by the host or hostess, engage in conversation without, however, monopolizing him or her. He or she has other guests to greet.

If drinks are served, follow your customary practice, provided that your customary practice is moderation. This is business. Not only do you want to remain sharp, you don't want to behave irresponsibly or recklessly. There is nothing wrong with drinking a soft drink, club soda, or seltzer instead of alcohol. As for smoking, don't even ask. Smoke only if others are.

A moderate approach applies to the issue of hors d'oeuvres as well. Gather a few on a small plate, if one is provided, or a napkin, then leave the hors d'oeuvre table. Hovering there is very bad form, as, indeed, is hovering anywhere. Work the room, circulate, and do not exclude spouses from your conversation.

Be aware of the time. When significant numbers of people begin to leave, it's time for you to leave as well. The very next day, write a brief thank you note to the host or hostess.

Some observations regarding office parties: Depending on the "culture" of your place of business, office parties may walk closer to the wild side than evening cocktail parties outside of the office. Even if things do get pretty hilarious, it behooves you to avoid offensive behavior of any kind. Instead, *use* the office party to network. Just don't ambush your colleagues, subordinates, or bosses into a heavy business conversation.

World View

When Superman started out in the late 1930s and early 1940s, his range of operations was pretty much confined within the city limits of Metropolis. Over the years, however, Superman's gone national, international, and, ultimately, intergalactic. American business hasn't gotten quite so far, but, these days, even a modest corporation can expect to do business internationally, with customers, vendors, or both. We don't have the space to go into country by country, culture by culture specifics, but be aware that the style of business, including business etiquette, varies significantly from one global place to another. When you know that you are going to do business in a foreign country, research the business customs. However, if you find yourself in a foreign country or dealing with a foreign client or vendor and you get stuck, uncertain of how to behave in a given situation, stop what you're doing, smile, and ask for help. Don't be concerned that your questions will be taken as signs of ignorance. On the contrary, they will be interpreted as tokens of respect and a desire to please. Above all, watch and learn. It's what Superman would do.

SUPERMAN SUITS UP

FROM HIS OWN FORTRESS OF SOLITUDE ON THE SHORE OF WALDEN POND outside of Concord, Massachusetts, the nineteenth-century philosopher-naturalist Henry David Thoreau warned, "Beware of all enterprises that require new clothes." Well, as Joe Shuster first drew him in 1933, five years before the publication of *Action Comics* #1, the character he called "the Superman" hardly appears to have any clothes at all, new or otherwise. An inked cover is all that survives from this "Science Fiction Story in Cartoons," and it shows the super hero swooping down on a robber. The robber is about to be caught in mid caper, but the future Man of Steel not only lacks a cape, his torso appears to be bare, and his legs are so sketchily drawn that it is impossible to tell just what he is wearing over them.

According to Shuster's much-later recollection, as noted in Les Daniels's *Superman: The Complete History* (San Francisco: Chronicle Books, 1998), it was late the following year, in 1934, that he conferred with Siegel on redesigning the character.

"Let's put him in this kind of costume," Shuster said, "and let's give him a big S on his chest, and a cape, make him as colorful as we can and as distinctive as we can."

And the rest, as the saying goes, is history. Superman's costume has been tweaked over the years and has varied slightly from artist to artist, but, overall, it has been unchanged since its published debut in 1938. While no one would claim that Superman's appeal is exclusively due to his costume, it is doubtful that he would have gotten as far as he has—and for so long—without it. In any case, it is impossible to imagine Superman without his blue, red, and yellow outfit. It is his trademark, and the almost ritualistic transition, when duty calls, from Clark Kent's street clothes to Superman's tights and cape unmistakably signals that the Man of Steel has entered the building and is ready for business.

Power Suit

Popular magazines periodically publish feature articles devoted to "power dressing," and, over the years, innumerable "dress for success" books have appeared on store shelves. This is a perennial topic because, while the desire for success is eternal, fashion is fickle. No twenty-first-century business person would rely on a 1938 guide to dressing for success. Indeed, even as Superman's costume has violated all fashion rules by remaining in style since 1938, Clark Kent's wardrobe has significantly evolved over the years. The double-breasted suit that was de rigueur in the late 1930s and 1940s began to yield to two- or three-button, single-breasted cuts in the 1950s. The fedora, indispensable to the male wardrobe sixty and seventy years ago—and especially important for a reporter (you need a hatband to hold your press pass)— was often omitted by the mid 1950s, whereas, beginning in the 1960s, Clark was typically hatless. In a January 1971 story, "Kryptonite Nevermore!" (*Superman* #233), artists Curt Swan (pencils) and Murphy Anderson (inks) gave Clark Kent a wardrobe so stylishly contemporary that, as Daniels notes in *Superman: The Complete History,* it merited mention in *Gentleman's Quarterly,* while script writer Denny O'Neil earned an interview on TV's *Today Show.*

Between them, the Superman costume and Clark Kent's suits represent the ideal in dressing for business. Together, they combine a timeless expression of values associated with the wearer *and* an awareness of changing fashion. The Superman costume suggests an adherence to distinctive principles, which are both highly individualistic (*Superman's* trademark) yet partake of universal values ("Truth, justice, and the American way"), while Clark Kent's evolving suits reflect an engaged awareness of changing trends, fashions, and ideas. As an Office Superman, the image you project, in part through what you wear, should similarly balance an expression of who you are and even what you believe with an acknowledgment of the changing ways of the world. This is the essence of business dressing. It consists of wearing clothing that helps you to achieve the balance we spoke of in Chapter 6, "On Changing the Course of Mighty Rivers," the balance between fitting in and standing out.

Action Suit

Superman's costume has been described variously as an "invulnerable uniform," an "action costume," a "super-uniform," and an "action suit."

There are very good reasons for these characterizations. Through the years, accounts of how Superman's costume came into existence have varied. In *Superman* #5 (Summer 1940), the Man of Steel says that his outfit was "constructed of a cloth I invented myself which is immune to the most powerful forces!" In "The Mighty Mite," however, published in December 1951 (*Superman* #73), we are told that Clark Kent's foster mother, Martha Kent, made the costume out of the brightly colored blankets the infant Kal-El (Superman's Kryptonian name) had been wrapped in as he rocketed to Earth. Some later accounts depart from this—for instance, "20,000 Leagues Under the Sea with Superman" (*Superman* #81, April, 1953), which says that the costume had been created out of "a rare material from Krypton." However, most later stories resume the Martha Kent tale, and one, "The Story of Superman's Life" (*Superman* #146, July 1961), even explains how she worked with indestructible cloth, which, because indestructible, must have been impervious to scissors. After unraveling the loose ends of the blankets, Martha coaxed the infant Superman to use his X-ray vision to snip the unraveled threads, so that she could sew a playsuit. Later, Martha unraveled the playsuit to get the thread with which she sewed the celebrated costume. (And for those who don't have better things to think about, "The Origin of Superman's Costume"—*Superman Annual* #8 (Winter 1964)—explains that the young Superman made his bright red boots himself, using "strips of rubber padding" saved from the wreckage of the rocket that had transported him to Earth.) Most recently, in *Superman: Birthright* #3 (November 2003), Clark Kent and his foster mother are depicted as collaborating on the costume. "It's not like I can take this project to a *tailor*," Clark observes with dry humor.

However the chronicles vary on the details of how Superman's costume came to be, they all agree on one point: that it is essentially indestructible—or, more precisely, that it possesses the same degree of invulnerability Superman himself enjoys. Like Superman, it is not impervious to kryptonite radiation, and, were the suit to be returned somehow to a Kryptonian environment, it would cease to be superdurable, just as Superman would cease to have superpowers in such a place.

As Clark Kent, Superman wears his remarkable costume under the mild-mannered reporter's street clothes. These, however, despite their ordinary appearance, are by no means ordinary. According to "The End of Clark Kent's Secret Identity" (*Action Comics* #313, June 1964), Kent's clothes are "made of super-compressible material." When Kent tears off his suit to become Superman, "with one squeeze of his mighty fingers, he compresses Clark Kent's resilient clothing and special fibre shoes into a compact ball!" The next moment, Superman thrusts his compressed Clark Kent clothes into a secret pouch in the lining of his cape ("The Menace of Metallo," *Action Comics* #252, May 1959).

Like Superman's costume, Kent's suit is essentially indestructible, as are his "indestructible super-glasses" ("The Super-Luck of Badge 77," *Superman* #133, November 1959), which young Clark had fashioned from the "plexiglass shield" of his wrecked rocket ship. "These super-plastic lenses don't melt when I project my X-ray vision through them," Clark observes in "The Curse of Kryptonite," (*Superman* #130, July 1959).

In addition to dressing in a way that proclaims who he is while also demonstrating how well he fits into the prevailing styles, Superman/Clark Kent dresses with great practicality in a costume and a suit that are both entirely appropriate to his line of work.

Dress Code

The Office Superman seeks both individual and collective style, but, above all, he ensures that what he wears is appropriate to his position and the particular work environment in which he finds himself. This does not mean that he mindlessly dons a corporate uniform, but he does make sure that he understands the unspoken, unwritten, but nevertheless quite real "dress codes" that govern his office and his industry. Effective business dressing is a combination of what makes you comfortable, what expresses how you feel about yourself, *and* what is appropriate to the office and industry in which you work.

Before we consider the "dress code" concept further, let's make sure there is no misunderstanding about the meaning of the word "comfortable." For many of us, "comfortable" means the jeans and T-shirt we wear, at home, in front of the TV. In the office, however, most of us would be decidedly *un*comfortable in such an outfit. Comfort has emotional and cultural dimensions as well as physical dimensions. Always consider all three dimensions when you choose your business wardrobe. Being underdressed or overdressed in comparison to those all around you can be a most stressful experience.

The "comfortable" concept also flows two ways. Your business wardrobe should make you—*as well as those around you*—comfortable. You may relish a touch (or more) of the unconventional in your appearance: a bright red shirt, perhaps, a wild paisley-print necktie, a lavender jacket. In some offices and industries—a hip interior design firm, say—such accents may be entirely appropriate. But in other offices—for instance, a Wall Street brokerage—this attire would cause acute discomfort in bosses, coworkers, and clients alike. And be assured that if they are uncomfortable, you will be also.

You can generally achieve appropriateness and true comfort by observing two rules of thumb.

First, determine the prevailing "dress code" by gauging how the people in your office dress. This done, ratchet up your attire just a *notch* higher. Some business fashion gurus actually try to put a number on this notch, advising us all to dress no more than "5 percent better" than our peers.

Second, the best business "look" is the safest look, which translates as a conservative or traditional or, if you prefer, *classic* look. While Clark Kent's wardrobe was substantially revised in 1971, it remained rooted in 1938 and, of course, was always counterbalanced by the unchanging look of the super costume underneath.

"Conservative" does not have to mean dull, and you should depart from conservatism if your office or industry calls for doing so. Even if you do adopt a conservative look, you can add dash with tasteful accessories such as a colorful tie, a pocket square handkerchief, or a subtly patterned shirt. But, generally speaking, it is best to establish a conservative base, a style that keeps the attention focused on you, not your clothing. Think of the word "conservative" not as describing a political or cultural attitude, but as expressing a desire to *conserve* your image and to be seen as something more than the sum of your flashy clothes. Make too bold a fashion statement in the office, and you risk being written off as an empty suit.

The Celebrated Spit Curl

Even if his complexion weren't chalk white and his face a faceted block of stone, you'd be able to tell Bizarro apart from Superman in an instant. Whereas Bizarro's crop of hair is matted and unkempt, Superman's is always neat—superneat, in fact, his trademark spit curl always perfectly in place, even when he is flying faster than a speeding bullet.

The "safe" look appropriate to just about all business environments extends to personal grooming as well as wardrobe. Respect yourself and everyone around you by ensuring that you come to work clean, showered, appropriately coifed, and either shaven or with your moustache and/or beard neatly trimmed.

The issues of hair length and facial hair wain and wax in importance, depending on political and cultural forces. Your best guide is the prevailing appearance of others in your office and industry. In some stories during the 1990s, most notably "The Wedding Album" of 1996, Superman is depicted with a substantial mane, which Clark Kent gathers into a then-fashionable ponytail. Your best style guide is to focus on those who are demonstrably the most successful and emulate them, but do, in all cases, avoid extremes. Really long hair suggests sloppiness and rebellion to some people, including, perhaps, your bosses and clients. On the other hand, these same folks may associate a buzz cut with a neo-Nazi cult or other extremists. Similarly, at one time, a full beard was regarded as a token of business success, while, much later, it was seen as a symbol of radical rebellion. Be sensitive to the standards that prevail around you.

We are blessed in the United States with a strong set of hard-won civil rights laws, which prohibit (among other evils) discrimination in employment based on such factors as race, gender, and age. Despite this, many employers continue to place a premium on youth or, at least, the appearance of youthful vigor. Weigh this in your mind when you consider whether or not to dye gray hair. Depending on your particular office and industry, the appearance of age may put you at a disadvantage or it may give you an edge—if, for example, you are working in a situation in which gray hair conveys a priceless store of experience and wisdom.

Beyond these changeable tonsorial considerations, some other grooming issues are universal. For example, avoid dousing yourself in deodorant, cologne, or aftershave. At the very least, overindulgence in these things conveys the subtle message that you are trying to "cover up" something very unpleasant. Worse, many people find strong scents annoying and those who use such cosmetics even more annoying. Some people are actually allergic to the scent of cologne and aftershave. You don't want to annoy your colleagues, let alone make them sick. Should you therefore avoid colognes and the like altogether? There is no harm in doing just that, but if you enjoy a certain scent, do use it—just do so sparingly, to create a pleasant, inviting, clean, and polished aura.

Progressive Dressing

In your bid to fit in, be aware of what you are trying to fit into. By all means, scope out the "look" of the office and adjust your wardrobe accordingly, but it is often best to set your sights on the level of employment just above your current level and dress appropriately to it, the level to which you aspire, rather to the level you currently occupy. For example: You are an executive assistant in an office in which most people at your level wear a sport jacket, shirt, tie, and jeans. Invest in the best conservative-cut suit you can afford and wear it at least once a week. Once a week, you'll look as if you belong at the next salary level.

Upwardly mobile, the Office Superman takes periodic stock of his professional wardrobe. As he sorts through the closet, he asks himself two questions:

1. Do I have the appropriate clothing? (Appropriate to my current position and the next higher position? Appropriate to my office and industry?)
2. Is my wardrobe in excellent condition—neat, clean, and in perfect repair?

The first question we have already considered. The second deserves a bit of elaboration, because it matters little how carefully you have selected your wardrobe and how much you have paid for it if what you choose to wear is not sharp and clean. Visit the dry cleaner frequently. You don't have to dry clean a good suit or sport coat every time it starts to look a little rumpled. In fact, even the best-made garments lack the indestructible durability of Superman's costume, and the dry cleaning process does take its toll on fabrics. Unless you suffer a mishap—a burst taco, say—dry clean a suit only two or three times a year, but take it in as often as necessary for a pressing only. As for shirts, they should be freshly laundered, preferably by a professional. Light to medium starch is best.

Like Superman, the Office Superman may have to do a lot of flying. According to "The Coward of Steel" (*Action Comics* #322, March 1965), Clark Kent's suit is specially treated to make it "friction-proof," so that, in an extreme emergency, Superman can fly or perform other feats without changing into his costume and without fear of burning or otherwise damaging his suit as a result of friction with the surrounding air.

It would be nice to have something like that for what the rest of us wear. Air travel can be pretty hard on a business wardrobe. Preserve it by folding what you pack neatly and carefully. These days, it is usually impossible to hang your garment bag in a full-length closet aboard a crowded airliner, so, you'll have to fold suits in half. The best tactic is to keep suits in the plastic bags the dry cleaner delivers them in. Professionally laundered shirts are best transported in the boxes most cleaners provide. If you don't have the cleaner's plastic bags and must fold suit jackets into a suitcase, fold them in half, lengthwise, *away from* the lining (in other words, so that the lining shows). This fights wrinkling.

Think ahead before you do business on the road. Make use of the hotel's pressing service the evening before to get your suit ready for an important meeting this next day. In a pinch, you can steam out wrinkles by hanging clothes in the bathroom while the shower is running full hot. Two things to be careful about: First, don't scald yourself. Second, don't end up soaking your clothes.

Suit Yourself

Fashions change and vary widely, so any cookie-cutter formula for successful dressing would have a very short shelf life. However, like Superman's costume, general principles change very little, if at all, through time.

Set as your objective dressing in a way that communicates reliability and attention to detail. This means not allowing any one article of your outfit to be singled out as the subject of special attention or discussion. Remember, *you*, not your clothes, should be the focus of those you work with.

As a rule of thumb, dark colors suggest authority, and dark blue conveys the greatest degree of authority. (There is a reason that most police departments dress their officers in this color.) Black may be going too dark, since it strikes many as overly formal or even funereal. Most people tend to find brown suits unattractive.

Favor natural fabrics (especially wool) or blends with a high percentage of a natural fibers. Synthetic fabrics tend to have a sheen and texture that makes them look cheap—even if they aren't—and they don't "drape," hang, or conform to the body as attractively as natural fabrics do. They also tend to show wear more readily than natural fabrics, and they retain body odors stubbornly.

Solids and subtle patterns are always good choices for suits and sport coats. So-called "banker stripes"—muted, narrow pin stripes—are typically associated with conservative finance firms and power politics, which may well be the message you want to convey. If it is not, however, consider avoiding this pattern. To be shunned under all circumstances are "loud" checked patterns. No one wants to do business with a disreputable used-car salesman.

Few of us can claim a physique that approaches Superman's, but, fortunately, most businesses don't call for the wearing of tights. If you have an appropriately slender build, smart European cuts look great, but most of us are safer with a more generous—and conservative—American cut.

Beneath the Clark Kent suit is the Superman costume. Beneath your suit is a shirt. In most offices, long-sleeved, button-front shirts are always most appropriate. French cuffs, fastened with simple and plain cuff links, convey an extra measure of attention to detail, but ordinary button-fastened barrel cuffs are fine, too. The best color choices are white or very pale blue.

Some people think a monogram is a surefire sign that they have "arrived." The fact is that many people interpret the presence of a monogram not as a mark of individual distinction and prosperity, but as sheer ostentation, even vulgarity. If you feel the need to wear monogrammed shirts, put the initials on your left sleeve, at the top of the cuff and never above the breast pocket.

Are You Fit to Be Tied?

Experts are divided over the question of which article of a man's wardrobe draws first notice. Some say it's the shoes. Others insist on the tie.

Your first decision is whether or not to wear a tie. Take your cue from the standard set in your office. If the other men wear ties, yours is not to reason why, just go ahead and wear a tie.

A small minority of men favor bow ties over long ties in the belief that it makes them look different and distinctive. Indeed it does, but not necessarily for the right reason. Wear a bow tie and you'll forever be known as "the guy with the bow tie." *That* is not a particularly distinguished achievement.

The wrong necktie can make even an expensive suit look cheap, whereas the right one can elevate modest attire. For virtually all business purposes, only one fabric is acceptable: 100 percent silk. Linen wrinkles right away, wool is too casual, and synthetics do not lend themselves to beautiful knots.

If you play it safe by wearing a white or very pale blue shirt, coordinating shirt and tie won't be a problem. With regard to the suit, your tie should complement it rather than match it. If your suit is patterned, don't wear a patterned tie that fights the suit pattern. People will rub their eyes and stare at the conflict between suit and tie while you yourself disappear into the background.

Wide or narrow? Necktie widths swell and shrink with the ever-changing tides of fashion, but one rule of thumb seems never to change: The width of the tie should approximate the width of the suit lapels.

In keeping with the slightly-conservative-is-best philosophy, select the traditional patterns: foulards, stripes, and muted paisley prints, in addition to solids. Bold "power stripes" can make a strong statement. Also capable of a strong statement are polka dots, pictures (hound's heads, cartoon characters, etc.), and sporting images (golf clubs, polo mallets, etc.). Unfortunately, the statement is hardly the one the Office Superman wishes to make. Deep six these silly ties—along with that designer-logo tie your buddy talked you into buying. Many businesspeople feel that designer ties broadcast your insecurity even as they broadcast the designer's name, logo, or monogram.

If you don't already know how, learn to tie a beautiful knot. It's the kind of detail that suggests you value careful attention to quality in everything you do. If the necktie is sufficiently long, a "full Windsor" is the knot of choice, but many ties are too short for this and should be tied with a small, tight knot. However you tie your tie, the "fat" end should never extend below your trouser belt and should always be longer than the "skinny" end.

Does Superman use steroids? Perish the thought! Nor should the Office Superman even *think* of wearing a clip-on tie.

On Your Feet

Red boots of Kryptonian rubber look mighty fine on the Man of Steel, but the Office Superman favors shoes of black or brown leather, always well polished, and with unworn heels. Supervisor types have long tended toward lace-up wing tips, while executives and accountants tend toward slip-on dress shoes. Those in so-called "creative" positions—such as advertising copywriters and designers in various fields—often sport Italian loafer styles that are priced commensurately with Italian sports cars.

The color of your socks should complement the color of your suit, and the socks should be long enough to permit you to cross your legs without revealing a startling expanse of hairy skin.

Accessories Included

Your belt should be leather and should match or complement your shoes. Buckles borrowed from the U.S. Cavalry, a singing cowboy, or a Hell's Angel should be avoided. Suspenders (or "braces") reached the height of their popularity in the late 1980s as symbols of executive wishes and CEO dreams. As of the early twenty-first century, they're still around, although in less profusion. Be aware that some people find suspenders a bit pretentious.

Many business folk are squeamish about male jewelry. Wedding bands, school or college rings, and military service rings are always acceptable, as are simple cuff links (if your shirt has French cuffs). To be avoided are neck chains, stick pins, and bracelets. A pinky ring is almost certain to offend someone.

Earrings, though hardly uncommon in the male earlobe as of the early twenty-first century, are still considered an aggressive cultural statement and certainly turn off as many people as they impress. Best to avoid.

A Proclamation

Clothing is a physical and cultural necessity, but it is also much more. Most of us think of what we wear as a proclamation of who we are. That position is a good place from which the Office Superman may start, but, as usual, he always wants to go a bit farther. The Office Superman understands that business clothes proclaim not only who he is, but how he feels about what he does and about those with whom he works.

Maintaining a wardrobe that reflects who you are while also embodying something of the values shared by coworkers and clients demonstrates a combination of self-respect and respect for others that never goes out of fashion in the world of business.

CHAPTER

17

KAREER KRYPTONITE

COMIC BOOK SUPER HEROES COME AND GO, BUT SUPERMAN IS FOREVER. Though fans and scholars may endlessly debate the sources of Superman's longevity, one explanation trumps them all. Superman partakes as much of humanity and human nature as he does of comic book ink.

Super Humans

Over the years, we've learned more about Superman than we ever get to know about most flesh-and-blood human beings. We know that he was an infant refugee from the doomed planet Krypton, that he arrived on Earth in a space-age version of the basket that floated baby Moses into the bulrushes, that he was found and adopted by the kindly Kents of Smallville, that he grew into youth and young manhood, discovering—as all of us, one way or another, discover—certain talents and powers. We know that he formulated a career plan, a double life designed to help him best apply his talents and powers. We know that he left the small town for big-time Metropolis and a job as a newspaperman with the *Daily Planet*. We know that he fell in love with, and finally married, Lois Lane. We know that he lives in Metropolis, but maintains his Fortress of Solitude, a kind of vacation home to end all vacation homes.

About Superman, in fact, there is very little we do not know.

Clark "Superman" Kent is more fully familiar to us than any other fictional character ever created—Hamlet, Captain Ahab, and Holden Caulfield included. This creature of popular fantasy seems utterly human. In part, surely, this is because the Superman story has been told so well, so long, and so richly in comics, on television, and in the movies. But the remarkably rounded reality of Superman is also doubtless due to the way the character was created. Unlike much that is stamped out of the Hollywood studio mill, Superman evolved, developed, and matured over time.

Take the matter of his superpowers. In June 1938, when he first appeared in *Action Comics* #1, Superman more closely resembled a Paul Bunyan tall-tale folk character than he did a super hero. He couldn't fly, exactly, but he could "leap an eighth of a mile" and "hurdle a twenty-story building." To be sure, he could "raise tremendous weights," and he was fast—"faster than a streamline train," which is better than a slow freight with a string of boxcars, but by no means faster than a speeding bullet. As for invulnerability, "nothing less than a bursting shell could penetrate his skin." Mighty durable, but not absolutely indestructible.

Over many decades, Superman's chroniclers have steadily augmented his powers, even as they have presented him with increasingly formidable challenges. The Superman of today has demonstrated that he can penetrate safely to the very core of the Sun without so much as a dab of Coppertone, and that he can fly at many thousands of times the speed of light without so much as a nod to Albert Einstein.

Yet as Superman has become more superhuman, he has not become less human. Just as Superman has grown in his fictional life, he has developed as an artistic creation—and nothing is more human than development, growth, and maturity. Each of us changes with age. The best of us, like Superman, improve. We grow into the fullness of our powers and talents. In the most profound sense, we advance, acquiring and honing new abilities to meet increasingly formidable challenges and to compete for higher and higher stakes.

Super Flaws

But growth and development are not sufficient in themselves to explain the enduring human appeal of Superman. While the superpowers of the Man of Steel have increased in magnitude and variety over the years, one important thing has remained constant: not his invulnerability, but his ultimate vulnerability.

It boils down to single word: *kryptonite*. At various times and in various stories, Superman has experimented in his Fortress of Solitude in search of some means of rendering himself immune to the one substance in the universe that can destroy him. So far, he's failed. And the odds of his ever succeeding weigh heavily against him.

The earliest heroes we know, the strongest, the bravest, the smartest, have always had a single flaw, a weakness without remedy. For heroes, that goes with the territory. Think of the granddaddy archetype of them all. Son of the mortal Peleus, king of the Myrmidons, and the immortal sea nymph Thetis, Achilles was the bravest, handsomest, and greatest warrior of the army of Agamemnon in the Trojan War. When he was newborn, Thetis dipped him in the waters of the River Styx to render him invulnerable. Unfortunately, she held him by one heel, which remained dry and, therefore, vulnerable. And so we speak today of a person's "Achilles' heel," an otherwise strong man's vulnerability. No one's immune. Not even Superman.

Especially not Superman.

The Greeks, who gave us Achilles, also gave us the so-called tragic hero, a dramatic character whose greatness consists of the very qualities that ultimately undo him. Take Oedipus. His quick intellect and bold decisiveness elevated him to royal prominence, but also made him overly confident, reckless, and rash, propelling him into acts that destroyed him and brought down on his kingdom of Thebes a terrible plague. Superman's vulnerability to kryptonite makes him the symbolic brother of Achilles and Oedipus because his weakness, like theirs, is part of the very thing that makes him strong.

Superman's superpowers came from his origin on the planet Krypton. There are actually two accounts of just how this happened. In *Action Comics* #1, Siegel and Shuster took pains to offer a scientific explanation: "Kent had come from a planet whose inhabitants' physical structure was millions of years advanced of our own. Upon reaching maturity, the people of his race became gifted with titanic strength!" Seems plausible, and the boys from Cleveland made it even more so: "Even today on our world exist creatures with superstrength! The lowly ant can support weights hundreds of times its own. The grasshopper leaps what to man would be the space of several city blocks." This general explanation held for about the first decade of Superman stories, but, then, in the late 1940s, the comics began to describe Kryptonians as pretty much ordinary people—as long as they stayed on Krypton. Put a Kryptonian on Earth, however, and the vast differences between the gravitational pull and atmosphere of the two planets confer superhuman powers on the transplant. Hence Superman.

Whichever explanation you prefer, the point is that Superman's special powers are associated with his origin on Krypton, and so is the source of his vulnerability. As reviewed in Chapter 2, the infant Superman was sent rocketing to Earth by his parents, desperate for his survival as Krypton was on the verge of exploding due to a "cataclysmic chain reaction originating at the planet's core." The baby escaped the end of his world, but the explosion of the planet fused all of Krypton's atomic elements into kryptonite, chunks of which were scattered throughout the universe, some even falling to Earth as meteorites. The substance comes in five varieties: red, gold, blue, white, and green. All are quite harmless to Earthlings, but, although produced by his native planet, red, gold, and green kryptonite are harmful or fatal to Superman. Contact with or proximity to red kryptonite temporarily produces bizarre and unpredictable, albeit temporary, symptoms. (Red kryptonite once divided Superman into twins and, on another occasion, transformed him into a giant ant.) Gold kryptonite is far more dangerous. Exposure to it would permanently rob Superman of his superpowers. But worst of all is green kryptonite, the effects of which are highly toxic. Exposure brings on lassitude, weakness, and inertia followed by death unless the exposure is of short duration. (Blue kryptonite, by the way, is harmful only to the other-dimensional version of Superman known as Bizarro Superman, and white kryptonite is harmful only to plant life.)

Kryptonite is essential to the Superman story just as the fatal flaws of Oedipus are essential to his story and the undipped heel of Achilles is the key to his fate. Such vulnerabilities drive our interest in the doings of these super heroes because they allow us, vulnerable as we mere mortals are, to identify with them. The flaws in our super heroes allow us to share in their fate and they in ours. We understand that these characters are not alien, but have something valuable to teach us.

The Kryptonite Within

The stories of Superman, Oedipus, Achilles and those of other mythic heroes all contain the same warning. The personal assets that make you an exceptional achiever—even an Office Superman—can also be the liabilities that bring you down. The mediocre conformist may be doomed to a lackluster life, but the person whose head rises high above the crowd runs the risk of getting it lopped off. There is a fine line separating attractive self-confidence from obnoxious arrogance. Narrow, too, is the border between a productively decisive approach to the business of life and sheer impulsive recklessness. The most elementary of business principles is that there is no reward without risk. Successful people possess a willingness to take risks. Yet it is not always easy to see the difference between a calculated risk and a foolish chance.

Superman cannot fight kryptonite (he's tried and failed), and he cannot guarantee that he won't ever encounter it (in fact, it pops up in story after story). What he *can* do is become and remain aware of its existence. Self-awareness and vigilance won't eliminate the danger, but they help make it manageable.

For the Office Superman, avoiding risk and accepting mediocre conformity are not viable options. But neither is willful ignorance. Be aware of the dangers of allowing self-confidence to become blind arrogance, of allowing drive and decision to become reckless action on impulse, and of allowing risk-taking to become nothing more than a crap shoot. The dangers are always there, but so is the choice to be mindful of the feelings and needs of others, to prepare carefully before acting, and to assess with realistic objectivity the proportion of risk to reward before making any decision. Neither Superman nor the Office Superman can be content to avoid the inherently risky desire for achievement, but both learn to manage the desire as well as the risk.

Political Kryptonite

The "Kryptonite Within" is one variety of vulnerability, but just as the kryptonite that threatens Superman comes in different colors, Kareer Kryptonite presents itself in several guises. Political Kryptonite is one of the most common. You can recognize its presence by these telltale signs:

- You deserved and expected a promotion, but a clearly less-deserving coworker copped it instead.
- You discover that you've been dropped from a certain e-mail routing list, so that you no longer routinely receive management memos.
- You are hit in a meeting by a missile of gratuitous criticism launched from left field.
- You are no longer invited to certain management-level meetings.
- You aren't invited to the boss's birthday bash.
- You discover that you are the subject of office gossip.
- You are scapegoated—blamed for things that aren't even remotely your fault.
- You find that you can no longer rely on the cooperation and goodwill of your colleagues.

If you recognize any of these telltale signs, it's pretty obvious that you've become the victim of office politics. Don't panic. Accept the signs as a wake-up call to get in touch with the political situation that, like it or not, you are now in.

The phrase "office politics" has a distinctly negative ring, especially when you find or feel yourself a victim of it. However, you can turn the situation around if you act promptly to get a handle on the prevailing politics. Don't shun or run from office politics. Regard office politics as nothing more or less than a set of strategies people use within an organization to further their careers. True, when you're on the receiving end of such strategies used against you, office politics is a dirty, rotten business and potentially a career killer. But take up these strategies yourself, use them to your benefit, and office politics can become neither dirty nor rotten, but savvy business.

If you feel yourself being pushed out of the office loop, get yourself back in by making yourself more influential. The more influential you can make yourself, the more powerful you will be perceived to be and, in fact, the more powerful you will become.

Begin by *selling* your influence to others. The more ideas and initiatives you sell to others, especially to bosses, the more influential you will become.

Start with one idea. Just don't squander it. Instead, identify someone in your office who has the power to help you. Regard this person as the lever on which you can lift your idea. Sell the idea to him, and he'll sell it to others. Promoting an idea to an influential person multiplies your influence, just as a lever multiplies the effect of your arm muscle, however puny it might be.

Sell your idea by selling its benefits. Don't point out how the idea will benefit you or even benefit the company. Instead, show how the idea directly benefits your prospect, the person you're trying to influence. For instance: You have an idea for starting a special customer support group. You identify George as someone with the clout to get your idea heard in the larger organization. "George," you tell him, "starting the customer support group will certainly give *you* a bigger voice with upper management."

No idea sells easier than one the other guy thinks he already owns. Once you present your idea to your prospect, start referring to it as "our" idea rather than "my" idea. Recruit support by sharing ownership.

Don't expect a smooth sale, but don't shy away from whatever resistance you meet. Don't back away from your critics, and don't argue with your critics. Instead, recruit your critics. "George, your comments on the customer support idea really gave me food for thought. I need your input on developing the support group so that we can make it work." Co-opt the opposition by inducting it into your service. If you can't beat 'em, make 'em join you.

Finally, don't overlook the most obvious antidote to political kryptonite. There are plenty of people in business who are naive enough to believe that ideas and individuals are promoted strictly on their merits. Good ideas and competent people, they believe, just naturally float to the top in business.

Nonsense.

The world of business is a community, and, like any other community, it is built on many kinds of relationships, including those cemented by nothing more or less than personal affection. Make friends. You are far better off professionally if the people you work with like you personally. Cultivate warm personal relationships with the people who hold the power and influence in your office. This isn't sucking up. It's doing business like an Office Superman.

The Kryptonite of Rumor

The existence of kryptonite is an unpleasant fact Superman cannot deny. Here's another: No office shared by more than two people is without gossip and rumor.

This particular lump of kryptonite radiates in two directions: *from* you and *against* you. So, first and foremost, avoid trafficking in rumor and gossip. Don't start rumors, and don't spread them. They can come back to destroy you. Moreover—and this may be harder to do—refuse to become a party to or conduit for gossip. This takes a measure of tact, because you don't want to come across as priggish or holier-than-thou, but when Joe Blow asks you if you "heard the latest about Sally and John," opt out of the exchange with something in this vein: "Joe, I have to get this report out. I'm on a tight deadline." You don't need to take the matter any further. Joe will get the message that you are just not interested in hearing his gossip. Now your only problem is maintaining the self-discipline to deny yourself the guilty pleasure of running after Joe to find out all about Sally and John.

Next, what do you do when the kryptonite shines on you?

If you discover that you've become the subject of malicious rumor, don't cover your ears and hope the thing will just go away. Chances are, it won't.

If you can identify the source of the rumor, seek him or her out. Avoid accusations. Instead, ask for help:

You: Sarah, I don't know if you've heard this rumor going around about Jane and me.

Sarah: Uh, well, er, I, uh, yes, I may have heard something . . .

You: Well, look, you can really help me out. You know that this kind of thing can be very destructive, even when there is absolutely no truth to it. You have a lot of influence in the office. People listen to you. So, please, do me a big favor and spread the word: There is nothing at all to this gossip. I'd like to save Jane and myself anymore needless embarrassment. Could you help us out?

Of course, not all rumors are groundless. Many are distorted versions of the truth. In this case, try identifying the source of the rumor, then get confidential with him: "Hey, Sam, what's your take on the buzz that's been going around about what I'm doing with the Halsted account? From what I've been hearing, everybody's got it all wrong. Let me tell you what's *really* happening." Now, take Sam by the arm, draw him closer to you, and, in hushed tones, tell him what you want him to hear. Make it sound like a secret, and you can *depend* on his spreading the word.

Some rumors are too distorted, outrageous, or hurtful to counteract subtly or indirectly. In these cases, consider distributing a corrective e-mail to everyone in the office. Begin straightforwardly: "It has come to my attention that a rumor is circulating to the effect that I have . . ." Summarize the rumor, then continue: "Misinformation like this can be very destructive. We all deserve the truth, and here it is." Then deliver the facts. Don't editorialize, don't accuse, and don't indulge your emotions by letting off steam. Stick to the facts.

The Bully's Kryptonite

Think you left your last bully back in the schoolyard? Don't count on it. Most office bullies are easy to spot by the three B's they manifest: They bluster, they bellow, and they berate. Some bullies, however, operate more subtly. Instead of indulging in openly abusive language, they find other ways to belittle you. For instance, you propose a certain approach to a particular project. The subtle bully will avoid commenting on the merits or faults of your proposal, but will focus instead on you personally: "You've *got* to be kidding. Who would even *think* of doing it that way?"

Admittedly, it can be difficult to stay poised and confident under an attack aimed squarely at your ego. But in coming on strong like this, the bully reveals his fatal weakness: a complete absence of logic. His is a hollow assault. Puncture the bully's bubble by replying, in a calm, quiet tone of voice, with the facts: "This approach will accomplish such and such while reducing costs by so much and so much . . ." The bully takes aim at personalities. He is powerless against facts.

Remember that no bully is a solo actor. He needs a victim. Refuse to play the victim's role, and the bully deflates into nothing more than an ill-mannered lout.

But what about the not-so-subtle bully, the guy who rants and rails? No job description ever requires enduring abuse. If you've got a bully in your china shop, avoid him or her whenever possible. Substitute e-mail and memos for face-to-face contact. If you find yourself caught in one of the bully's verbal explosions, just let it happen. Remain silent while the bully carries on. When the eruption fizzles out, respond with the facts. If the verbal storm continues or resumes, remove yourself from the line of fire. "We can talk about this later." Then walk away.

Bullies are emotional parasites. They require your strong emotion—fear or anger—to function as a bully. Deny them this nourishment.

Passive-Aggressive Kryptonite

Passive-aggressive people come on as easygoing, maybe even meek, but beneath their placid exterior lurks the soul of a saboteur. Their monkey wrench of choice is unreliability. Ask for some critical task to be performed, and the passive-aggressive colleague will promise to perform it. Sure enough, however, it will remain undone. Maybe you'll confront him with the fact. "Oh," he'll reply, "it will get done. Don't worry."

That, of course, is your signal to start worrying. More to the point, it's your cue to start monitoring this individual closely. Check his performance. Watch his work. Prod him. Furnish a deadline for everything you ask of him. Remind him of each deadline you set. Repeat instructions as necessary. Repeat them again. It is a waste of time to try to counsel the passive-aggressive subordinate or colleague. Instead, focus on the tasks at hand. Furnish schedules. Make instructions clear. Review progress. Do not be tempted to walk away and hope for the best. It just won't happen unless you make it happen.

Whining Kryptonite

Every office has its chronic complainers. Some grumble but get the job done anyway. Listen politely to these folks, then let them get on with their work. Others, however, use complaining as a way of avoiding assignments. They protest that such-and-such is impossible or that it can't be done in the time allotted. And they are very insistent.

Your first step, always, must be to determine if the complaint has any basis in fact. Don't reject complaints out of hand. The whiner may have identified an actual problem that needs to be fixed. However, once you decide that the problem is the complainer and not the task at hand, stand firm. Avoid discussing the merits of the complaint. Express no sympathy—sarcastic or sincere—for the complainer. Repeat the importance of the task or assignment. Repeat that it is necessary to do the work, to accomplish the task, to solve the problem. Then *tell* the complainer to dig in and tackle the project. Assure him that you will review the results and will offer suggestions and help as necessary.

Whiners typically complain about burdensome workloads, the hot weather, the cold weather, rule breakers, sticklers for rules, a slow morning commute, speeders, how others behave. Whether the whiner is a subordinate, a colleague, or a boss, you can't just ignore him.

If there is something you can do to address the subject of his complaint, do so.

"The coffee in the break room is undrinkable. Who buys this stuff, anyway?"

"Well, Helen, *you* can. I agree that the coffee could be better. Tomorrow morning, before you come in, stop by the supermarket, look for something more appealing, buy it, and I'll reimburse you out of petty cash. Let's all start enjoying the coffee around here."

If you perceive that the whining is really nothing more than a plea for attention, respond with kindness.

"I am so sick and tired of this lousy snow and miserable cold weather."

"That's a good-looking coat, George. Is it new?"

If the whiner, a subordinate, complains about another employee, don't insert yourself in the middle. Avoid comment. Don't take sides. Instead, reduce the tension by arranging a meeting—in your presence—between the whiner and the object of his complaint. Encourage the two to talk about the relevant issues.

Ethical Kryptonite

It is easy, even for basically honest people, to act unethically on occasion. And that is a frightening fact, because a single lapse in business ethics can be the greenest of green kryptonite: rapidly fatal. Consider the following scenarios.

You feel overworked and underpaid. Sometimes you order office supplies on the company account and use them at home. Overworked and underpaid as you are, you're still a thief.

You've returned from a business trip. You sit down to make out your expense report. Earlier, the talk at lunch was about how *absolutely everybody* in the company pads their expense reports. "It's expected!" a colleague chirps. So you add a few dollars here and there. Everyone does it. But you're still a thief.

You finish a client's job in three hours flat. The estimate you gave him was for a five-hour job. He agreed to the estimate. You bill him for five hours. Thief.

Unethical conduct is unethical, regardless of how you may seek to justify it, regardless of how many others engage in it, regardless of whether or not you can get away with it. Unethical conduct creates an unethical environment, which tends to spread throughout the organization, then into the business community, and out to the community generally. Sooner or later, your reputation and that of your firm begin to suffer. Sooner or later, your career will suffer and maybe even die.

Dodging the Fatal Dose

There are no guarantees that you won't ever have a close encounter with Kareer Kryptonite in one form or another. This chapter has suggested some ways of surviving contact. However, as with most bad things, the best cure is prevention.

- Cultivate good corporate karma. This means that you should always act ethically by giving good value for the value you receive. Fair value for fair value is the essence of good business.
- Make it your business to be liked and respected at work. Be friendly. Demonstrate supreme consideration for the needs of others.
- Greet by name those you work with. Be generous with small talk. Express interest in family, hobbies, whatever.
- Make friends and allies. Begin from day one on the job. Do it.
- Do your job so well, every hour of every day, that you become indispensable: *the* Office Superman.

C H A P T E R

18

HOW TO BE
A MAN OF STEEL

THE CHARACTER OF SUPERMAN IS PROTECTED NOT BY SUPERSTRENGTH and supertough skin, but by copyrights and trademarks. Yet, of course, Superman is much more than this. Even when his likeness appears on merchandise, his value derives not from a group of corporate executives and salespeople, but from a long line of artists and writers who understand that the compelling appeal of Superman is rooted deeply in human psychology and mythology. Although clearly an invented commercial character, Superman has assumed a place in American popular culture and folklore. A super hero, he is also a folk hero, with whom, in various ways, we all identify.

In this respect, Superman taps into the same tradition that produced another familiar legendary figure, long the subject of folk tales, popular ballads, and work songs. John Henry was an African-American laborer who is celebrated for his heroic competition against a steam hammer in a desperate race to lay railroad track. As the ballads and folktales tell it, John Henry was a "steel-drivin' man"—a steel driver—a highly skilled laborer who used a hammer and a steel chisel, called a drill, to punch holes in rock face for the setting of explosive charges. When railroad bosses brought in a steam hammer to replace John Henry and those like him, the laborer vowed that he could outperform the machine. The contest was on, and John Henry made good on his pledge, beating the steam hammer—only to collapse in death at the moment of his triumph, his mighty heart having burst.

Most folklorists trace the historical origins of the John Henry legend to the Big Bend Tunnel, which was constructed in West Virginia during the early 1870s, but the appeal of the legend is timeless. Generations have identified with it as a tale of the working man's soul and will versus the soulless bosses greedily eager to bring in machinery to deprive hard-working human beings of their livelihood.

This was a big issue in the nineteenth century, when all sorts of machines were beginning to take over work traditionally assigned to people, but the issue has persisted through successive eras of automation and computerization, and it is still relevant today. The most recent steam hammer many American workers confront is "outsourcing," the practice of sending jobs ranging from customer service to accounting to computer programming off-shore, to countries where labor costs are a small fraction of those here. But while outsourcing may or may not remain a specter of menace for years to come, many of us are and will always be haunted by other on-the-job fears: the fear that we'll make a catastrophic mistake, the fear that, somehow, we'll fall short and fail to deliver what the bosses want, the fear that, when tested, we just won't measure up.

Insecurity affects all of us to one degree or another, which is why many folks find it so hard even to hear criticism, let alone make constructive use of it. Fearful of failure, worried about our adequacy to the task at hand, the last thing we want is confirmation of failure and inadequacy in the form of criticism from an outside authority.

Even Superman Gets the Blues

Oh, to be Superman! To be perfect, failure-proof, and immune to all critics and criticism!

But if Superman really were perfect, it is doubtful that our interest in him would have lasted so long. Consider a story called "The Super-Key to Fort Superman," published in 1958 in *Action Comics* #241. In it, Superman is tormented by a puzzle that resists all of his efforts at solution. The puzzle is this: Someone, somehow has penetrated the impenetrable Fortress of Solitude and has purposely left behind tantalizing clues to his presence. The puzzle gnaws at the Man of Steel, ultimately undermining his confidence so thoroughly that he nearly makes a catastrophe of one of his routinely superhuman feats.

The narrator introduces a panel showing Superman the next day, having resumed "his super-chores," lofting with one hand a great luxury liner, flying the "disabled ship home to port." But all is not well. Someone aboard ship cries out, "Superman! Watch out!" to which the Man of Steel stammers out a reply, "Wh-What?" In the next panel, another passenger explains: "Y-you're rocking the boat! This voyage is more dangerous than the one you rescued us from!"

There can be no more damning criticism than to be told that your efforts to improve a situation are actually making it worse, and poor Superman can manage only a most pathetic reply: "I'm (gulp) sorry!" The internal monologue that follows this weak apology makes it clear that he understands why he has mishandled the rescued ship: "I can't concentrate on anything else . . . except the intruder! I wish it were night . . . so I could go back to the Fortress!"

The cruelly insidious thing about self-doubt is that it tends to give you more and more reason for even greater self-doubt. Fearful of criticism, you may perform in ways that make criticism inevitable.

By the end of "The Super-Key to Fort Superman," the Man of Steel solves the puzzle—it all turns out to be a good-natured prank perpetrated by Batman—but we are left with a disquieting glimpse of Superman's very human aspect. In his monumental encyclopedia, *The Great Superman Book*, Michael L. Fleisher suggests that Superman is, in fact, gravely afflicted by self-doubt, that "despite his vast powers, Superman sees himself as weak and inadequate."

> If it is difficult to comprehend how a being so nearly omnipotent as Superman can possibly feel so impotent and powerless, [Fleisher writes,] it must be remembered that Superman is not an Earthman, but a Kryptonian. On the planet Krypton, where he was born, Superman had no special powers. He acquired his superpowers, the powers that transformed him into a "superman," only by virtue of having been transplanted to the alien environment of Earth.

Fleisher compares Superman's situation to that of an ordinary man in Gulliver's Lilliput, who "may be a giant to the Lilliputians, but he will continue to see himself as ordinary, for the standards by which he measures himself will not be Lilliputian standards, but rather the standards of the country from which he came." Where Superman came from, Fleisher continues, he was a helpless infant. "The one time in his life when power really mattered, Superman was an impotent witness to planet-shattering events." He now suffers from what psychologists call survivor guilt, for "as the planet Krypton shuddered and rumbled toward the doomsday cataclysm, Superman was not really 'super' at all; he was cringing Clark Kent, spinelessly fleeing the scene of terrifying events he could not even hope to control." Indeed, Fleisher concludes that Clark Kent is not just a convenient alter ego for Superman, but is the Man of Steel's psychological projection of "deep inner feelings of worthlessness and self-loathing," a person "who continually reinforces and confirms his own lowly estimation of himself by arousing the loathing and contempt of others through his cringing, unmanly behavior."

The point is that all of us, even the apparently strongest among us, have vulnerabilities that increase our sensitivity to criticism and prompt us either to accept it passively or to react to it defensively instead of taking the far more productive third alternative, which is to listen to our critics and learn from them.

Making a Constructive Response

It is too much to expect that you will ever actually welcome criticism, but it is reasonable to create strategies for responding to it constructively.

The first step in a constructive response is to accept criticism as an opportunity. All criticism, even if it is undeserved and unfair, can be useful to you. Criticism may show you things you are doing ineffectively or poorly—things you could do better— and even unmerited criticism can suggest how you might be creating the false impression of a problem, even when no problem really exists. In either case, criticism can be a first step toward greater achievement. Taking this step, however, requires that you suppress your very human impulse to respond defensively. Nothing stops the ears and closes the mind more effectively than defensiveness. Let down your guard, so that you can listen, hear, and learn.

Understand that criticism is the expression of a perception, nothing more. Compare all criticism to objective measurements—sales figures, costs, production numbers, and so on. If such objective yardsticks bear out the critical perception, you have your work cut out for you. However, if it is clear that perception and objectively measured reality differ, explore, with yourself and your critic, the reasons behind the erroneous perception. It is important that you produce excellent results, but it is also important that you perform in such a way that others invariably perceive these results as excellent.

While you should not be defensive and unreceptive to criticism, neither should you accept it passively, especially if you believe the criticism to be either unjust or mistaken. Instead, listen, then respond, point by point. Don't feel pressured, however, to make an immediate response. Buy the time you need by saying, for example: "You raise an interesting point, which I am going to have to think about for a while before discussing it further."

Demonstrate Active Listening

Superman possesses super-sensitive hearing. While listening to criticism, the Office Superman does his best to demonstrate his own brand of super auditory perception. It is called active listening, and it is a way of visually demonstrating to your critic that you value what he says and are taking it in.

Create positive visual feedback by making and maintaining eye contact with your critic. Take care to monitor your own non-verbal signals of resistance. The most common signals include placing your hand over the mouth or on your forehead, as if to shade your eyes. Arms folded across the chest send a strong signal that you may be listening, but you are not *hearing*.

It is a good idea if both you and your critic sit during the discussion, since standing both suggests and tends to provoke a face-to-face confrontation. However, if you must stand, keep your hands at your sides, not folded across your chest or positioned, akimbo, on your hips.

If you are summoned to your boss's office and feel that you are about to be exposed to criticism, good body language may help establish a more favorable emotional climate. When you enter, don't rush to be seated. It is better if you linger a moment or two standing in front of the boss's desk, so that he or she must look up at you. This establishes you in a position of power, which you can reinforce, after you are seated, by shifting eye contact from time to time to your boss's forehead. Periodically focus your gaze just above his eyes. This is unconsciously perceived as dominant and conveys your strength.

Once you are seated, sit upright and keep your hands visible. Use them to underscore key points, but keep them away from your face, neck, hair, and mouth. The most powerful hand gestures are made with an open, slightly upturned palm.

Avoid cringing. Half opening the door and timidly poking your head into the boss's office is a terrible way to start the meeting. Also to be avoided is looking down or to the side. Look at your boss. As you should avoid slumping or slouching in the chair, you should also avoid nervous or fidgety leg movements when seated. This suggests your eagerness to "get away." All aggressive gestures, including pointing, stabbing gestures, making a fist, pounding the desk, should be avoided.

A Scenario or Two

Your boss ambushes you with unexpected criticism. Your initial response will determine a great deal about how you'll emerge from the encounter. Try to convert criticism into constructive advice and a critic into a collaborator.

Boss: Say, it seems to have taken you an awfully long time to process the last batch of orders. You need to get better organized.

You: I understand. I'm always looking for more efficient ways to get the orders in and out of here. I'm open to any suggestions you might have.

Take the spotlight off personalities and put it on issues. If what the critic says hurts, offends, or threatens you, try to put those feelings aside while you tackle the issues instead.

Boss: A cost overrun of 10 percent is just way too high. I cannot and will not tolerate it.

You: I agree, and I'd like to discuss it with you. I have a plan to bring down costs, and it would be great to get your take on it before I make a full formal presentation.

Blameless But Blamed

Clark Kent knows what it means to be unjustly criticized. It happens to him all the time, beginning with the very first Superman story in *Action Comics* #1. To protect his secret identity as Superman, Kent must continually act the part of the meek, even cowardly reporter, and he takes plenty of heat for it, most scorchingly from Lois Lane, the woman he loves.

You should never passively accept criticism or blame for performance problems, accidents, or errors that are not your fault. However—and this may be almost as difficult to accept—you should *always* take responsibility.

Blamed when you are blameless, your first impulse will be to defend yourself. Act on this impulse, but do not stop at your defense. Explain to your critic that you are not the cause of the problem, but also assure him that you *will* help to solve the problem. This does not mean that you have to take on the whole of somebody else's burden, but do set about identifying and locating the person who is responsible for the problem and discuss the matter with him, always focusing on constructive solutions rather than on blame. Direct him to appropriate action. Motivate him to find a solution. If the responsible person cannot be identified, offer to collaborate with your critic to resolve the problem.

Sometimes you find yourself in a situation in which a snafu is clearly not your fault, but is—rightly—your problem. For instance, someone who reports to you may perform poorly. As this person's boss, it is up to you to resolve any negative results from the subordinate's performance.

The ideal resolution of such problems is to address them yourself, immediately, efficiently, and effectively, without resorting to higher authority. If you must make a report to a boss, however, heed the motto President Harry Truman kept on his Oval Office desk: *The buck stops here*. While your report *should* accurately and factually assess fault—your subordinate neglected to do something, a supplier failed to deliver, whatever—what you say to your boss *must* also make clear your willingness to take ultimate responsibility for the solving the problem.

Lemons into Lemonade

If it weren't for catastrophe and the ever-present risk of failure, Superman would be just another strongman. Maybe he could find work in a circus.

The fact is that problems—hard problems, entailing the risk of poor performance or outright failure—leave Superman, as well as the Office Superman, perpetually open to criticism. The fact is also that such problems give both Superman and the Office Superman meaningful, rewarding careers.

Properly handled, even the harshest criticism can be turned into a benefit. How you respond, both verbally and in the actions you take to resolve the issues in question, can identify you not as the guy who made a mistake, but as a committed problem solver, an Office Superman who won't get off the case until the job is done and done with excellence.

CHAPTER 19

DEALING WITH MR. MXYZPTLK

DURING HIS LONG AND ILLUSTRIOUS CAREER, SUPERMAN HAS FACED DOWN A LEGION OF SUPER-VILLAINS. Most famous is Lex Luthor, a mad scientist capable of almost infinite evil and infinite power, who made his debut in *Action Comics* #23 (April 1940) and of whom we shall see much more in the next chapter.

No enemy of Superman "is more terrible than the space villain, Brainiac," according to "Brainiac's Super-Revenge" (*Action Comics* #280, September 1961). As originally depicted when he debuted in *Action Comics* #242 (July 1958), Brainiac is a hairless green-skinned humanoid with green eyes, who resembles the other inhabitants of the planet Colu, but who is really a kind of android, a flesh-encased super computer created by the "computer tyrants" who had seized control of the planet. The computer tyrants were ultimately overthrown on Colu, but their creation remained at large, a consummately evil "master of super-scientific forces" ("The Super-Duel in Space," *Action Comics* #242, July 1958).

In May 1959 (*Action Comics* #252), Metallo first clashed with the Man of Steel. Journalist, thief, and murderer John Corben, catastrophically injured in a car wreck, is rebuilt as a bionic man, clad in flesh-like metal armor, a Superman look-alike capable of destruction on a massive scale.

In *Superman's Pal Jimmy Olsen* #134 (October 1971), Darkseid took his first bow. Ruler of the enslaved planet Apokolips, Darkseid has designs on conquering the rest of the universe, starting with Earth, which, he believes, is the source of the "Anti-Life Equation," key to absolute power over all living things.

Even more recently, a whole series of super-villains have marched through the chronicles of Superman. These include, among others:

• Mongul (*DC Comics Presents* #27, November 1980), a kind of Attila on galactic steroids, who made his way through outer space as a cosmic conqueror

• Cyborg (*Adventures of Superman* #466, May 1990), the spirit of injured astronaut Hank Henshaw as embodied in virtually any mechanical device; he shares Superman's DNA and has partnered with Mongul to kill millions

• Doomsday (*Superman: The Man of Steel* #17, November 1992), a toothy giant bred to be genetically perfect, but who became the perfect destroyer of life

• Dominus (*Action Comics* #747, August 1998), formerly a being of peerless devotion and holiness who becomes a fantastic destroyer of worlds after he is disappointed in love

• Encantadora (*Action Comics* #760, December 1999), a beguiling enchantress who uses the Mist of Ibella (contained within the necklace she wears) to cast a spell on even the most powerful of men

• Imperiex (*Superman* #153, February 2000), the being who lit the fuse on the Big Bang, an entity therefore older than time itself, and now in command of a legion of world wreckers

Imp

It's all pretty overwhelming, this horrific Rogues Gallery, and the ante is continually upped through the introduction of one villain more supremely powerful and supremely evil than the last.

And yet, of all the titanic and terrifying evil-doers Superman has confronted, perhaps the most intriguing is a diminutive creature, about half Superman's size, who first appeared in *Superman* #30 (October 1944), attired in nothing more formidable than a purple suit and vest, chartreuse bowtie and matching spats over blue shoes, the ensemble topped off with a purple derby several sizes too small even for *his* almost hairless pate. In "Dimensions of Danger" (*Superman* #33, April 1945), Superman calls him the "sappy sprite with the slaphappy sense of humor." He is Mr. Mxyztplk.

Comical in appearance and downright absurd when seen side by side with the mighty Man of Steel, Mr. Mxyztplk has been described as a mischievous imp, but, in fact, is extraordinarily powerful. If Superman's birth on Krypton and subsequent transplantation to Earth have endowed him with powers and abilities far beyond those of mortal men, Mxyztplk's origin in the fifth dimension confers on him extraordinary power over those of us confined to a strictly three-dimensional world.

Unlike Superman's other adversaries, Mr. Mxyztplk is not evil, but impish, a cosmic practical joker. To wit: In his debut appearance, he is hit by a truck and apparently killed, for he has no heartbeat. Small as he is, the ambulance attendants discover that he is far too heavy to be lifted on their stretcher. While several men struggle to lift him, he suddenly springs to life.

"But he can't be alive! His heart don't beat!" exclaims one of the attendants.

"Confusing, aren't I?" Mxyztplk beams.

"Come back here, you," calls out the ambulance attendant. "You're going to answer some questions!"

"Catch me if you can!"

With that, Mxyztplk steals the ambulance and drives it vertically up the side of a skyscraper, then continues with it into space until the vehicle "explodes into many fragments in a blur of blinding color."

Mxyztplk pulls off one bewildering—and silly—stunt after another. At an unveiling in the Metropolis Museum, he brings a priceless statue to life, then walks off to the municipal swimming pool, where he fakes a drowning, only to fly off, instantly taking all the water with him and leaving his three muscular would-be rescuers gaping foolishly as they stand in the empty pool.

"Ha! Ha!" one of them says wildly. "If this wasn't just a dream, I'd think I was going crazy! Ha! Ha!"

That is precisely the effect Mr. Mxyztplk has: either to drive people crazy or, at least, to make them seriously question their sanity.

The story continues from one absurdity to another, with Superman always a step behind, unable to nab the little imp. Throughout all his chronicles, we have seen Superman in many moods and facing many dangers, but only when he is in fruitless pursuit of this silly creature do we see Superman *frustrated*. At one point, Mr. Mxyztplk brings down on Metropolis a rain of paper, which he generates by blowing his breath into the headquarters of the General Waste Paper Corp. Superman, who sees only the paper storm, races about in an effort to clean up.

"I've worked like a Trojan," he says through gritted teeth, shaking his clenched fists, "but all my labor will be in vain unless I learn the source of this paper deluge . . . and bring it to a halt!"

He quickly discovers Mr. Mxyztplk at the root of it all.

"I thought it would be fun to sabotage the city's Clean-Up Week Campaign!" Mxyztplk explains. "Aren't I just as mean as mean can be? Hee hee!"

In the end, and after more of what Superman calls "absurd shenanigans," the Man of Steel succeeds in sending Mr. Mxyztplk back to his native dimension only by stooping to the imp's own level. He tricks Mxyztplk into saying the magic word "KLPTZYXM"—"Mxyztplk" backward—which causes him to disappear in a flash.

Mr. Mxyztplk, A Real-World Villain

The end of the story is not so much a victory for Superman as it is a defeat for Mr. Mxyztplk, who loses on *his* terms, not as a result of the Man of Steel's superpowers. Nor is he finally defeated, of course. Mr. Mxyztplk can return to Earth to plague Metropolis and Superman at any time. And, through the years, he does just that. Silly though he most certainly is, Mr. Mxyztplk has stood the test of time and changing tastes, proving to be a most resilient character in the chronicles of Superman. Among a cast of far more spectacularly menacing villains, this little imp has continued to be popular among fans of the Man of Steel. The reason?

In a word: *realism*. In two words: *realism* and *relevance*.

Few of us face or ever contemplate facing a consummate evil analogous to a Lex Luthor or a Brainiac, but all of us deal with Mr. Mxyztplk on an almost daily basis. Accidents happen. Things go wrong all the time. It may be your fault. It may be her fault. It may be his fault. It may be no one's fault at all. In 1785, Robert Burns put the situation into verse:

> The best-laid schemes o' mice and men
> Gang aft a-gley.

And, if a U.S. Air Force legend is to be believed, in 1949 a Captain Edward A. Murphy put it into the form of a law. Murphy was an engineer assigned to a USAF project dedicated to determining how much sudden deceleration a human being can stand in a crash. One day, while analyzing a completed test, he discovered that a transducer had been wired incorrectly, invalidating the results. Cursing the tech responsible, he declared: "If there is any way to do it wrong, he'll find it." Apparently, the contractor's project manager kept a list of what he called "laws," random pronouncements that struck a chord with him. The project manager duly added this one: "If anything can go wrong, it will." He dubbed it Murphy's Law. Since then, it has become very familiar.

MISTER MXYZPTLK

Debut: *Superman* #30, October 1944
Real or Full Name: Unknown

A mischievous imp who visits Earth about once every 90 days, Mr. Mxyzptlk makes it his business to challenge the Man of Steel with mind-bending illusions and cosmic pranks born of his origin on the fifth-dimensional world known as Zrfff. When the fifth-dimensional Mxyzptlk operates on three-dimensional Earth, the results defy logic as well as physics, producing outcomes that are both hilarious and potentially catastrophic.

No one knows what Mr. Mxyzptlk "really" looks like, as human beings cannot perceive entities in five dimensions; however, while on Earth, Mr. Mxyzptlk adopts an absurdly gnomelike body. He is not evil, but, rather, the uncontrollable incarnation of mischief. His stunts have included animating the *Daily Planet* building, turning Lois Lane into a mannequin, and grotesquely altering Superman's physique.

No Loopholes in Murphy's Law

Things go wrong all the time. You can grit your teeth and clench your fists as Superman does when Mr. Mxyztplk finally gets on his nerves, or you can accept the truth of Murphy's Law and manage—as creatively as possible—its effects and its fallout.

Nobody *wants* things to go wrong. But the fact is that almost everything that happens in the workplace, even bad things, can serve as an opportunity for communication and constructive interaction with your boss and the others you work with. The good news is that most mishaps and mistakes are neither fatal nor irreversible. Make a bad decision, and you can usually make another decision to correct it. Problems lay the foundation for solutions. They are opportunities to get together with others and create answers.

Typically, the real enemy when things go sour is not the mistake or the misfire itself, but the *feelings* associated with the mishap. Ill-will, panic, and discouragement can be truly destructive. Communicate effectively, and you can usually minimize the damage caused by emotion. Moreover, almost all accidents and errors contain at least one valuable ingredient: the opportunity for forgiveness. Think it feels good to point the finger of blame? It feels a lot better to forgive.

Snafu Strategies

There are three steps to take in dealing with any snafu. First: Acknowledge the error. Fans of the old Three Stooges short subjects will remember a frequent gag. For some reason or other—though invariably due to the trio's stoogery—a hole opens up in the floor. The Stooges' solution? Throw a rug over it. The result? Invariably, a slapstick disaster. Covering up a mistake or mishap may seem like a good idea at the time and, indeed, may seem—at the time—like the *only* viable option. But, invariably, a cover-up will only serve to enlarge the original error, sometimes resulting in disaster.

The second step is to let your boss know that he or she would be justified in getting angry, then thank him or her for understanding and patience. Defuse the emotional reaction to the event by acknowledging the grounds for anger while simultaneously reinforcing the option of understanding and patience. Empathizing with your boss is a far more effective tactic than attempting to deny his emotions. The object is to deal with the feelings so that they can be separated from the objective issues at hand. You, your boss, and any others involved in this situation need to see beyond emotion so that you can all act on the problem, not merely vent your strong feelings.

Finally, propose a course of action. Offer positive suggestions for working together to make things right and to repair any damage.

Speed without Panic

Superman's actions are always swift, but they are also sure. Although he moves faster than a speeding bullet, Superman is never propelled by panic. Likewise, the Office Superman never delays in reporting an error or snafu.

It is always better that the bad news should come directly from you than if your boss discovers it for himself or, even worse, if someone else makes the revelation. Your reporting the problem conveys that, whatever has happened, you still exercise a significant measure of control and are on top of the situation. Moreover, it demonstrates your willingness to take responsibility and to accept consequences.

While you should report without unnecessary delay, don't run, panic-stricken, into your boss's office. Whatever emotions you convey will powerfully influence how your boss receives, interprets, and responds to the news.

Let's pause a moment to consider the phrase "unnecessary delay." Prompt reporting is crucial, but, before you barge into an office with tidings of disaster, try to take some time to assess, accurately, the nature and the degree of the problem. You cannot make a full-scale study, of course, but you want to report as accurately as possible, with neither undue pessimism nor inflated optimism. If possible, you should also take the time to sketch out a course of action, a proposal for controlling and repairing the damage. It is always best to report a problem while you are armed with some possible solutions.

Balance the need for speed with the amount of information you deliver. Exercise judgment before you deliver your assessment of the situation at hand. Sometimes it is best to report the particulars of an error minimally, giving your boss the feeling that she is assessing the damage for herself and not being subjected to your "biased" take on it.

Facing Failure

The actions of Murphy's Law are by nature day-to-day occurrences, and that, actually, is fortunate, since it means that the vast majority of snafus are relatively minor bumps in the road. We find ways to roll over them. But sometimes the stakes of failure are far higher, as when a product line you've developed doesn't sell, a client you've pitched doesn't bite, or a contract you've negotiated goes to someone else.

Is your job on the line? That depends on your track record and your employer. But one thing's for sure: Your ego *is* hanging right out there. While embarrassment makes it doubly difficult to communicate in strong and positive ways, it is more important than ever that you manage to do just that. The object is to salvage from the wreckage as much as possible, so that, at the very least, you can gather data that will help you learn from any mistakes that have been made. Ideally, you are salvaging nothing less than the future, and at this time it is the future that should be the focus of discussions with your boss, colleagues, and subordinates.

Focusing on the future is not an abstract exercise of mind, but a concrete use of language. Jettison such phrases as "should have," "wish I had," and "if I had only." Instead, use phrases like "next time," "in the future," "we [not "I"!] learned a lesson for the future," "we won't do it this way next time," and so on. This does not mean that you should attempt to evade responsibility for *present* circumstances, but don't let go of the future. Embrace potential and opportunity.

Here's a scenario to chew on. You've just received a very disappointing report on sales following the introduction of a promotional program you authored. Instead of waiting for the boss to receive and read the report you already have, you personally walk the figures over to him.

"I'm not going to tell you that I'm happy with this performance," you say. "We worked hard on this, and it's rough on the whole department when disappointing figures like this come in. I'd like to schedule a meeting with you and the development team to review the program and see what we can learn from it. I want to make sure we'll all be happy with the results next time out."

This approach assumes responsibility and simultaneously demonstrates a willingness to learn. No excuses are offered, but perspective is maintained, as is a resolutely forward focus.

I'm (Gulp) Sorry!

It's a rare thing to catch Superman in a lame moment, but, as we saw in the last chapter, that is precisely what happens in "The Super-Key to Fort Superman" (*Action Comics* #241, 1958), when, in the process of rescuing a big ocean liner, the Man of Steel almost wrecks it. About all he can say is "I'm (gulp) sorry!" Now, this is better than saying nothing at all, but it is hardly the most effective of apologies.

Like many of us, Superman finds it difficult to apologize. No one looks forward to saying sorry, yet there is an up side even to apologies. There is never anything to cheer about in the *reason* for making an apology. Success, after all, does not call for making amends. But the apology itself can be a valuable opportunity for building and strengthening relations with those among whom you work. Work relationships are stressed and tested by crisis and disappointment. How you manage emotions during such situations can help you and your group to emerge from them stronger than ever.

An apology should be, first and foremost, timely. When an apology is called for, don't wait to be asked. Take the initiative. Seek out those affected by the mishap, and apologize to them. But don't leave it at that. In addition saying that you are sorry, offer whatever help you can to make things right again. This will not only expedite repair and restoration, it will build positive relations between you and others.

Apology is a process. It consists of saying that you are sorry and then continues through an expression of empathy, a demonstration that you understand and appreciate the other person's feelings. As you propose a remedy for the situation, try to guide the conversation away from words like "you" and "I" and move instead toward "we." Finally, bear in mind that as much as your apology may be appreciated, what is most needed now is your help. Provide positive, effective aid, and you stand an excellent chance of being restored as a super hero in the estimation of all.

Under the Volcano

Superman is adept at containing explosions. In any number of stories, he saves lives by covering bombs with his body and absorbing the blast. Despite your best efforts to defuse highly charged snafu situations, emotions may well explode. Expressions of anger in the workplace range from disturbing to downright frightening. The Office Superman acts to keep himself and others from getting hurt.

To the uninformed observer, explosions seem like evidence of pure chaos. Ask any physicist, however, and you'll learn that even the mightiest blast follows certain physical laws and can be analyzed and understood. So it goes with emotional explosions. Despite appearances to the contrary, they don't just happen at random. Sometimes, events at the office are sufficiently provocative to touch off an angry emotional response. But even when the immediate cause is not apparent, count on there being a cause. Remember, the people you work with are *people*, with lives outside of the office. An argument with one's spouse, a struggle with one's children, a lingering dispute with someone else at work, a horrendous bumper-to-bumper morning commute—all these and more can contribute to an explosion some time during the work day.

Obviously, you cannot eliminate all the stressful and enraging factors in your colleagues' lives, but you can recognize that an enraged response from you in return will only fuel any expression of anger, whereas a calm, businesslike, empathetic response will tend to make it harder for the other person to maintain his rage.

A key to managing the rage and the potential for rage in others is to reduce the causes of stress in your own life. Do you get enough sleep? Fatigue erodes both patience and tolerance. Whenever possible, handle potentially emotional situations, such as apologies, after breakfast or after lunch—not when you or others are likely to be hungry. The American workplace is typically awash in coffee. Consider moderating your intake. Be aware that caffeine heightens anxiety and rage levels. Do what you can to make yourself more comfortable at work. Fix that buzzing fluorescent tube, get rid of the clock that ticks too loudly, and by all means turn up the air conditioning. Summer heat can be welcome, but too much heat for too long makes most people irritable.

So, you're rested, lunch was great, you've had only one cup of coffee, and the ambient temperature is 72 degrees. Suddenly, Joe Blow storms into your cubicle, fuming because *you* neglected to tell him about yesterday's meeting. He's right. You forgot to mention it. You apologize, but the explosion is just beginning.

Let it begin. Give Joe Blow room to vent. It may be hard to sit and take it, but doing so will allow Joe to bleed off some of his pent-up energy. Resist the temptation to tell Joe to "calm down." That is sure to fan the flames. In fact, at this point, don't *tell* Joe to do anything or to feel or behave in a certain way.

Once Joe has vented, "play back" to him the essence of his angry message—minus the rage: "I understand you're angry about not having been at the meeting . . ." This demonstrates that his message has gotten through to you. Next, propose a remedy, if you can: "Joe, next time I'll send you an e-mail right away. I won't let this happen again." Of course, another response might be, "Joe, I'm not your secretary. You could have found out about the meeting the same way I did, which is to check in with Mary." But this is not the time for criticism, even if it is warranted.

It is also possible that, in a given situation, a quick fix is impossible. In such a case, lay the burden—gently—on the other person: "Joe, how do you want to resolve this?" Try to remember that rage is directly proportional to the enraged person's feeling of powerlessness. Ask him to tell you what he wants, and you give him power. If he proposes something you can agree to, assure him that you will take the necessary action. If, however, you are unsure about the proposed remedy, ask for some time to think through to a solution. Suggest a specific time and place for a follow-up discussion. If, however, it is clear to you that the proposed solution is unfeasible, negotiate an alternative: "I can't do that, but here's what I *can* do."

In most cases, these actions will restore calm. However, if anyone at work becomes abusive or threatening, remove yourself from the situation: "Joe, this is getting out of hand. I'll be back in an hour. Maybe we can discuss this productively then."

Living with Mr. Mxyzptlk

Superman first encountered Mr. Mxyzptlk in 1944, six years into his own career. Today, the imp is still going strong, returning to Earth from his dimension every three months or so, intent on creating chaos and, most of all, irritating our super hero. Through trickery, the Man of Steel manages to send him packing each time, but Mxyzptlk is always sure to return. Over the decades, therefore, Superman has come to accept that he has no choice about whether or not to learn to live with Mr. Mxyzptlk. He is a fact of life, a fixture of the super hero business.

As Murphy's Law implies, much the same applies in every aspect of life, including any business. Accident, disappointment, and outright disaster take different forms in different offices and industries, but they are inevitable. The Office Superman learns to live with them—and, what is more, to live with them productively.

CHAPTER 20

LIVING WITH LEX LUTHOR

DID YOU CATCH THIS STORY IN THE *DAILY PLANET*?

November 8, 2000—METROPOLIS. *The votes have been tallied across the nation and the poll results are in: Alexander Joseph Luthor will be the forty-third president of the United States. His actions as innovator, peacekeeper and philanthropist are known by Americans at home and overseas; from his instrumental role in assisting the Justice League in recharging the sun during "The Final Night" to his assimilating and sharing of the alien technology "upgrade" of Metropolis last year, Luthor is a man who knows how to create "Tomorrow Today."*

Maybe you'd better start reading the newspaper. Keep yourself informed. If you stopped following the Superman chronicles a few years ago, the Lex Luthor *you* know hardly seems presidential timber. Not that our nation has always been overly concerned about a candidate's resume. After all, we've put actors, pro wrestlers, exterminators, the singing partner of Cher, and—ugh! —a whole lot of lawyers in high office, but it's true that *President* Lex Luthor is pushing it.

During his very first years, beginning with the beginning, 1938, Superman faced some pretty lame adversaries—garden-variety gangsters, mostly, bullies and toughs, few of them truly memorable. Then came *Action Comics #23* (April 1940). At the time, Europe and Asia were engulfed in World War II, which had yet to touch the United States, but had certainly fired the American imagination, including that of Joe Shuster and Jerry Siegel. They sent the *Daily Planet's* Clark Kent and Lois Lane as correspondents to Europe to cover the war between Galonia and Toran. With the two nations about to begin peace negotiations, a car carrying Toranese peace negotiators explodes on its way to the conference.

"Another example of Galonian treachery!" a Toranese official exclaims, and the war "resumes with renewed bitterness."

Clark Kent, as Superman, investigates the source of the "treachery," which leads him to the Galonian general Lupo, whom he persuades ("Either answer my question, or have your brains dashed out against that wall!") to tell all. What General Lupo confesses to is much worse than merely conspiring to perpetuate a conflict between two rival nations.

"Momentarily a squadron of unidentified planes are to invade and bombard a nearby neutral country. Luthor's plan is to engulf the entire continent in bloody warfare."

"But who is Luthor?" Superman asks.

Who Is Luthor?

Who indeed? In this debut appearance, we see him as a figure powerful enough to hold court (from a throne, no less) in a hall that is part of a small city perched on platform suspended from a "gigantic dirigible . . . high above Earth in the stratosphere." He exercises hypnotic power over a legion of henchmen, and his plan (as he reveals when Superman confronts him) is "to send the nations of the Earth at each other's throats, so that when they are sufficiently weakened, I can step in and assume charge!"

In a world under the shadow of a Hitler and a Mussolini, Superman could not afford to spend all his time fighting mere mobsters. In a single bound, the Man of Steel had found an adversary truly worthy of him, and Lex Luthor would figure in the Superman chronicles from this time on.

There would be some confusion about the history. After being introduced as a mystery man in 1940, a new backstory emerged in the 1960s, which put the childhood of Lex Luthor in Smallville and had him growing up with Clark Kent. Later, we were told that he was the impoverished product of the big city, the "Suicide Slum" of Metropolis, and was, in fact, a boyhood pal of Perry White. When Luthor's parents were killed—quite mysteriously—in an automobile accident, young Lex reaped a $300,000 insurance benefit, which catapulted him out of Suicide Slum and gave him seed money to found the sinister industrial empire that became the mighty conglomerate LexCorp.

A redhead at the time of his April 1940 debut, Luthor had purple-gray hair in his next appearance (*Superman* #5, Summer 1940), then, from 1941 onward, has been seen as totally bald. In November 1962 ("The Kryptonite Killer," *Action Comics* #294), Superman explained that Luthor "lost his hair in an accidental explosion and blamed me for his baldness! In his bitterness he became Earth's most evil criminal scientist." Aside from this spasm of silliness—suggesting that the menace of Luthor could be ended with a rug, plugs, or dash of Rogaine—Lex Luthor has been depicted throughout the chronicles as "one of the most dangerous evil-doers in the universe" and "an enemy of humanity" ("The Kryptonite Killer," *Action Comics* #294, November 1962).

Luthor's many diabolical schemes to defeat Superman and achieve local, national, world, and universal conquest by means of a myriad catalogue of secret rays, infernal machines, mind games, and synthesized kryptonite are far too numerous to list here. Suffice it to say that he is never destroyed nor does he ever fully triumph, but he *does* attain the White House (until forced out by scandal) and even a measure of success as a diplomat and wartime leader.

Lex Luthor is perhaps the greatest of all comic book villains. At times one dimensionally evil, he has evolved into someone much more complex, and his roots run deep, all the way back, really, to the prehistory of Superman. Recall from Chapter 2 that, in January 1933, Siegel and Shuster created the "The Reign of the Superman," featuring a kind of modern Frankenstein's monster, whose superpowers, used for wickedness, are entirely mental—in contrast to the powers of the later Superman, which are primarily physical and always used for good. Lex Luthor, in effect, revives the reign of that earlier incarnation (whom he even resembles in appearance), bringing into the world a new diabolical mind.

Siegel and Shuster, as well as the writers and artists who followed them, recognized that Superman needed a truly worthy foe, one whose powers were commensurate with his. They understood that the opposition of good and evil is essential to any story with epic aspirations precisely because this opposition is at the core of all human mythology, belief, faith, and history. No religion, no mythology, no world view survives on a vision of good alone. There is always an opposite and equal force at work. For Superman, it is any number of villains but, paramountly, it is Luthor.

The Engine of Opposition

If all this seems a little too cosmic or philosophical to be of practical value, just turn your focus back to the world of business. It's no secret that the engine of business is competition, the opposition of one firm against another, one industry against another, one product or brand against another. Within a firm or a department, the

LEX LUTHOR

Debut: *Action Comics* #23, April 1940
Full Name: Alexander Joseph Luthor

Over the years, the creators of the Superman chronicles have offered several accounts of Lex Luthor's origins. In the current account, he is portrayed as the son of rapacious parents who raised Luthor in isolation to exploit his budding genius for what they hoped would be their eventual profit. Luthor emerged from his boyhood a psychopath, who engineered the "accidental" death of his parents in order to collect on their life insurance.

Using the insurance proceeds, young Luthor founded LexCorp, which he quickly built into a giant technology company. Wildly successful and extravagantly wealthy, Luthor, presenting himself publicly as the great benefactor of humankind, became politically powerful–the most important man in Metropolis, until the appearance of Superman. The Man of Steel accused Luthor of being a criminal mastermind and thereby became Luthor's arch foe.

Ultimately, it was journalist Lois Lane who exposed Luthor's criminal life. Once revealed as a villain, Luthor turned his fantastic weapons on Metropolis, which he destroyed. After Superman and other super heroes rebuilt the city, the battle between the Man of Steel and Lex Luthor resumed, and Luthor was able to manipulate not only the citizens of Metropolis, but those of the entire United States to win for himself election to the office of president. Although his intention was to gain sufficient power and prestige to bring Superman down at long last, Lex Luthor, astoundingly, proved a highly able chief executive and, indeed, a great leader in successfully rallying the nation to resist the potentially planet-destroying Imperiex invasion. However, in the pages of the *Daily Planet*, Lois Lane and Clark Kent exposed the fact that Luthor had prior knowledge of the Imperiex invasion, and the resulting scandal drove him from office.

competitive opposition is typically one individual against another. After all, there can only be one man or woman at the top.

Of course, business also works through cooperation and collaboration, through mergers, teamwork, and so on, without which any enterprise suffers. Yet competition is even more critical to success. Without it—well, we all know what happened to Soviet Communism in the late 1980s and early 1990s. In the absence of competition, business dies and with it goes the entire economic structure.

The election of Lex Luthor to the office of chief executive does not signify his rehabilitation or the elimination of evil. Instead, it acknowledges the reality, the inevitability, the *normality* of opposition and competition in our lives. Luthor is no longer portrayed as some strange, external force of evil, but as an American institution. Superman lives with Lex Luthor, just as capitalism prospers on the fierce competition of interests, and just as the Office Superman thrives among his opponents. There is nothing wrong with this picture. It is real, it is inevitable, it is normal. It is business as usual.

Playing the Game

The cornerstone of the so-called "dismal science" of economics is the principle of scarcity. In society, there's just not enough of everything to give everyone everything they want. The result? Competition for scarce resources.

Like society at large, any particular workplace is governed by the principle of scarcity. At some time—maybe all the time—you will find yourself directly competing with others for a certain position, a certain office, a certain set of resources, or a certain salary. This is normal. It's the way of business life. Just don't let the rivalries get personal.

Avoid criticizing colleagues on a personal level. Take aim at what the competition produces, not at the person behind the product. Show your results, and criticize the results others show. *Results* are what interest your bosses. Personality is beside the point.

Of course, your competition may not play the game this way, and the fact is that when you and a colleague actively compete for the same job, the situation can get most uncomfortable, quite personal, and even downright nasty. Your best option is to behave in a civil manner, even if the other person does not. Instead of descending to his level, do what you can to redirect focus from egos to issues: "Hey, Bill, I know we're going for the same job. You want it as much as I do. But I just want to let you know that whoever is picked, this is nothing personal. It's just a business decision. I have no intention of being an enemy."

Will you become best buddies? Not likely. But, whatever happens, you are going to have to learn how to get along as colleagues. Today's rival may be tomorrow's boss or tomorrow's key subordinate, a person on whom your authority and advancement depend.

Sabotage

Even if your competition does choose to play above board, without resorting to personal attacks, be assured that they are still very much in the game.

A favorite move among the hyper-competitive is the one-up. You've seen it happen, and maybe it's even happened to you. You're in a meeting and have just completed your big presentation. Now comes the Q&A session. A coworker pipes up: "Well, Ed, that's nothing much. Our division was able to turn a project like this around in under *two* weeks."

How do you respond?

To begin with, on the plus side, most people recognize the one-upper for what he is—a competitive craver of attention. The best way to deal with such people, therefore, is to give them what they want and then move on.

"Yes," you say, "that's terrific—a real accomplishment. But let's get back to my report. . . ."

It is possible that the one-upper will persist, but she does so at her peril. If you can get the conversation to move past her, she'll just look foolish standing still.

Another competitive ploy is to douse your ideas with a splash of cold water. No matter what you suggest, snide Sue will look for a way to suck the enthusiasm right out of the room.

The best defense against this is to anticipate it. Thoroughly prepare your presentation, arming yourself with counterarguments to any objections you can possibly think of. You may find it useful to send up a trial balloon *before* the big meeting by running your idea past the colleague from whom you anticipate the cold-water bath. At the very least, this will give you an idea of where you stand and allow you to predict more accurately the objections she is likely to raise. Also, by consulting this person, you effectively offer her an ownership stake in the idea, thereby heading off or at least blunting the expected criticism. She won't easily criticize something she's already bought into.

Another effective tactic is to erect a bulwark against anticipated criticism by first appealing to less critical colleagues. Recruit allies who will help you build a coalition of support that may intimidate even the most determined of critics. Once Sue understands that her objections will be challenged by more than one person, she may well moderate her approach, keep silent altogether, or—who knows?—even jump on your bandwagon.

If you cannot preempt your critic, then challenge her, but never do so on a personal level. The moment criticism gets personal, both you and your critic lose. Don't respond to criticism with a personal counterattack: "You're always like this—a wet blanket!" Instead, respond to such (wet) blanket remarks as "It can never be done" with a polite request for specifics: "Sue, I'm interested in hearing your perspective. Precisely which aspects of the plan won't work and why?" It is important that you focus this challenge exclusively on the issues at hand.

Although it is key to focus on issues rather than personalities, it is also important to try to understand where your critic is coming from in a personal sense. She may well be masking her own insecurity. Perhaps the two of you are competing—directly—for the same job, or perhaps the critic was just born jealous. Take a moment to analyze motives and sources. This may help you preempt or avoid criticism.

A final strategy for dealing with critics is the if-you-can't-beat-'em-join-'em approach. Try co-opting the critic by bringing her into your camp: "Sue, you have some strong opinions about this, so I'm wondering if you would consider, for the next phase of the project, working with me from the start. I'd like to get your perspective early on." Disarm your rival by giving her an ownership stake in the work.

The Suicide Saboteur

Not every critic aims his guns at you. Some are apparent self-critics, who habitually put themselves down in the hope that others will take pity and "spontaneously" offer praise. It is always a good policy to praise genuine accomplishment, even if the author of the achievement is a direct competitor; however, don't be lured into the trap of doling out *undeserved* praise just because you feel sorry for a colleague. This puts you on the receiving end of a highly manipulative ploy that will do you no good. You are judged not only on your performance, but on how you evaluate the performance of others. It is never in your interest to inflate the stock of anyone else in your organization.

Reign of the Rude

A lot of us have been raised on the motto, *The best defense is a good offense.* Unfortunately, many of your office competitors interpret the last word in this sentence with appallingly narrow literalness. They are *offensive*, using bluff, bluster, and downright rudeness to silence, pre-empt, and intimidate others, including you.

Perhaps surprisingly, the best counter to rudeness is an application of the Golden Rule: *Do unto others as you would have them do unto you.* You are interrupted, you are needled, you are pointedly ignored, you are provoked, but, if you're an Office Superman, you successfully resist the temptation to return such behavior in kind.

The most effective response to frankly rude behavior is to excuse yourself politely from the scene and offer to come back at a later time. This defuses tensions and communicates to the offender that you will not collaborate in his display of ill manners by offering yourself as a willing victim.

The *filibuster* is a common form of competitive rudeness. It consists of rambling verbiage designed to prevent or, at least, discourage you and others from speaking. Break into the monologue by converting it into a dialogue. This is done by interrupting with specific questions.

"Yes, Bill, but how does what you're saying impact the budget we're discussing right now?"

The more specific you can make the question—the more sharply it is focused on the subject at hand—the better the chances that the offender will fall silent. At the very least, everyone present, perhaps even the filibusterer himself, will realize that time is being wasted and that we must now get back on track.

Shakespeare's Hamlet says, "One may smile, and smile, and be a villain." Duplicitous praise, the back-handed compliment, may be the unkindest cut of all.

"Hey, great presentation, Fred. It's good to see that things are finally looking up for you."

As usual, the Office Superman avoids responding in kind to such undermining tactics. Instead, he approaches the smiling villain privately and says: "Thanks, Sarah. I worked hard on that presentation. But I'm not sure I understand what you mean by 'things looking up.' Things have been just fine with me. Is there something we need to discuss?"

Most likely, Sarah will deny that she meant anything by the comment. If she's more perceptive, however, she may try to deflect your question by suggesting to you that you're "overreacting." In either case, continue along the high road of the Office Superman by replying: "Oh, I am glad to hear it, because if there's something I've done to upset you, I want to address it as soon as possible."

However you defend yourself against critics, always remember that the critic's motive in putting you down is to raise himself up. This equation requires a *pair* of variables. Allow a critical or condescending remark to wound you, and you've penciled yourself into the equation. Instead, never allow anyone else to define your self-worth. Listen to genuinely useful criticism, but acquire the equally important habit of tuning out the background noise of mere negativity. Direct your energy toward producing the positive results that will demonstrate, consistently, your value.

Spies and Whispers

Every office has its snoops, who make it their business to ferret out information they believe they can exploit to accumulate power. Your best protection against such competitors is to be discreet and to take confidentiality, privacy, and security very seriously. Ensure that sensitive phone calls and conversations are not overheard. Don't leave important documents out on your desk for others to read. Most of all, don't become the snoop's accomplice. These people will pepper you with questions, and they won't let up until they have what they want. Deflect them with, "I think it's best if we dropped the subject." Or, without comment, simply change the subject. Respond consistently in this way, and the snoop will soon seek his information elsewhere.

Gossip happens in any office staffed by more than two people. You can stem it or, at least, opt out of it by declining to tolerate talk behind people's backs: "Frank, I'm really not interested in talking about that. If I want to know more about Jane, I can always ask her in person. I don't think she'd like the fact that you're talking about her this way."

Look in the mirror. Sometimes the rude behavior of others may be a response to signals you are not even aware you're sending. Examine how you deal with others. Do you let them finish sentences? Do you thank them for a job well done? Do you ask them politely to do certain tasks? Ask a friend—one who won't betray your confidence—for an honest assessment. The personality of a group is largely derived from the perceived personality of its leader. Are you behaving as you want others to behave?

Long Knives

Just about every office has its schemers. These are people who automatically opt for under-the-table plots rather than play by the rules. Do not ally yourself to schemers. In business, the great majority of shortcuts are dead ends.

If you have reason to believe that someone is secretly working against you in the office, try to checkmate the offender by bringing to bear the one weapon he chooses not to use: the rules. Make an effort to document anything and everything suspicious. When the time is right, present your case to management calmly, rationally, and with all the evidence in hand. The point to make is that an attack on you is an attack on the organization.

"Bob," you say to your boss, "I recently learned that a 'private memo' had been circulating saying that I made several mistakes on the Smith project. I got hold of the memo. I don't know if you've seen it yet, but I wanted to bring it to your attention and go over it point by point before people actually start believing the nonsense it contains."

Vaulting above the schemer to the level of management (to which both you and the schemer report) is the best means of cutting him off at the knees. However, sometimes your only practical recourse is to confront him directly. Hold on to the facts, and avoid expressing unproductive anger: "Sam, there's no law that says we have to be the best of friends, but I don't think we need to be enemies, either. If you have a problem with something I've done or said, I am eager to talk about it with you and try to resolve the problem. But I can't just stand around and hear about what you've been saying behind my back. I don't do this kind of thing to you . . ."

Another useful tactic is to heed the advice of every successful tactician since Sun Tzu wrote his *Art of War* some 2,500 years ago: "The only people I keep closer than my friends are my enemies."

Without revealing what you know or suspect about his scheming, recruit the schemer to *work* with you on some project you can control. Not only might this neutralize the ongoing scheme, it may even convert an adversary into an ally. At the very least, you can use this approach to signal that you are on to the schemer's game and that you don't intend to be ambushed.

As you maneuver, you must assume that the schemer is also working to gather allies and co-conspirators. Stay alert to the alignments and alliances that are being formed. Work hard to hold on to your present allies, contain your current enemies, and win over neutral parties.

By definition and by their nature, schemers go for short-term gains. They are tacticians rather than strategists, winning battles, but often losing the war. Dealing under the table may win temporary gains, but, in the long run, those in authority usually come to recognize dangerous patterns of behavior when they see them. In contrast, the Office Superman is a strategist, who plays for the long term. He operates to outlast the schemers, to be there long after they have come and gone.

Role Call

Sometimes Superman is Superman, and sometimes he is Clark Kent. No one knows better than the Man of Steel what it means to play a role—except, perhaps, for the Office Superman. He understands that a business professional wears many hats, plays many roles, without having to sacrifice his essential integrity or deny who he really is. The Office Superman maintains the flexibility of mind required to distinguish between personality and the roles we all play at certain times and under certain circumstances as required by the varying contexts of business. He deals first and foremost on the level of role rather than personality. He rolls, as it were, with the roles rather than attempting to pin colleagues, subordinates, clients, and bosses to this or that "personality."

In short, the Office Superman learns the great lesson of Lex Luthor. Yesterday's evil scientist can become today's president. Yesterday's adversary can become today's ally. That's business, and, within the brackets of sound ethics, the Office Superman keeps his options wide open. Live with Lex Luthor? Sometimes it's the best way, and sometimes its the *only* way.

21

SOME LAST THOUGHTS on SUPERMAN'S FORTRESS of SOLITUDE

SUPERMAN'S FORTRESS OF SOLITUDE is not mentioned by name until June 1949, in "The Case of the Second Superman" (*Superman* #58), some eleven years after the Man of Steel's debut. There are, however, hints and foreshadowings of the Fortress as early as January 1941, a reference to Clark Kent's "laboratory" (*Action Comics* #32), and, throughout the 1940s, various allusions to a "mountain retreat" and a "secret citadel." It is as if Superman's writers and artists gradually came to recognize that the Man of Steel *needed* a place of contemplation, a place to dream, a private space. It was called a "laboratory," then a "retreat" and a "secret citadel," but, finally, it was named just what it *had* to be: a Fortress of Solitude.

The Superman backstory and plot line don't absolutely cry out for the existence of such a place. After all, it is clear that Superman and Clark Kent are one and the same, and that Clark Kent lives in Metropolis, in an apartment identified in "Superman's Neighbors" (*Superman* #112, March 1957) as number 3-B at 344 Clinton Street, located in a high-rise building according to "The Boy from Outer Space," (*World's Finest Comics* #92, February 1948). So the storytellers don't have to go out of their way to establish Superman's place of residence. Indeed, Kent's apartment even incorporates aspects of the Fortress of Solitude. It is located not near his workplace, the Daily Planet building, but "across town" from it ("The Super-Scoops of Morna Vine," *Superman* #181, Parts I-II, November 1965), just remote enough, presumably, to afford a desired degree of privacy. On the other hand, the apartment is near the home of Lois Lane ("The Mxyztplk-Susie Alliance," *Superman* #40, June 1946), the dearest person in Kent's and Superman's private life. An entire room in Kent's apartment is given over to his collection of antique clocks, just as portions of the Fortress of Solitude are dedicated to Superman's collections, trophies, and hobbies ("The Hobby Robbers," *Action Comics* #73, June 1944). The apartment has a "secret closet" accessible via a door that slides open at the touch of a concealed button ("Superman's Toughest Day," *Action Comics* #282, November 1961). The closet holds several robots Superman has fashioned ("Superman's Lost Parents," *Action Comics* #247, December 1958), trophies and mementos, and even experimental samples of kryptonite ("Superman's Hunt for Clark Kent," *Superman* #126, January 1959).

Both before and after the Fortress of Solitude made its first appearance in June 1949, Clark Kent's apartment served the key Fortress function as a private, secret space. Even before the Fortress, Superman's creators recognized a need for something like it. If this had little to do with plot, it had everything to do with the character of Superman. The Superman story line didn't require the Fortress of Solitude, but the Superman psychology did.

A Mighty Fortress

In some ways, the Fortress of Solitude is mainly a super—super-sized, super-secret—closet. As many Superman stories reveal, much of it is devoted to mementos and trophies that have special meaning for the Man of Steel as well as a vast array of special weapons, equipment, and robots. But, of course, the Fortress of Solitude is much more than a closet. It lies "deep in the core of a mountainside in the desolate Arctic wastes" ("The Super-Key to Fort Superman," *Action Comics* #241, June 1958), a "secret and solitary home" ("The Oldest Man in Metropolis," *Action Comics* #251, April 1959), a "secret sanctum" ("The Legion of Super-Creatures," *Action Comics* #326, July 1965). Over the years, it has been variously described and even presented in architecturally detailed diagrams, cross-section elevations, and floorplans. It is a place of multiple levels, a place of infinite security, but also a repository for some of the most dangerous things in the universe: poisons, viruses, strange weapons, even samples of kryptonite. Although the details have varied over the years and from one description to another, all accounts agree that the Fortress included, at one point or another, a trophy room; highly advanced laboratory facilities (in which Superman pursues his apparently endless quest for an antidote to kryptonite); a gym and other recreational facilities; an interplanetary zoo; memorials to the vanished planet Krypton and Superman's parents, plus "memorials" honoring his living friends, including Lois Lane and Jimmy Olsen; the miniaturized and bottled-up Kryptonian city of Kandor, stolen by Brainiac and rescued by Superman; and communication devices for contacting the lost city of Atlantis, the Phantom Zone (the twilight dimension to which Krypton's criminals were banished), remote planets, and various alien dimensions and realms.

A dazzling array. Let's break it down: In the Fortress of Solitude, Superman has created a place for rest, for recreation and fitness, for devoting time to those he loves, for education and intellectual growth, and for coming to terms with his deepest fears; he experiments with the deadliest weapons in the universe and, most important of all, with kryptonite.

With the Fortress of Solitude, the creators of Superman recognized that the Man of Steel has a life outside of work, a life that cannot be narrowly defined by his vocation, even one so exalted and consuming as that of super hero. The Fortress of Solitude is one of those extraordinary elements in the Superman chronicles that add a dimension of depth and realism rarely found in any fictional character, let alone a comic book character.

Don't Forget Your Fortress

Extraordinary realism for a comic book character, yes. But perfectly normal for a flesh-and-blood person, right?

Well, it *should* be. It *should* be quite unnecessary to point out that we all have lives outside of the workplace and beyond career. Superman is super, but he's also only a comic book hero, and if *he's* entitled to a Fortress of Solitude, shouldn't all actual, living, breathing human beings enjoy the equivalent?

Apparently, many of us think not. Legions of would-be Office Supermen believe that career success requires an exclusive focus on work—*exclusive*, as in to the exclusion of everything else. It's as if Superman had decided to plant a big bomb in the middle of the Fortress, set the timer, walk out the door, seal the place up, and let it blow—just so that he could focus *exclusively* on being a super hero.

Superman is a deeply ethical being, who acts from a deeply rooted need to make himself indispensable by helping others. Yet also at his very core is a lie (however benign), an identity divided between Clark Kent and Superman. He understands, profoundly, that he plays roles, different roles at different times and in different contexts. Similarly, the Office Superman has deeply ethical roots and an inborn drive to excel. Yet he also recognizes that different contexts call for different roles. Moreover, each role energizes the other. The role of the ethical businessman informs the role of the ethical person, even as the ethical person role drives that of the ethical business-man. The role of indispensable Office Superman is modeled, in part, on the role of family provider and all-around good citizen, just as the drive to achieve excellence in the office informs the ways in which the Office Superman relates to those who mean the most to him outside of work, including family and friends.

Clark Kent and Superman are not Jekyll and Hyde, opposites in a single body. Quite the contrary, despite their differences, they are truly "one and the same." They represent different roles, but they are very much the same person. Sure, the dual identity often creates problems for Clark as well as for the Man of Steel, but, ulti-mately, the two identities, the two roles, complete each other. Likewise, anyone who has to juggle the competing commitments of business and family knows that these two roles can create problems. Yet they, too, complete each other.

Any job that requires machine-like endurance, focus, and efficiency is best done by a machine, not a human being. However, the most important jobs are done not by accountants or salesmen or art directors or systems analysts, but by human beings who, at the appropriate time, take on the identity of accountants or salesmen or art directors or systems analysts.

Build Your Fortress

Dedicating yourself to a new job or a new career should never require you to jetti-son what is precious to you. While you may well have to manage your time in inno-vative and flexible ways, your job should never force you to stint on your family or friends, nor should it demand that you give up hobbies, passionate interests, com-munity and civic projects, and intellectual or spiritual growth.

In fact, the demand of any truly worthwhile work should be just the opposite. Superman builds his Fortress of Solitude not only as an *escape* from the pressures of his most demanding career, but also to *advance* his career. The narrow view would dictate that he should be spending every waking hour rescuing those in need. *That*, after all, is the number one item on the super hero job description. Superman real-izes, however, that the more he studies, experiments, and invents in his Fortress, the better he becomes at fulfilling the requirements of his job description. The time he spends in the Fortress of Solitude makes Superman more worthy of his calling—and not only because of his study and experimentation, but also because of his dedica-tion to friends and loved ones (symbolically memorialized in the Fortress) as well as his dedication to his own well-being (his hobbies, his physical health, his fun).

Worthwhile jobs require worthwhile people to do them. No worthwhile job requires you to become less worthwhile, less of a human being. On the contrary, the more worthwhile the job, the more worthy the worker should be. Even the most time-